LOCAL GOVERNMENT IN INDIA: POLICY AND PRACTICE

Local Government in India: Policy and Practice

With Special Reference to a Field Study of Decentralization in Kerala

RASHMI SHARMA

MANOHAR
2009

First published 2009

ISBN 978-81-7304-805-0

Published by
Ajay Kumar Jain *for*
Manohar Publishers & Distributors
4753/23 Ansari Road, Daryaganj
New Delhi 110 002

Typeset by
Kohli Print
Delhi 110 051

Printed at
Salasar Imaging Systems
Delhi 110 035

For

Saba and Pravesh

Contents

Tables and Boxes

TABLES

BOXES

Acknowledgements

This book literally 'emerged', as one thing led to another, beginning in the middle. The second part of this book, i.e. the study of decentralization in Kerala, is based on a project sponsored by the Centre for Public Policy and Government (CPPG), Institute of Applied Manpower Research (IAMR), Delhi. I am indebted to H. Ramachandran, Hiranmay Dhar and Shailendra Sharma for supporting this work, and providing valuable comments throughout. Extremely valuable inputs were provided by Meenakshi Sundaram, N.C. Saxena, George Mathew, Indira Rajaraman, and especially S.M. Vijayanand and Vimala Ramachandran. The staff at CPPG were extremely helpful and obliging, for which I am grateful. I also thank the Centre for Education Management and Development, Delhi especially Jayshree Oza, Bina Rai and Binoo Sen for their continuous support, because of which this book could be written.

The Centre for Socioeconomic and Environmental Studies (CSES), Kochi, contributed enormously. I specially thank K.K. George, for some very helpful suggestions. I am grateful to the people from the CSES team as well as the small team at Thiruvananthapuram, who conducted the panchayat case studies. I am particularly indebted to Krishna Kumar and Mini Sukumar for their insights and help.

Faculty at the Centre for Development Studies, Thiruvananthapuram, were generous with their time. R. Kannan and K.N. Harilal gave some extremely helpful advice. Discussions with several members of the Kerala Shastra Sahitya Parishad were educative. In fact, in Kerala, so many people gave time and valuable insights that it is difficult to mention all by name.

Some findings of the study were discussed at seminars organized by CPPG and by the Ministry of Panchayati Raj, Government of India. I am grateful to the participants of these seminars for their helpful comments. I also thank Alok Sheel, Aditi Mehta, Harsh Sethi and Bishnu Mahapatra for their comments and help.

Finally, many thanks to Pravesh Sharma for several valuable comments throughout this whole project, and also for rescuing this book from computer collapses more than once. My mother was encouraging and supportive. Saba contributed to this book by checking up on the progress off and on, and by asking questions, which was flattering. In the end I wish to reiterate that all the views expressed in this volume are personal and mine alone.

RASHMI SHARMA

PART 1

CHAPTER 1

Introduction

The word 'panchayat' conjures up, for many Indians, the idea of the Gandhian *gram swaraj*. *Gram swaraj* was based on the concept that centralization could not be sustained and defended without adequate force and was therefore inconsistent with a non-violent society. For democracy to be successful, it had to be decentralized, leading to the participation of the people. The village, in *gram swaraj*, was envisaged as independent of its neighbours for vital wants, growing its own food crop and cotton and possessing an adequate infrastructure for community life: a village theatre, school, community hall. It was to be governed by five elected persons with people's participation. Society in this village republic would be free of state oppression and people would cooperate for various common activities. The village republic was to form the basis of a decentralized state, wherein villages would elect district administrations, the district administrations would elect provincial governments and the latter would elect a president. For Gandhi, in this decentralized Indian state, power would be transformed into legitimate government (Bhattacharya, 1969; Parel, 1997). In India, the discourse on decentralization or 'panchayati raj' carries with it the aura of Gandhian ideals.

This powerful image coexists with a bewildering support for decentralization in the current context, from the right as well as the left of the political spectrum. Since the late 1980s, many governments in the developing world, representing a great diversity of regimes, have attempted decentralization.[1] Parallelly, decentralization has been promoted by international funding agencies,[2] experts and non-government organizations (NGOs) of various types (Conyers, 1986; Manor, 1999; Rondinelli et al.,1989). The reasons for promoting decentralization are as varied as are the actors who promote it. Commenting on the growing popularity of decentralization, Crook and Manor point out:

> Economists . . . influenced by neo-liberal ideas saw it as a way of shifting power away from the centralized state which had discredited itself in their eyes through voracious rent-seeking and other abuses. Advocates of pluralist, competitive politics regarded it as a device for prying open closed systems, to give interest groups space in which to compete, organize and otherwise assert themselves. Enthusiasts for efforts by village communities to achieve things through co-operation rather than competition viewed it as a means to that end. The leaders of some autocratic regimes in Asia and Africa saw it as a substitute for democratization at the national level, as a safe way to acquire much needed legitimacy and grassroots support. Democratic politicians in less developed countries regarded it as a way to make government more responsive to local needs and preferences. (Crook and Manor, 1998: 1)

As can be seen, not all the above reasons for decentralization are mutually compatible. For instance, decentralization is the favoured strategy of those who seek to promote co-operative action by village communities as well as those who favour greater market competition so that individuals and local governments can 'choose' as they buy goods and services. The term 'decentralization' is an umbrella-like concept beneath which a wide variety of goals and strategies can take cover.[3] In general, it has emotive overtones and positive connotations (Conyers, 1986). In India, the Gandhian aura that panchayati raj carries heightens these positive connotations which, in combination with the wide-ranging endorsement from a variety of actors, often impede the sketching of a more accurate picture. At the same time, decentralization functions as a label for a very wide variety of policy thrusts and strategies, and the positive connotations of the word get transferred to many of these. The picture in the end is of an ill-defined policy thrust, promoted by several actors (some of who disagree on many other issues), riding on general enthusiasm and multiple (often mutually contradictory) expectations.

WHAT THIS BOOK IS ABOUT

In fact, such powerful ideational thrusts and policy prescriptions demand a detailed and dispassionate analysis, and the umbrella-like idea of decentralization needs to be replaced by a more rigorous understanding of what it means and entails in specific contexts, in order to promote more strategic and effective policies as well as action. This is what this book attempts, in the context of India. The 'decentralization' that forms the topic of this book pertains to elected local government, i.e. panchayati raj, and not other types of administrative and financial decentralizations, or decentralization from the national to the state government. The analysis is further confined to rural local governments or panchayati raj institutions (PRIs), and does not extend to urban local bodies. This book does not attempt to draw general conclusions about decentralization that may hold across countries, but instead, the goal is to understand panchayati raj in the Indian historical and socio-political context, in which it has acquired its particular significance and form.[4] The focus is on policy *vis-à-vis* the PRIs, and identifying the possibilities for the future.

Such an analysis promises to be especially fruitful at this point of time, as panchayati raj has got an important boost since the 73rd Constitutional Amendment in 1993. Before the constitutional amendment, though some states took initiatives to empower PRIs, the very existence of local government was tenuous, and elections to these bodies were simply not held for long periods in many states. The constitutional amendment, an initiative of the central government, makes it mandatory for state governments to hold elections to PRIs every five years. Consequently, the *existence* of local elected government has been ensured across the country. At the same time, expectations from PRIs have risen, and the pace of decentralization has quickened in several states. This is clearly an important point of time at which to move away from mere hopes and generalizations and examine expectations, policies and strategies realistically.

It is necessary to clarify here that a 'realistic' assessment of expectations from PRIs is not a prelude to a recommendation that the idea needs to be abandoned. Nor is a detailed probe a step to listing out unaddressable problems and shortcomings. The purpose rather is the opposite. If PRIs have potential, as this author thinks they do, then the potential has to be understood accurately to be exploited to its fullest. On the other hand, uncritical endorsement (that the 'emotive' character of decentralization can produce) sets the scene for failure, because utopian agendas are favoured over realistic possibilities, or because the possible pitfalls have been glossed over rather than addressed. Moreover, through a realistic assessment, there is no attempt to rob the initiative of its ideas of deepening democracy, participatory government, etc., but rather to identify key steps that lay the basis for moving towards them.

In this book, the scrutiny of panchayati raj takes two considerations into account, i.e. the *reasons* for which various policies are adopted and the actual *effect* that they have. While reasons and effects have a relationship to each other, they are not the same. Decentralization may be promoted for various (stated as well as unstated) reasons, but the ultimate effect may be quite different from the one anticipated at the time of initiation of policy. For example, the stated reason for promoting decentralization may be to encourage people's participation in decision-making. However, whether or not decentralization actually results in participation would depend on a host of factors, some of which may be related to policy, such as the creation of appropriate mechanisms and environment, and others may lie outside the sphere of policy, such as the fact that individuals may not be able to, or be willing to, participate. A policy can be said to be 'comprehended' only when this whole dynamic of stated and unstated reasons, the formulation and operationalization of the policy, and its effects have been explored thoroughly.

Importantly, comprehending the reasons and motives of governments for promoting (and blocking) decentralization is not just an academic question, but also has some very direct implications for policy. First, decentralization policies vary a great deal, and to a fair extent, the specific features of a policy are shaped by the reasons for which the policy is promoted. For example, if a major motive for decentralizing is to encourage participation, then decentralization is likely to be close to the grassroots. On the other hand, if the motive is to increase efficiency, then decentralization may focus on levels where technical and administrative competency is high. Second, reasons may not vanish once the initiative is put in place, but can continue to form an important background of the initiative. For instance, an argument in this book is that since the mid-1980s, one important reason for pushing the PRI agenda has been the problems within the state apparatus. These problems continue to form the background in which PRIs exist, even though they are expected to counter it. For example, if bureaucratic ineptitude is an issue, then PRIs are also saddled with it, and it affects their functioning. Reasons thus provide important insights into the context in which PRIs are situated. Finally, the stated reasons for promoting a particular policy are also the yardstick against which their success is measured, though unanticipated successes are also possible.

While reasons help us comprehend policy thrusts, the actual effects of policies provide the most vital information about future needs. The manner in which a particular policy succeeds or fails provides important information about the dynamics on the ground, which ultimately have to be taken into account in order to formulate realistic and do-able policies. The 'effect' of panchayati raj policies is a complex dynamic, which can be understood at two levels. The first of these is in terms of organizational outcomes, i.e. the institutional characteristics of PRIs, such as the extent to which these are elite dominated or inclusive, technically capable, accountable and so on. The second level at which the effect of policy can be understood is in terms of the larger social impact, e.g. reduction of poverty and socio-economic development, that PRIs may have.

In this book, the focus is on the former dimension, i.e. the organizational outcome, as the possible larger social impact of PRIs is dependent to a large extent on their institutional or organizational characteristics. Too often, the tendency is to look for the larger social or economic impact without examining the nature of the organization that comes into existence. Yet, institutional characteristics have a vital influence on the types of interventions that are made as well as the manner in which these are made, and hence influence the 'socio-economic impact'. For instance, whether PRIs, as institutions, are aligned to powerful social groups or to the marginalized sections of society would impact how they address inequities and poverty. Consequently, as far as 'effects' are concerned, the understanding of institutional or organizational dynamics is a key concern.

Institutional outcomes, in turn, depend on various features of policy, as well as the context in which these policies are implemented. The two important aspects of panchayati raj policies are the extent of devolution on the one hand, and institutional design, i.e. issues such as how PRIs should be structured and financed, what processes should be promoted, etc., on the other. These form the 'content' of panchayati raj policies, and are examined in detail in this book. However, it is important to understand that, along with the specific policies that address devolution and institutional design, institutions are also shaped by specific socio-political contexts, and it is the dynamic interaction of policies and contexts that results in the development of one type of institution or the other. In India, as varying policies have been followed in different states with different socio-political contexts and at different points of time, several types of interplays of policies and contexts can be observed. This book attempts to capture this dynamic.

The above analysis leads to the final goal of this book, i.e. delineating key policy initiatives for the future, based on the understanding of the nature of institutions that have developed as a consequence of various policies implemented in a range of contexts. While delineating the key steps, it is not assumed that a particular policy will result in the type of institution envisaged, but the focus is on understanding a range of outcomes that are possible in varied contexts. This leads to a more realistic understanding of what needs to be done, than would an analysis that does not take the context into account. The attempt here is to identify key strategic steps, looking at the broad goals of decentralization as well as the actual experience.

STRUCTURE OF THE BOOK

This book is structured into three parts. In the first part, which comprises this and the next two chapters, the development of panchayati raj policies and ideas about devolution and institutional design across India are examined. This discussion extends to central as well as state policy, as both have impacted panchayati raj, and each has also drawn upon the other. While local government is essentially a state subject, and the state level is critical for examining policy, the central government plays an important facilitating role. The influence of central recommendations on state policy is by no means straightforward, as state governments adapt these to their own ends, but it is a powerful influence all the same. Parallelly, national recommendations are influenced by outcomes in states, especially by successes of particular state initiatives. The initiatives of Maharashtra, Gujarat, West Bengal and Karnataka have influenced central policy a great deal, and continue to be the 'models' around which the discussion on decentralization in India takes place. Special attention has consequently been given to the policies of these states.

A few other important points regarding this analysis need to be stated. One, 'panchayati raj' is not a single policy but a *set of policy thrusts* that vary temporally as well as spatially within India. The emphasis in central and state policies varies, and these have also shifted over time. Second, in analysing the development of policy, this book focuses a great deal on the pressures and considerations *within* governments.[5] Research across developing countries shows that decentralization is rarely driven by demands and movements from the grassroots, but is rather, a decision taken by politicians for various reasons, though once decentralization has taken place, popular pressure may well become important (Eaton, 2001; Manor, 1999). As the following chapter shows, a similar situation exists in India and panchayati raj initiatives have emerged at various times mainly because decision-makers have found it to be the most appropriate strategy.

The second part of the book, comprising the next four chapters, focuses on a detailed analysis of panchayati raj in Kerala, examining not only policy but also outcomes. The state of Kerala is selected because, in the post-73rd Constitutional Amendment scenario, it has undertaken extensive decentralization (the most extensive in India so far). The Kerala initiative has been much admired nationally as well as internationally. As this book is written, Kerala's decentralization is often presented to other states as an example. It therefore demands a detailed scrutiny. Additionally, the fact that decentralization in Kerala has been extensive and innovative allows for an exploration of a new range of questions about institutional design and outcomes, which emerge only in the context of a significant devolution.

The analysis of Kerala's decentralization includes the findings of a study conducted in 2003 and 2004, based on detailed and intensive fieldwork in a small number of PRIs. The fieldwork was aimed at eliciting the institutional and organizational characteristics of PRIs in terms of structure, capacities and dynamics as well as examining the plans and projects (see Box 1). This study raises some new questions about panchayati raj, and also throws new light on the old ones.

The last part of the book, i.e. the final two chapters, addresses the question of organizational outcomes and dynamics in the wider Indian context, and from this analysis, key policy thrusts for the future are identified. In the analysis of organizational dynamics, panchayats are seen as situated in socio-political contexts which share some broad similarities, but also vary across different states. An analysis of the varied set of organizational/institutional patterns that have emerged as a consequence of a range of panchayati raj policies followed in these different contexts provides insights into the dynamics of decentralization in India. This lays the basis for addressing the last question of this book, i.e. of future policy, bringing the discussion about panchayati raj policies that begins in the following chapter, full circle.

Box 1: Design of the Field Study of Kerala PRIs

The study encompassed 3 district panchayats, 3 block panchayats and 12 village panchayats. These panchayats were located in three districts, selected to capture socio-economic and historical variations across the state. These districts, i.e. Wayanad, Thrissur and Thiruvananthapuram, belong to north, middle and south Kerala and also to the Malabar, Kochi and Travancore regions respectively. Wayanad has a significant tribal population and as per various indices of backwardness estimated by the State Planning Board, is the most backward of the 14 districts of Kerala.

To understand the functioning of PRIs and the nature of their projects, three sectors were selected for special focus, i.e. agriculture, school education and drinking water. While the study was not confined to these three sectors, they provided important reference points for more detailed analysis, in terms of the relationship of institutional capacities with project outcomes as well as the differential performance of PRIs across these sectors.

In each of the three districts, the district panchayat, one block panchayat and four gram panchayats (GPs) were studied. The blocks studied were representative of the districts as per the percentage of Scheduled Caste (SC) and Scheduled Tribe (ST) population and female literacy rates. Four GPs were selected from each district on the basis of two criteria: three GPs were selected on the criterion of the social and gender category of the GP president, while the fourth GP was selected to represent one of the 'best' panchayats in the district. As far as possible, GPs were selected from within the selected block (so as to allow the study of the relationship between the GP and the block). However, where a particular type of GP did not exist in a block, a neighbouring GP in another was selected.

The fieldwork was based on the study of panchayat records, interviews with key actors, focus group discussions (FGDs) with the community and observation. Interviewees included a range of persons associated with the PRIs, i.e. panchayat representatives (PRs) from different social and gender categories, panchayat secretaries and departmental officials dealing with the three sectors mentioned. The interviews and FGDs were semi-structured. Additionally, the field work included brief case studies of community-based associations such as a farmers' associations or a parent-teacher associations (PTA), women's self-help groupses (SHGs), etc., at the GP level as well as of projects undertaken by village and district level PRIs (for more details see Annexes 1 and 2).

NOTES

1. According to Manor (1999), decentralization policies have been promoted in developing countries as a result of a widespread but vague notion that centralized government has failed. Slater (1989) argues that decentralization has been ideologically indispensable in the Third World as claimants have emphasized decentralization as a unifying force in the consolidation of new identities, remedy for rapacious centralized bureaucracies and as a policy to soften the resistance to changes brought about by development.
2. The World Bank situates decentralization in the agenda of 'good governance', promoting 'exit' and 'voice'. Exit is promoted by increasing the options (other than the state) for the public delivery of services, including private actors and NGOs. Voice is promoted through popular participation. Decentralization is seen to lead to improvements in efficiency and effectiveness by reducing overload on central governments and improving access to participation and decision making at lower levels (World Bank, 1991). A critique of the World Bank approach is that decentralization is promoted to 'reach out, incorporate and monitor', as privatization and marketization can create potentially explosive social and political situations, and the 'mystique' of decentralization is used for forming a consent (Slater, 1989).
3. An important distinction that Samoff (1990) makes is between 'administrative decentralization' and 'political decentralization'. In administrative decentralization the focus is on institutional reform to improve implementation. The language here is of 'service delivery', 'efficiency', 'behavioural incentives and rewards' and 'cost recovery'. On the other hand, 'political decentralization' has the goal of transfer of decision-making authority to previously under-represented or marginal groups. The language here is 'effective participation', 'empowerment', 'conscientization' and 'collective action'. Manor (1999) draws a distinction between decentralization that occurs with simultaneous democratization and that which occurs without, and argues that only devolution, i.e. democratic decentralization is genuine decentralization.
4. To quote Bird and Rodriguez (1999): 'The essence of decentralization is that it does not occur in general but rather in a particular context—in a country with its own history and traditions and its own specific institutional, political and economic context. Moreover, decentralization has taken many different forms in different countries at different times, and even the exactly the same variety of decentralization may have very different effects under different conditions' (p. 300).
5. A similar position is taken by Ghosh and Kumar (2003) as they analyse panchayati raj policies in four Indian states.

CHAPTER 2

The Question of Existence

At Independence, India inherited two legacies of local self-government. The first of these came from the colonial government, prompted by a mixture of financial prudence and liberal impulses. After the Indian mutiny of 1857, as imperial finances came under strain, and as the colonial government sought to extend its influence through public works (Spear, 1973), Lord Mayo got a resolution passed to bring about administrative efficiency and finance local services through local taxation. In 1882, Lord Ripon, a liberal, who saw local government as an instrument of political education, and a way to vent the aspirations of a growing class of educated Indians, got passed a resolution that provided for local boards that comprised large majorities of elected non-official members. In 1909, the Royal Commission on Decentralization elaborated these principles further, arguing that it was desirable to constitute and develop village panchayats for the administration of local affairs. In actual practice though, steps to develop local elected bodies remained tardy (Khanna, 1999; Mathew, 1996; Shiviah et al., 1976).

The second legacy arose from the national movement, which seized the panchayats for its own struggles. Panchayats became part of the challenge to British authority as in 1909, the same year as the Royal Commission completed its report, the Indian National Congress adopted a resolution urging the government to make all local bodies elected and strengthen them with financial resources. During the national movement, the pre-colonial panchayats were often projected as idealized village governments, indigenous institutions destroyed by the colonial power.[1] Though the focus on panchayats was strategic to begin with, its socio-economic and politico-philosophical dimensions became more explicit in Gandhian ideas over time. The more concrete opportunity came in 1919 when some responsibilities of government, including local self-government, passed on to Indian ministers elected on the basis of limited franchise. Subsequently, a spate of panchayat legislations followed, and village panchayats—representative institutions with jurisdictions in civic matters—were established in a number of provinces. More legislation regarding village panchayats followed when the Government of India Act of 1935 widened the scope of provincial governments, and when Congress ministries assumed office in the provinces in 1946 after a break of seven years. However, preoccupation with national politics and the freedom struggle resulted in a neglect of local bodies, and they lacked manpower, were poorly financed, could not ensure efficiency and fell prey to corruption (Khanna 1999; Mathew, 1996; Shiviah et al., 1976).

We have visited briefly, in the beginning of this book, Gandhi's vision of a radically decentralized political and economic order with the village as its basic unit. But this was not the vision of the modernistic elements led by Nehru, and did not form the basis of the Constitution that India adopted after Independence. In October 1945, before the Constituent Assembly started its discussions, Gandhi attempted to settle differences with Nehru, arguing that truth and non-violence could be realized only in the simplicity of village life. Nehru's reply was that he did not see any special virtue in villages just because they were villages, and he underlined instead, the advantages of science and technology. These views were largely shared by the Constituent Assembly, and when the draft Constitution was completed in 1948, the word 'panchayat' did not appear in it even once. Instead, the draft Constitution document envisaged a federal-parliamentary structure with a bias towards centralism, with the individual, and not the village, as the basic unit of the political system. National development was visualized in terms of modern science and technology and not a village movement. During the constitutional debates, Ambedkar was famously to describe the village as a 'sink of localism, den of ignorance, narrow mindedness and communalism'. Other members argued that unless village people were educated and politically conscious, panchayats would do more harm than good and local influential classes would take over (AVARD, 1962; Shiviah et al., 1976). Ultimately, the basic structure of the draft Constitution was retained, but panchayats were not wholly abandoned, and the Directive Principles stated that: 'The state shall take steps to organize village panchayats and endow them with such powers and authority as may be necessary to enable them to function as units of self-government.'

Subsequently, from its ambiguous place in the Directive Principles, the idea of panchayats has been promoted, relegated to the background, and retrieved at various points of time in public policy in India, till in 1993, close to half a century after the Constitution was framed, panchayats were given constitutional status through the 73rd Constitutional Amendment. During this period, there have been several shifts in the meanings and connotations of the idea, as well as its context. An analysis of these shifts that follows below is useful in understanding what panchayats stand for today, and the possibilities that they embody.

PANCHAYATS FOR DEVELOPMENT

Post-Independence, in national policy, panchayats emerged as a component of the rural and agricultural development policies,[2] which were themselves a sub-text in the overall policy of *centrally planned rapid industrial development* through the public sector, with the bulk of investment planned in heavy industry. In the rural sector, the goal was advancement of justices and equity among agricultural producers on the one hand, and increased agricultural production on the other, without diverting resources from the priority goal, i.e. heavy industry. An 'institutional strategy' for agriculture that included land reforms, farm and service cooperatives and village government at the local level was adopted (Rudolph and Rudolph, 1989; Varshney, 1995). At the same time, rural development was promoted through the National Extension Service (NES) and the Community Development (CD) projects,[3] a broad-based programme for holistic rural reconstruction that laid emphasis on development of self-reliance in the individual and initiative in the community. The programme encompassed several aspects of village life including agriculture, irrigation, animal husbandry, health, education, transport and communication, rural industries, housing, social welfare for women and children and supplementary employment (Dantwala and Barmeda, 1985; Mishra, 1981).

The ideas about local government coalesced in the form of 'panchayati raj', or three tiers of local elected bodies in the report of the Balwantray Mehta Committee[4] of 1957. But the logic of constituting panchayats at various tiers had already been articulated in the Second Five Year Plan as a necessary institutional mechanism in the context of the expanding role of the state in rural and agricultural development and agrarian restructuring (GoI, 1956).[5] Subsequently, the Balwantray Mehta Committee, set up to review the CD project as it completed five years, found that 'one of the least successful aspects of the Community Development and National Extension Service work is its attempt to evoke popular initiative' (GoI, 1957: 5). The reasons for this failure were located in the limitations of the popular bodies at the block and district levels, which had nominated members and were advisory in character. Consequently, the Committee suggested a well-organized democratic structure of administration, i.e. a three-tier system of panchayati raj at the village, block and district levels. The most important concern of the Balwantray Mehta Committee regarding panchayati raj was the creation of institutions that would ensure community engagement with rural development, i.e. CD projects. While the Committee acknowledged the possibility that several functions could be assigned to the panchayati raj structure, it clarified that 'the immediate objective is to ensure that the development of the countryside is carried out as rapidly and efficiently as possible and through democratic processes' (GoI, 1957: 12).

The Committee considered the village to be too small an area to create a body that would 'take charge of all aspects of development work' (GoI, 1957: 6). Consequently, the focus of democratic decentralization was shifted away from the village to the 'block'. The block was a new administrative unit, identical to the *taluk* in some states and smaller in others, that had become the operative unit in the NES and CD projects. The block was staffed with a block development officer (BDO), extension officers for agriculture, animal husbandry and co-operation, social education organizers, an overseer and village-level workers and had a advisory committee with nominated persons (Dantwala and Barmeda, 1985). The Balwantray Mehta Committee recommended that the 'panchayat samiti', an elected body at the block level, replace the advisory committee and become the central agency for implementing development programmes. The case for the block-level panchayat samiti was strengthened by the fact that in several blocks personnel for development administration had already been provided. The panchayat samiti was to work 'with and through' (GoI, 1957: 8) the village panchayats, and at the district-level, zilla parishads were expected to play an advisory role[6] (GoI, 1957).

Apart from its emphasis on panchayats as agencies of development, three ideas that run through the Committee's report need to be highlighted. The first of these is actually an absence, in that that the Committee made no recommendations about the gram sabha (village assembly), that was the bedrock of the Gandhian vision of *gram swaraj*. Later, the Diwakar Committee was set up to go into this issue, and as it gave its report in 1963, it gave qualified support to the gram sabha. The Diwakar Committee pointed out that there were deep divisions within the community and an integrated village community did not really exist. Moreover, gram sabhas were not active in states where the legislation did provide for them. However, the Diwakar Committee recommended that in the future, the gram sabha be statutorily recognized and developed as a body to which the gram panchayat could be made accountable (GoI, 1963).

The second idea concerns politics and the role of political parties, about which the Balwantray Mehta Committee was ambivalent. Though the Committee iterated the value of democracy, it viewed competitive politics at the village level as deleterious, and said that 'one of the banes of democratic village administration in some areas has been the intensification of factions and feuds. . . . The system of electoral contests at the village level has often added to these' (GoI, 1957: 18). Consequently, direct elections were recommended only for one tier of panchayats, i.e. the village panchayats, while the block and district panchayats were to be constituted through indirect elections. Additionally, the Committee endorsed consensual panchayat elections where 'membership of the village panchayat should be regarded as an opportunity for service to the people which should be taken by the best men in the village' (GoI, 1957: 18). The Sanatham Committee that gave its report in 1965, concurred, recommending that no political symbols be used in the panchayat elections and no representations from political parties be entertained by the PRIs. It further went on to recommend the direct election of sarpanches (panchayat presidents) to the village panchayats, so that able and popular leaders could emerge at the village level.

Both the Balwantray Mehta and the Sanatham Committees showed keen awareness of the fact that PRIs were situated in a context marked by wide social inequities. Though they favoured election by consensus, they were also ambivalent about it, as they perceived that it could reinforce traditional authority, and the PRI structure was susceptible to capture by elites, while the most marginalized groups were likely to be left out. Consequently, both Committees recommended measures to include SC and ST representatives as well as women. However, from today's perspective, these recommendations appear benign, but naïve and imprecise, as they depend on co-option rather than reservation. The Balwantray Mehta Committee recommended, for instance, that 'These (panchayat samiti) elected representatives will co-opt two women who are interested in work among women and children' and 'Where the population of SC exceeds 5 per cent of the total population of the panchayat samiti area, one person belonging to a Scheduled Caste shall be co-opted; and similarly, one member of a ST' (GoI, 1957: 10).

The third idea in the Balwantray Mehta Committee's report was an implicit faith in a centralized bureaucracy controlled by state governments, which was a corollary to its distrust of local politics in the context of an iniquitous society. For instance, even though the Committee envisaged that the panchayat samiti would become the main developmental agency, it did not recommend that the panchayat samiti recruit its own personnel. Instead, it recommended that all its officers be drawn from state cadres. Further, the Committee sought to minimize the interference of local politicians in the functioning of the bureaucracy by separating the policy and executive functions of the PRIs, the former the domain of elected representatives and the latter of state government employees (GoI, 1957).

It can be seen that the idea of panchayati raj that evolved in the Balwantray Mehta Committee report was not an articulation of Gandhian principles, and the chief intention of recommending panchayati raj was not to promote *gram swaraj*, but to develop a viable institution for rural and agricultural development. The focus on the panchayat samiti at the block level with its growing development bureaucracy, rather than village-level democracy, and the ambivalence about the gram sabha highlight this point. Thus Jayaprakash Narayan, an eminent Gandhian, was to say in his speech at the Local Self Government Conference held at Bangalore in 1960:

> It is . . . a matter of great satisfaction to me that you (the national government) are coming back to Gandhi, not because of any ideological prejudices or bias, but because you are faced with the problem of development. (Narayan, 1970: 62)

In tune with the Gandhian vision, Jayaprakash Narayan visualized the three-tier panchayati raj structure differently, with the district-level panchayats creating the state assembly, and the state assemblies the national legislature (Shiviah et al., 1976). This vision stood in sharp contrast to the panchayati raj structure that was emerging in national policy, in which state and national legislatures were elected through individual votes, not 'built-up' from the panchayats. Moreover, panchayati raj was promoted in the context of extreme centralization of the economy, in which the powers of the central government were enormous through its control on industry in the public sector as well as its powers of licensing for private sector industry. In contrast, Jayaprakash Narayan argued for a decentralized, small machine and labour-intensive economy (Narayan, 1970). Clearly, the post-Independence panchayati raj was not the communitarian democracy of self-sufficient villages envisaged by Gandhians.

After the report of the Balwantray Mehta Committee, there was a renewed interest in panchayats across the country. By 1959, all states had passed Panchayati Raj Acts and by the mid-1960s, three tiers of panchayats (called the 'first phase panchayats'), had been established in 15 out of 22 states (Mathew, 1994). However, these first-phase panchayats, as feared in several reports and other documents of this time, were often captured by local elites. Important for the panchayats was the failure of land reform, for though intermediaries were abolished, redistribution of land did not take place on a large scale. Land reform encountered stiff resistance at the state level, where landed property interests were entrenched and powerful. As agriculture was a state subject, the result was flawed, easily-evaded land legislation and ineffective implementation. At the same time, the district and *taluka* level landlords and substantial landowners became influential in politics (Hanumantha Rao, 1992; Rudolph and Rudolph, 1989; Varshney, 1995). Consequently, the rural elite got elected to positions of power in PRIs, as they were seen as people who could get the best possible bargain from state and national authorities, or because there were no secret ballots in some panchayat elections, or even where there were secret ballots, poor people did not believe these to be so. There were several instances too of intimidation and violence in elections (Bailey, 1965; Chaudhri, 1969; GoI, 1965; Gray, 1969).

The first phase panchayats did not become popular institutions, and the poor had little reason to support them. For instance, Gray (1969) recounts in the case of panchayats in Andhra Pradesh (AP) that 'unanimous' elections in villages were dominated by politically active landlords. In the context of CD programmes in two UP villages, Dube (1969) shows that in the case of activities undertaken with voluntary labour, the village elite played a supervisory role and got praise from outsiders, while the hard labour was done by the poorest people, who did not get any praise from outsiders, lost wages for the day, and came to regard voluntary work as forced labour. Chaudhri (1969) notes in the case of the panchayats in Rajasthan that panchayati raj did not result in any perceptible increase of flow of funds to weaker sections of society.

It is not very useful to go into the question of the 'effectiveness' of PRIs *vis-à-vis* development in this phase, because as described below, the first phase was brief, and support for PRIs began to wane from the mid-1960s onwards. But panchayati raj developed with some vigour in two states: Maharashtra and Gujarat. Ghosh and Kumar (2003) show that in Maharashtra, along with the establishment of an elaborate structure of credit, input and marketing cooperatives, PRIs became the mechanism through which the ruling party expanded its base in the countryside and promoted rural development, focusing on the interests of big farmers. Maharashtra chose to empower panchayats at the district level, i.e. zilla parishads or panchayats (ZPs)[7] through which the political ambitions of several local elites could be accommodated, and they could access state resources and power to dispense patronage. In Gujarat too, panchayats helped the ruling party to consolidate its hold on the countryside. However, since many of the leading figures of panchayati raj hailed from the state, there was also a strong ideological support for the institution. Learning from Maharashtra, the Gujarat state government vested the ZP with maximum powers and functions, but panchayats at all three levels were given due recognition and taxation powers (Ghosh and Kumar, 2003).

While these two states developed the most robust and effective panchayati raj systems, two other legacies of the first phase were important even for states where PRIs remained dormant. First, the structure of panchayati raj with its multiple tiers of interlinked local governments, that could play a significant role in rural development, spread across the country. In most states, parallel legislation was also put in place. Second, in the NES and CD projects, a new administrative unit, the 'block', and an administrative structure that focused on development, i.e. the development bureaucracy, separate from revenue administration, was created. This development bureaucracy got linked to PRIs, and would form an important background to the whole decentralization process in the future.

CENTRALIZATION AND DECLINE OF PANCHAYATS

From the mid-1960s onwards up to the mid-1970s, PRIs were increasingly marginalized. Regular elections to PRIs were not held and in several states there was a gradual development of subsidiary legislation and orders that curtailed the power of the panchayats. There are numerous examples during this period of state governments encroaching on the powers of the panchayats regarding sanction of projects as well as transfers of government personnel such as health workers and teachers, including in the two successful states. In Maharashtra, planning work was entrusted to a body chaired by a minister. And in Gujarat, the state government interfered on many occasions and passed several orders on subjects already transferred to the PRIs. In many states, staff given to local bodies was withdrawn and resources tapered off (GoI, 1978; Jain, 1985; Mathew, 1994; Pandya, 1981).

As this phase is characterized by a decline of PRIs, panchayati raj literature often gives scant attention to it. But in fact, there are very good reasons for taking stock of the developments at this time in order to understand local government in India. To begin with, it is important to understand, as part of the chequered history of panchayati raj in India, why this project was marginalized, just as it is important to understand the reasons for which it was promoted. Even more critical is the fact that some very significant developments took place in the Indian polity and society at this time, which shaped the *context* in which the future (second phase) panchayats would function. For instance, the future panchayats would deal and work with a bureaucracy that began to deteriorate sharply at this time. Additionally, the developments of this phase set the stage for the resurgence of panchayats in national policy in 1977, so that this phase is a formative one for the second-phase panchayats as well.

One context in which the marginalization of panchayats took place was that of a substantial shift in the agricultural and rural development policy. The economic situation of the country deteriorated in the mid-1960s as a result of the war with China and Pakistan and the droughts of 1966 and 1967, with the Gross Domestic Product (GDP) in these two years falling in absolute terms. Moreover, till the mid-1960s, grain shipments from United States had made adequate amounts of food available at relatively low prices, but this aid ceased thereafter. This, coupled with the rise in population and agricultural stagnation, made the issue of increasing agricultural production urgent, and the direction of the agricultural policy shifted. In 1959–60, when India had faced a severe food crisis, an alternative strategy, proposed by the Ford Foundation, of concentrating efforts to increase food production through intensive use of technology in a few districts in the country was tried out. An Intensive Agricultural District Programme that demonstrated the potentialities of higher food production through a package of practices in areas that were especially endowed with water supply, good infrastructure facilities, good soil and so on was launched initially in three districts, and later extended to cover one district in every state. This programme laid the foundation for the wider adoption of a new strategy of agricultural modernization. Instead of the earlier 'institutional view' that had informed agricultural policy, the focus now was on improved technology and price incentives for farmers which, with the introduction of high yielding variety of seeds, ushered in the Green Revolution (Dantwala and Barmeda, 1985; Dhar, 2003; Hanumantha Rao, 1992; Mathur, 1996; Varshney, 1995). At the same time, funds available to PRIs through the CD programme dried up.

It has been argued that the tempo of development administration at this time required intensive efforts for which the PRI structure was not suitable, and that the staff at lower levels had to be requisitioned back to the departments, and hence PRIs were marginalized. However, this does not seem an adequate explanation. It is difficult to understand how panchayats could have impeded the modernization of agriculture *per se*. Conceived as agencies for development, they could, in fact, have been extremely useful in the speedy implementation of programmes, as the case of Maharashtra would suggest. The need to look for other explanations is also reinforced by the mode of implementation of anti-poverty programmes that began in the 1970s. Briefly, in the 1970s, as it became clear that the Green Revolution had not benefited the poorest sections of society, anti-poverty programmes, i.e. area-specific programmes such as the Drought Prone Area Programme, Desert Development Programmes as well as those targeted at the rural poor such as the Small Farmers Development Agency, Marginal Farmers' and Landless Labour Agency, Cash Scheme for Rural Employment and social welfare-oriented programmes such as the Minimum Needs Programme were started. But even in the context of these programmes, the strengthening of panchayats did not become a priority. In fact, for some of these programmes, as in the case of agriculture, separate agencies were established for implementation (Dantwala and Barmeda, 1985; Mathur, 1995). There is again, no reason for believing that panchayats could not have played a pivotal role in implementing anti-poverty programmes. In fact, as West Bengal was to show at a later stage, PRIs proved to be extremely effective in implementing such programmes.

The decline of panchayats was not a consequence of the types of policies and programmes undertaken, but needs to be situated in the nature of politics that developed in this period. This phase has been described as one in which there was 'the simultaneous rise of plebiscitary and personal politics' (Rudolph and Rudolph, 1987). About the developments in Indian politics, Atul Kohli writes:

> One important method of preserving power has been populism: to establish direct contact between the leader and the masses and to undermine those impersonal rules and institutions designed to facilitate orderly challenges. . . . The destruction of institutional constraints will leave more matters to the leader's personal discretion, enabling the leader to promote those who are loyal, while shunning aside anyone who is a political challenger with an independent political base. (Kohli, 1997: 388)

The erosion of state institutions which began in this phase, and continued subsequently, has been the subject of much study and comment (Kaviraj, 1988; Kohli, 1991; Kothari, 1988; Wallace, 1976). About the changing political ethos, Rudolph and Rudolph (1987) write:

> Nationalist politicians were gradually supplanted by professional politicians, who in turn were joined and to an extent displaced by condottierri seeking personal profit. (Rudolph and Rudolph 1987: 84) And . . . in the early 1980s, commitment and loyalty were not being interpreted in policy and professional terms. Instead many ministers behind the façade of policy concerns, were more interested in partisan and personal interests. Loyalty and commitment became willingness on part of civil servants to accommodate themselves to ministerial manipulations of this kind. (Rudolph and Rudolph, 1987: 80)

As the development of person-centric power bases as well as rent seeking could be carried out better in a centralized rather than decentralized system, the thrust towards panchayati raj vanished from central policy. At the same time, the central leadership began to intervene directly in state politics and the leadership of state governments slipped into the hands of persons 'nominated' by the centre, as compared to leaders with a genuine political base and following (Rudolph and Rudolph, 1987). As persons who lacked political base headed state governments, they feared the panchayats and postponed elections so as to reduce the influence of their more popular political rivals. For instance, as Ghosh and Kumar (2003) show, in Maharashtra the curtailment of the powers of the panchayats followed the instalment of a chief minister who lacked popular support.[8] In fact, the situation that was created in the states stood in sharp contrast to the one in which Maharashtra and Gujarat had promoted PRIs earlier, when panchayats had been used to build and expand the political base of the party.

Though this phase saw the decline of panchayats, its legacy for the future panchayats in terms of an overall deterioration in state functioning was critical. Along with the shifts in Indian politics noted earlier, important changes also took place in the bureaucracy. While the expansion of government activities after Independence had led to an increase in the number of government employees, now, a significant erosion of administrative ethos began. The relatively 'neutral' character retained by the bureaucracy till the mid-1960s, was replaced with increasing politicization, in which transfers and postings were used liberally as mechanisms of influence. This 'politicization' lent support to the proclivities towards dispensation of patronage and rent seeking in the bureaucracy too (Dwivedi, Jain and Dua, 1989; Kaviraj, 1988; Potter, 1996; Rudolph and Rudolph, 1987).

THE POLITICAL PANCHAYATS

The crisis in Indian politics culminated in the Emergency in 1975, whereby democratic rights were curtailed. The Emergency lasted up to 1977, when elections were held again. In these elections, the Janata Party, a coalition of parties, containing, like the Congress, left as well as right leaning elements, formed the first non-Congress national government in independent India and decentralization formed one of its main agendas. Importantly, the legitimacy of the Janata leaders derived significantly from the moral authority of Jayaprakash Narayan and his stature as a Gandhian (Corbridge and Harris, 2000). But while this ideological underpinning played its role, the focus on decentralization was also a response to two more immediate developments. One of these, in the post-Emergency scenario, was a heightened concern with liberal democracy and the need to guard against authoritarian centralism (Kothari, 1989; Varghese, 1977; Wallace, 1976). The other was a new focus on the rural sector.

The focus on the rural sector needs to be situated in the context of the increasing influence of agricultural producers on state policy through the 1970s. With the strategy of agricultural modernization, a more powerful farmer lobby had begun to emerge and wield political influence (Patnaik et al., 1996; Varshney, 1995). Through the 1970s, agricultural prices and subsidies on irrigation and power, rather than land reform, became the basis of agrarian unrest. The influence of this group was visible in the politics of subsidies, and in the agriculture price policy that became increasingly producer oriented (Varshney, 1995). About this phase, Rudolph and Rudolph write:

> The formation of the Janata government in 1977 marked the ascendance of a political coalition in which agrarian interests were senior partners for the first time. . . . As a result the Nehru-era policies favouring cities, centralization, bigness and capital-intensive industrialization were modified by policies that favoured agriculture and rural society, decentralization of the government and the economy, and small producers using labour intensive technologies that promote employment. (Rudolph and Rudolph, 1987: 51–2)

This heightened concern with the rural sector was reflected in the report of the Asoka Mehta Committee, which was set up by the government to examine the case for panchayati raj. The Asoka Mehta Committee observed that agriculture had become a complex operation. It saw Indian agriculture as highly dynamic, encompassing not merely farming and production of food grains, but also non-food crops, horticulture and allied activities such as animal husbandry, farm and social forestry, fisheries, poultry, and so on. Parallelly, it expected rural industry to expand and grow in the near future. It anticipated more government intervention and an increasingly complex and vibrant developmental scenario in rural India, and it attempted to 'discern the institutional requirements of development management in a changed developmental context' (GoI, 1978: 11). The report emphasized that state governments would simply not be able to take up the large number of development programmes without a significant decentralization of functions.

The concern of the Asoka Mehta Committee with agricultural modernization and rural industrialization, as against the CD Project background of the Balwantray Mehta Committee, led it to suggest a different structure for panchayati raj. The Asoka Mehta Committee suggested that the district panchayat or zilla parishad, rather than the block samiti, be the main tier of the PRI structure as departmental heads were situated at the district level and hence greater technical expertise was available. The success of the zilla parishads in Maharashtra and Gujarat in promoting agricultural and rural development strengthened the argument. In the report, state governments were urged to transfer substantial developmental and planning functions as well as funds to the zilla parishads. At the same time, the Asoka Mehta Committee recommended that the zilla parishad be strengthened administratively.

The report of the Asoka Mehta Committee, as it focused on the district level, also did not visualize the small village as a viable unit for 'the effective transfer of technology' (GoI, 1987: 39) and for services related to health, education, agriculture and allied sectors. It recommended, rather, the next tier of panchayat to be the 'mandal panchayat', smaller than the block, with a population of 10,000 to 15,000, which it saw as a viable unit for economic development and a 'growth centre'. The mandal panchayat was visualized as located in a central village, surrounded by a number of 'hinterland' villages and 'the relative isolation for the traditional village would recede into the background' (GoI, 1978: 43). Essentially, it recommended a two-tier structure for panchayati raj rather than three tiers, the appropriate tiers being identified in terms of their potential for growth and rural development.

In other words, panchayati raj, as envisaged by the Asoka Mehta Committee, was to be an institutional framework in which technical upgradation in agriculture and rural industrialization would take place. How distant these ideas were from the original Gandhian vision of *gram swaraj* is indicated by the dissenting note of Siddharaj Dhadda, a Gandhian and a member of the Committee, who pleaded for the recognition of the village, functioning through its gram sabha, as the primary unit of panchayati raj. Disappointed that the gram sabha did not find its vital place in the Committee's report, he explained:

> (The) purpose of decentralization is not merely to help development, . . . but the creation of an integrated structure of self-governing institutions from the village and small town onwards to the national level, in order to enable the people to manage their own affairs. (GoI 1978: 173)

Moreover, as against the original Gandhian vision of a non-party village democracy based on consensus, the Asoka Mehta Committee was concerned with strengthening and deepening liberal democracy, recently threatened during the Emergency. It commented that, 'if the edifice of democratic polity is to become secure in the country, the strengthening of democracy at the grass-roots is inevitable' (GoI, 1978: 32), and that PRIs would be 'like democracy at the national and state levels, both ends and means' (GoI, 1978: 35). Three decades earlier, the Balwantray Mehta Committee report had betrayed a great deal of hesitation about grassroots politics and political party competition in PRIs. Unlike its predecessor, the Asoka Mehta Committee endorsed an increased role of political parties in panchayati raj. It recommended direct elections to district as well as mandal panchayats, and also the formal participation of political parties in panchayat elections. Learning from the experience of postponement of panchayat elections in the previous decade in many states, it also recommended that panchayats be constitutionally recognized.

The Asoka Mehta Committee was aware that PRIs had not addressed the concerns of the socially marginalized, even in the success story of Maharashtra. Noting that the earlier system of co-option of SC/ST members as suggested by the Balwantray Mehta Committee had been manipulated to include persons who were allied to dominant interests, it suggested reservation of seats for SCs and STs in PRIs, proportional to their share in the population. It also recommended that specific programmes for SCs and STs be earmarked in district plans, committees to look into these issues be set up, and mechanisms such as social audit be developed to ensure equitable distribution of resources. An important dissenting note to the Committee's report was that of E.M.S. Namboodiripad, the communist leader from Kerala. In the context of 'weaker sections', Namboodiripad argued that parliamentary democracy was a powerful weapon for the exploited majority, and SCs and STs needed the support of the poor belonging to other castes, and that the criterion for reservation should not be caste but economic status. Regarding representation of women, the Asoka Mehta Committee shifted its stand only slightly from the Balwantray Mehta Committee, recommending the co-option of two women with the highest votes in the district.

If the Balwantray Mehta and Asoka Mehta Committee reports are compared, they are like-minded in their concern for socio-economic development, but quite different in perceptions of state functioning. In the Balwantray Mehta Committee report, the panchayat was the institution though which a coherent and relatively unproblematic state apparatus was seen as seeking collaboration from society in its rural development agenda. In the report of the Asoka Mehta Committee, on the other hand, panchayats were seen as a way of addressing problems *within* the polity and the state. The endorsement of political party competition in PRIs and giving them constitutional status arose from the perception that democracy was not automatically ensured through the benevolence of political elites, but had to be fought for and protected. The recommendations for reservation of seats for SCs and STs in proportion to their population as against the more ad hoc measures suggested by the Balwantray Mehta Committee too suggest a far more combative stance.

The Janata Party did not stay in power long enough to implement the decisions of the Asoka Mehta Committee, and reportedly, in an initial meeting, the recommendations of the Committee were not received well by the state governments (Sethi, 1989). But all the same, the influence of the report of this Committee has been significant.

The Asoka Mehta Committee report inspired the 'second phase' of panchayati raj in West Bengal, Karnataka, Andhra Pradesh and Jammu & Kashmir, the most vigorous initiatives coming from the former two states. In Karnataka, as the Janata Party won control of the government in 1983, its leaders wanted to demonstrate that they were more imaginative and radically democratic than their Congress counterparts, to revive their fortunes nationally. They also had next to no party organization in the state, and they believed that a new system of elected councils at the district level and below would provide a framework of party building[9] (Crook and Manor, 1998). In West Bengal too, the leadership wanted to broaden the political base through the panchayats, but panchayats were also to become important agencies for land reform and poverty alleviation programmes that the government undertook (Ghosh and Kumar, 2003; Tornquist, 1992; Westergaard, 1992). Panchayati raj initiatives in Karnataka and West Bengal developed 'models' (discussed in greater detail in the next chapter) which, apart from the gains made in these two states, would influence the shape of panchayati raj across India. And, during the 1980s, one of the reasons why support for panchayati raj gained ground was that the West Bengal and Karnataka initiatives were considered successes (Mathew, 1996).

THE 'NEED' FOR DECENTRALIZATION

Though a concrete initiative of the central government *vis-à-vis* decentralization was not visible until 1989, from the mid-1980s onwards, several policy-makers as well as experts who advised and critiqued government, began to see panchayati raj as a solution to the problems of rural development and poverty alleviation, and the 'need' for decentralization was recorded consistently in various government reports. This burgeoning support needs to be viewed against the exacerbating problems within the state, and the difficulties these created, described by Atul Kohli as the 'crisis of governability', leading to 'a steadily widening gap between institutional capacities and socio-economic problems' (Kohli, 1991: 384). Centralization and deinstitutionalization, on the one hand, and the increasing proclivity for patronage dispensation and rent seeking, on the other, reduced the capacity of the state to deliver effectively as per policy goals. This was visible sharply in the case of the unsatisfactory outcomes of anti-poverty programmes, and it was in this context that panchayats began to be discussed and promoted once again.

From the late-1970s onwards, the central government initiated new programmes targeted at the poor. These included the Integrated Rural Development Programme (IRDP) that provided productive assets through loans to those living below the poverty line, and the employment generating Food for Work Programme, which was later merged into the National Rural Employment Programme and the Rural Landless Employment Guarantee Programme[10] (Dantwala and Barmeda, 1985). The involvement of PRIs in these programmes, though it varied among states, was in general quite limited (GoI, 1980; GoI, 1985a). In fact, in 1980, a new agency at the district level, i.e. the District Rural Development Agency (DRDA), headed by a senior administrator and staffed by departmental employees, was set up to implement these programmes (Khanna, 1999).

The anti-poverty programmes, especially IRDP, the largest of such programmes, did not deliver as expected. There has been a great deal of debate about the conceptualization and design of specific programmes, but some common problems, important from the point of view of PRIs, were visible across all programmes. Evaluation studies of IRDP by the central government as well as studies by scholars showed it to be implemented extremely mechanically, without adequate attention to the context. Additionally, there was a substantial 'leakage' of benefits that did not reach the poorest sections of society (Bagchee, 1987; Dreze, 1990; GoI, 1985a, 1985b; Swaminathan, 1990). As a result, ideas about local-specific, decentralized planning, to design context-specific initiatives on the one hand, and the involvement of popular institutions to reduce corruption on the other, were voiced frequently. PRIs were seen as the appropriate institutional mechanism in this context. For instance, the Working Group on District Planning that gave its report in 1984 said:

> (T)he mechanisms for planning and decision-making should descend to levels where they can come to grips with the people and their problems, and where they can organize an appropriate package of programme activities with a measure of community support. (GoI, 1984: 22)

And so did the Committee to Review the Existing Administrative Arrangements for Rural Development and Poverty Alleviation Programmes (CAARD) comment:

> While central and state levels are important to determine broad social priorities, allocation of resources and ensuring technical support in terms of qualified personnel and resources, to carry central and state level planning for rural

development beyond this stage is unwise, unrealistic, wasteful and disastrous. (GoI, 1985: 12).

In the Seventh Five Year Plan, one of the causes for the wrong selection of beneficiaries for IRDP identified was the 'non-involvement of people's institutions in the survey and selection process' (GoI, 1985a: 53). And the document also said that that 'wherever this (involvement of PRIs) has happened, the quality of programme implementation has been decidedly better' (1985a: 64). Panchayats were now seen as a solution to the problem of delivering as per policy goals.

THE 64TH CONSTITUTIONAL AMENDMENT BILL

This growing 'need' for decentralization translated into a major central government initiative in 1989 in the form of the 64th Constitutional Amendment Bill, which sought to give constitutional status to panchayats and make elections to panchayats mandatory. This bill was in tune with the long-term policy considerations noted above and can broadly be placed in an overall agenda of the then Congress government to reform governance. Initially, the new government, formed in 1984, had sought to develop a new administrative style by inculcating new values of efficiency, technology and, speedy delivery of services, but the opposition to several of these measures had mounted (Dwivedi, Jain and Dua, 1989; Hewitt 1989). Around the same time, the Singhvi Committee, set up in 1986, had recommended that local self-government be constitutionally recognized and protected through the inclusion of a new chapter in the Constitution (GoI, 1986). Nearly four years later, Prime Minister Rajiv Gandhi, while introducing the 64th Constitutional Amendment Bill, admitted that though the government had initially looked for managerial solutions, it had now shifted to systemic ones, i.e. panchayati raj. In his speeches in the Lok Sabha and Rajya Sabha, Rajiv Gandhi emphasized the importance of panchayats in diminishing the role of 'power brokers' and in ending corruption (Lok Sabha Debates, 15.5.89, 8.9.89, 10.8.89; Rajya Sabha Debates 14.8.89, 16.8.89, 13.10.89)

There is another context in which the 64th Constitutional Amendment Bill needs to be situated. The increased influence of agricultural producers, i.e. the rich and middle-peasants, on public policy has been noted. This influence intensified during Janata rule with the mobilization of thousands of peasant rallies. Importantly, in these peasant rallies the battle cry of 'Bharat (rural India) *versus* India (urban India)'—

and not tenants *versus* landlords—made its entry into Indian politics, drawing a new cleavage between the peasantry as a whole on the one hand, and the urban-industrial interests on the other. At the same time, as the vast majority of the population remained rural, it was extremely difficult for any government to ignore the interests of the rural sector (Lindberg, 1992; Varshney, 1995). A new twist in the Bharat *versus* India divide developed in the mid-1980s as the government sought to reduce state controls on industry, and reduce import barriers, i.e. liberalize the economy. Not only did this move attract considerable opposition within the ruling party, but in the Bharat *versus* India cleavage, liberalization came to be seen as a measure that favoured the urban elite. The government acquired a pro-rich and pro-urban image and began to lose support among the middle and poor peasants. Subsequently, liberalization policies were slowed (Kohli, 1989). And, the 64th Constitutional Amendment Bill was introduced months before the ruling party faced a tough state election in 1989. In this light, the new thrust towards panchayati raj, along with the bid to improve governance, can also be seen as a balancing act in favour of rural producers, by sharing power with them. What is important here for future reference is that, when economic liberalization did take place in 1991, in the Bharat *versus* India dynamic, liberalization policies had come to be viewed as anti-Bharat, while panchayati raj appeared as a pro-Bharat solution.

Though no political party opposed decentralization *per se*, the proposed constitutional amendment lost bipartisan support in parliament. This happened as it got tangled in the growing 'centre *versus* states' confrontation. It has been noted above that during the early 1970s, states had come to be increasingly subordinated to Delhi. But the Janata rule had the effect of stimulating locally dominant groups, and enhancing the status of regional governments, even though the Janata government flatly ruled out the idea of more powers to the states. Subsequently, as they came to power in several states, the influence of regional parties increased. Through the 1980s, the state governments from non-Congress states were increasingly confrontationist, the conflict around centre–state relations and the nature of the federal polity sharpened and the issue of the 'encroachment of the centre into state autonomy' became a key point for political disagreement. This led to the appointment of the Sarkaria Commission in 1982 to re-examine centre–state relations (Corbridge and Harris, 2000; Ray, 1988 and 1982; Rudolph and Rudolph, 1987; Sen Gupta, 1988).

The proposal for the constitutional amendment was seen as an infringement by the centre on the domain of the states and the suspicion was that the central government was motivated by the prospect of creating a more pliable instrument of government through a nationally constituted prefecture of local governments, as compared to the more assertive state chief ministers. Two provisions in the bill, that it empowered the Comptroller and Auditor General of India, a central government agency, to prescribe the form of auditing and accounting of panchayat funds, and gave the National Election Commission, rather than State Election Commissions, supervisory powers over panchayat elections, were seen as strengthening central government control over the states (Lok Sabha Debates, 15.5.89, 8.9.89, 10.8.89; Rajya Sabha Debates, 14.8.89, 16.8.89; Mitra 2001).[11] And in fact, panchayati raj, without a significant restructuring of powers between the state and the centre, did imply a diminished role of state governments, while the central government's role and authority remained intact.[12] These perceptions were strengthened as the bill was preceded by a series of workshops with bureaucrats, i.e. District Magistrates (DMs), and the report based on this workshop recommended giving the DM an important role in the zilla parishad. The provision of 'district government' proposed in the bill was seen as an attempt by the centre to encroach on the states and an assertion of bureaucratic power (Chandrashekhar, 1989; Lok Sabha Debates, 15.5.89, 8.9.89, 10.8.89; Rajya Sabha Debates, 14.8.89, 16.8.89; Dhawan, 1989; Ghosh, 1989). As it was, much of the criticism centred on the perceived motives of the bill rather than its provisions *per se*, as some critics themselves admitted (Chandrashekhar, 1989; Ghosh, 1989).

Though the 64th Constitutional Amendment Bill was not approved by the parliament, its underlying thrust, to address the problem of institutional functioning through panchayati raj, was not lost. Moreover, decentralization was now seen as a 'popular' measure, as can be seen from the fact that in the parliament debates as well as elsewhere, the proposed bill was criticized as a gimmick, sprung in the election year, with the criticism that the ruling party aimed to take 'credit' for decentralization (Lok Sabha debates, 15.5.89, 8.9.89, 10.8.89; Rajya Sabha Debates, 14.8.89, 16.8.89, 13.10.89; Dhawan, 1989; Ghosh, 1989). The popularity of decentralization lay in the promise of sharing power with the rural sector as well as the reform of government by shifting power away from its existing centre. Panchayati raj had come a long way from the days of the Balwantray Mehta Committee report.

As against PRIs as agents of a relatively unproblematic state seeking societal participation in the rural development agenda, the panchayats were now seen as a solution to the problems in state functioning itself, visible in the ineffectiveness of anti-poverty programmes and corruption.

THE 73RD CONSTITUTIONAL AMENDMENT

The process of giving constitutional status to panchayats was halted only temporarily. After the Congress lost in the national elections, the new National Front government introduced another bill in 1990. It too was based on the principle of strengthening the panchayat structure, though it differed in some features from the previous legislation. However, as the government changed before the procedural requirements could be completed, it died a natural death. But a new Constitutional Amendment Bill was introduced again by a minority-led Congress government in September 1991. After a preliminary discussion in the Lok Sabha, it was referred to a select committee of parliament. The bill came up for discussion again in December 1992, and the 73rd Constitutional Amendment Act was passed by both houses of parliament with near consensus. It was ratified by the state governments in 1993, and following the constitutional amendment, states also passed conformity legislations.

In the short period between the introduction of the constitutional amendment bill that did not go through in 1989, and the one that did in 1992, remarkable changes had come about in Indian economic policy. In June 1991, the various pressures that had been building up in favour of economic reform came to a head. Dealing with a foreign exchange reserve crisis, the central government sought a structural adjustment loan from the International Monetary Fund, and put in place a substantial shift in India's economic policies towards greater liberalization of the economy. The main features of the new policy regime comprised a reduction in number of sectors reserved for public investment, dismantling of the 'license-permit' raj, reduction of import barriers and a tight monetary policy. Importantly, there was a sharp cutback in the government's budget, with the target of bringing down the fiscal deficit from 8.4 per cent of the GDP in 1990–1 to 5 per cent (Jha, 2002; Nayak, 1992; Patnaik et al., 1996).

It can be hypothesized that these developments added a sense of urgency to the pressure building up for panchayati raj. Important here was the apprehension that with economic reforms, living standards of the poorest sections of society would decline. This concern was visible not only among a part of the intelligentsia (e.g. EPW 1992; Basu, 1991; Ghosh, 1992; Nayak, 1992), but was a live point of contention in a vibrant, competitive democracy.[12] Additionally, from the point of view of the ruling party, the sequence that had played out in 1989, i.e. the fact that economic liberalization, with its pro-urban, pro-rich tag could cut away at popular support in the rural areas, could hardly have been missed. At the same time, with the fiscal disciplinary measures in 1991, policy measures that had so far been used to appease the rural sector, i.e. subsidies, poverty alleviation and unemployment schemes were not possible, and this implied a significant change of political strategy (Bijukumar, 2004; Chibber, 1995; Jenkins, 1995).

These pressures pushed the panchayati raj agenda. Manor (1995) has argued that the Indian political elite were concerned about the overall impact of the reforms, and aimed to manage reforms so as to retain the opportunity to distribute resources in some areas to gain political support from important interests, and also redistribute resources in ways that aid the poor and play a significant role in development. To this must be added the wide international endorsement of decentralization that we have noted in the previous chapter, which can only have strengthened the case. To sum up, in the post-economic reforms scenario, the need for addressing the rural sector became urgent, and previous strategies in terms of subsidies and government programmes could not be undertaken. Panchayati raj, which had been seen as a solution to the problems caused by the deterioration of state institutions, became a desirable as well as doable option.

The 73rd Constitutional Amendment ensures the existence of panchayats by making it mandatory for state governments to hold local government elections every five years. Though even in the post-constitutional amendment scenario, panchayat elections were stalled in some states[14] (GoI, 2001), the pressure of the constitutional amendment and judicial intervention make this nearly impossible for any length of time. This is a significant shift, as in the past it has been possible to whittle down even robust panchayati raj systems through the simple postponement of elections.

The amendment also lays down a few broad features of the structure of panchayati raj, but most of the major decisions are to be taken by state governments. Panchayats at three tiers, at the village, sub-district and district level, are mandatory and gram sabhas are recognized as part of panchayati raj. All seats to the PRIs are to be filled up by direct elections, with seats for SC and ST representatives reserved in proportion to their population, and a minimum of one-third seats reserved for women. The same reservation applies to chairpersons of PRIs too. The 73rd Constitutional Amendment has added an Eleventh Schedule to the Constitution, which suggests a list of functions that can be devolved to PRIs. But the extent to which devolution to panchayats actually takes place is up to the state governments. The governor of every state is obliged to constitute a Finance Commission every five years to review the financial position of the panchayats and make recommendations to the state government, but final decisions are to be taken by state governments.[15]

Thus, while PRIs will exist, their actual empowerment remains an open question. Though the national leadership across political parties has supported the constitutional amendment, there is no guarantee that the state governments will, in fact, devolve substantial powers and functions to PRIs, and in several states, there is little actual change in the post-constitutional amendment scenario (GoI, 2001a) after more than a decade. Backtracking is also possible in several other ways. Some features of a few state legislations are not in consonance with the constitutional amendment. Additionally, both the central as well as state governments have continued to set up implementation structures that bypass the panchayats (Buch, 2004; GoI, 2001).

But with all these problems, the constitutional amendment has changed the scenario substantially. In the past, where substantial decentralization has taken place, subsequent reversals have been frequent. For instance, there are clear instances of reversal of the process of empowerment of panchayats in three of the four successful decentralizing states mentioned above (the exception here is West Bengal, where the same political party has been in power for a long time) (Chandrashekhar, 1993; Ghosh and Kumar 2003). This is not surprising, given that panchayati raj has been driven by short-term political concerns as well as longer-term strategies. However, a major strategy of reversing panchayati raj initiatives, i.e. the postponement of elections, is nearly impossible.

Disempowerment of PRIs is possible in other ways such as reduction of functions and finances, but even this is likely to become difficult over the long term. With recurrent panchayat elections, a substantial number of elected PRI representatives will come into existence, and may form pressure groups of their own. At the same time, decentralization remains a popular idea, so that it is likely to be promoted not only by political leaders who believe in it or see it as a way of improving governance, but also by those looking for electoral gains, as an offer to share power is likely to be a vote getter. Parallelly, once substantial decentralization takes place, recentralization may be increasingly difficult and risky, as it is likely to be opposed by PRI representatives, who can no longer be made to disappear by withholding elections. A broad trend towards decentralization, with variations across states, though not assured, seems likely.

NOTES

1. There is evidence of the existence of 'sabhas' (village assemblies) as well as 'gramins' (assemblies of senior citizens) as early as 1200 BC, which disappeared during the Vedic period. Though in the national movement villages were often construed as having been 'governed' by 'elected panchayats' in pre-colonial India, in actual fact, during this long historical era, the panchayat as a phenomenon was neither universal nor clearly institutionalized. The actual hub of corporate activities was the social corporation, i.e. the caste. Village assemblies appeared in south India in the earlier parts of the Christian era, but had to contend with the narrower and stronger identities of caste. Moreover, though the village was a unit of administration, and enjoyed a degree of autonomy from the centralized state, the administrative structure at the village level was dominated by the village headman, appointed by centralized authorities. Such 'self-government' as existed in villages was governed by religion and custom, and by and large played second fiddle to caste associations as well as village headmen appointed by centralized authorities (Mathew, 1996; Shiviah et al., 1976).
2. In the period immediately after Independence several state governments enacted legislations that focused on strengthening village panchayats, as a consequence of Gandhian influence and concerns for socio-economic improvement and development (Shiviah et al., 1976).
3. The CD project, begun in 1952, was supported by the Ford Foundation, and was modelled after experiments in Marthandam, Sariniketan, Baroda, Etawah and Nilokheri. The National Extension Service was an organizational structure recommended by the Grow More Food Committee and was launched a year after the CD projects began. Though the goals of the two were stated to be identical, the CD projects involved intensive activities over three years, while the NES intended to cover the entire country within a short period of time (Mishra, 1981; Shiviah et al., 1976).

4. In fact, three tiers of panchayats linked to each other were introduced in Central Provinces and Berar (Madhya Pradesh) in 1948. This is mentioned in the Balwantray Mehta Committee report.
5. The Second Five Year Plan emphasized not only the establishment of a statutory body in every village, but also a well-organized democratic structure of administration at the district or sub-district level, linked organically to the village panchayat. These democratic structures were seen as important mechanisms for implementing the CD projects as also land reform and cooperatization (GoI, 1956).
6. However, the Balwantray Mehta Committee, in its report, admitted, that in some states, the district rather than the block could be the 'nodal' or most important panchayati raj tier.
7. The Naik Committee of Maharashtra, giving its report in 1961, differed from the Balwantray Mehta Committee. It argued for direct elections to ZPs, as much of the management of schemes was done by district officials and only at that level was the required qualified staff available (Vankatangaiya and Pattabhiram, 1969).
8. Panchayat elections were postponed in Maharashtra in 1984 and 1987, largely because of infighting within the Congress party and then held again only in 1992 (Ghosh and Kumar, 2003).
9. The president's assent to the Janata Party bill was delayed. The party then waited for an advantageous moment to hold the elections. When panchayat elections were held in 1987, the Janata Party secured a clear majority in 11 out of 15 districts. In 1993, the new panchayati raj legislation changed many provisions of the earlier bill (Chandrashekhar, 1993; Nair, 1987; Ray, 1987).
10. IRDP provided productive assets to persons living below the poverty line to enable them to start self-employment ventures. The assets were provided through a mix of government subsidies and institutional (bank) credit.
11. A similar dynamic has been illustrated in the case of Bolivia in 1994 and 1995, when the central government strengthened municipal governments, but did not share political power with the regional governments, which posed a greater challenge to centralized power. This allowed the central government to appear innovative and creative at the grassroots while undercutting the power of the regional elites (Slater, 2000).
12. The Asoka Mehta Committee had noted that there were many arguments for devolution of power from the centre to the states, but did not consider that this comprised its terms of reference. But it was willing to say that 'the transfer of substantial quantum of powers from the state governments to the local level has implications for distribution of powers between the Union and the states' (GoI, 1978: 34). E.M.S. Namboodiripad, a member

of the Committee, went further in his dissenting note, arguing strongly for a reconsideration of centre-state relations.

13. And, in fact, the thin sample survey of the National Sample Survey Organization showed that immediately after the reforms, in 1992, rural poverty shot up by 25 per cent, and by some estimates more. Though several economists attribute this rise to bad weather conditions, others maintain that economic reforms affect the rural sector directly because of the curtailment of government expenditure (Maheshwari, 2002).
14. In Bihar panchayat elections were held eight years after the constitutional amendment. In UP and Orissa panchayat elections were held after court intervention (GoI, 2001).
15. The 1992 constitutional amendment excluded areas in the Fifth and Sixth Schedules of the constitution (i.e. areas inhabited by STs). Subsequently, the special requirements of these areas were considered by the Bhuria Committee, and the Panchayats (Extension to the Scheduled Areas) Act, 1996 (PESA) was passed.

CHAPTER 3

Institutional Design

With the 73rd Constitutional Amendment, the focus of panchayati raj has shifted away from the question of the mere existence of PRIs, i.e. regular elections, to what may broadly be seen as the issue of institutional design, which forms the 'content' of panchayati raj policies. There are two aspects to this issue. The first is the extent of devolution from state governments to PRIs in terms of functions, powers, funds, the autonomy enjoyed by PRIs, and so on, or the degree to which PRIs actually function as local government, determining their own agenda and implementing it. The second aspect concerns the structure and processes within the PRIs, including the nature of political representation, administrative structure, technical capacities, processes of planning, decision-making and participation. As policy decisions regarding both these aspects are taken, state governments articulate their vision of local government.

In the post-constitutional amendment scenario, the question of institutional design is critical for the whole PRI project, and needs to be studied and deliberated on intensively. The extent of actual decentralization in a state has to be gauged from the details of the devolution of functions, functionaries and finances. Devolution on paper, but not in practice, is possible with an imprecise or vague articulation of functions, as well as a lack of administrative back up and finances. It is in this respect that some states have decentralized more successfully than others, i.e. the articulation of the functions to be performed by the PRIs has been clearer, and requisite funds and personnel have been made available to a greater degree. At the same time, there can be, and as the following discussion will show, have been, at various points of time in different states, important differences in the vision of the role, institutional structures and processes of PRIs.

The question of the institutional or organizational design of PRIs has been discussed to a fair degree in Indian policy since Independence, and in this chapter the major threads of this discussion are summarized. Different ideas about institutional design have arisen as governments have promoted PRIs for varying reasons, and some such broad ideas have already been highlighted in the previous chapter. For example, in the 1950s, as the Balwantray Mehta Committee linked PRIs to rural development, it suggested the empowerment of the block-level panchayat supported by a development administration bureaucracy, in contrast to the focus on the village panchayats with legislative, administrative and judicial functions in the communitarian democracy envisaged by Gandhians. While such overall policy goals have formed an important basis for recommendations with respect to institutional processes and structures, the need to create *effective* institutions has also played an important role. Twenty years after the Balwantray Mehta Committee, as the Asoka Mehta Committee suggested the empowerment of district level PRIs, it was influenced by the success of the Maharashtra and Gujarat panchayati raj patterns. In other words, ideas about institutional design have developed in the context of overall policy goals as well as the effectiveness of various organizational designs as these have been tried out.

As the previous chapter shows, panchayati raj policies have unfolded at the level of the central as well as state governments in India. Undoubtedly, central government policy, and its recommendations *vis-à-vis* institutional design, has been highly influential. For example, most state governments adopted the three-tier structure of PRIs, making the block level pivotal, as per the recommendation of the Balwantray Mehta Committee in the late-1950s and early-1960s. And in 1993, with the 73rd Constitutional Amendment, some aspects of institutional design, e.g. a three-tier PRI structure and representation of SC, ST and women candidates have become mandatory across the country. But at the same time, central policy has been influenced considerably by the successes of different states. In particular, the innovations and experiences of four states, i.e. Maharashtra, Gujarat, West Bengal and Karnataka, where panchayati raj has enjoyed long spells of success, have influenced central policy significantly. A fifth such influential state, Kerala, appears to be emerging in the post-73rd Amendment scenario. While other state governments have also made important headways, particularly Andhra Pradesh, Jammu & Kashmir and Madhya Pradesh, the experience of these five states has been discussed the most, and is easily accessible in various reports and studies.

The discussion in this chapter is based on considerations that have emerged in national as well as state policy, with a focus on the four preconstitutional amendment successes, i.e. Maharashtra, Gujarat, West Bengal and Karnataka, while the extremely important experience of Kerala is examined in much greater detail in the next four chapters. The best performing states have been selected because the most influential ideas about institutional design have come from the experience of these states. Moreover, insights about institutional or organizational design become available only in cases where individual state governments have been most serious and committed about decentralization. Where a basic commitment to decentralization has been lacking, ideas about institutional design have not developed either, and there is little to explore and understand. Consequently, in examining the question of institutional design in the above-mentioned four states, the focus is on points of time when panchayati raj has been at its zenith. The references in this chapter to panchayati raj in Maharashtra and Gujarat pertain to the 1960s, in West Bengal to the late 1970s onwards, and in Karnataka during the late 1980s. While such a focus does not present a 'true' picture of panchayati raj in these states over time, it does provide the richest material available *vis-à-vis* policy considerations about institutional design.

While considering institutional design, an important background that needs to be kept in view is the nature of the Indian federal structure, which is characterized by a strong centre. The import of this aspect of the Indian polity for panchayati raj can be gauged from the fact that the 64th Constitutional Amendment Bill of 1989 lost bi-partisan support in parliament because it was perceived as an infringement by the central government on the domain of state governments. There have been strong arguments that unless the centre devolves more power to the states, panchayati raj will remain ineffective, as the polity will remain fundamentally centralized (Kothari, 1990; Mukharji, 1996). Moreover, decentralization in the form of panchayati raj, without a parallel devolution from the central government to state government, implies a decline in the importance of state-level actors, and the balance of power tilts towards the centre. Panchayati raj continues to be placed in this asymmetry.

Another point to be noted is that thrusts towards panchayati raj have, in general, remained fairly tentative. A majority of the state governments have simply not decentralized substantially. Where substantial decentralization has taken place, it has usually been followed by at least some reversals. As a result, panchayati raj has, by and large, been seen as a temporary development, liable to be reversed or weakened at any point of time. This tentativeness has co-existed in a context of the continuity and seeming permanence of a highly centralized bureaucracy on the one hand and the practice of centralized planning whereby funding is made available through schemes that stipulate predefined activities and costs, on the other. Questions about the institutional design of panchayats have been posed in this setting and the overall focus has been of fitting in panchayats, which may or may not last, in a more permanent bureaucratic structure and planning scenario of centrally designed schemes.

The considerations in Indian policy regarding institutional design may be divided in seven broad areas, i.e. what the role or functions of PRIs should be, how many tiers of PRIs should exist and which should be the nodal tier, the political structure and processes, the bureaucracy, people's participation, finances and the issues of control and accountability. Below, the major ideas and debates regarding each of these in policy discussions and critiques are summarized briefly.

ROLE AND FUNCTIONS

The role of local government as envisaged during colonial rule was largely that of discharging functions such as village sanitation, construction of minor roads, building and management of schools and disposal of petty civil and criminal cases. On the other hand, in the Gandhian vision, the village panchayat was to be a basic unit of the polity, combining legislative, executive and judicial functions. But as the previous chapter shows, this idea was marginalized early, and with the Balwantray Mehta Committee report, socio-economic development in the countryside was planted firmly as the central aim of the PRI project. In subsequent reports and other policy documents, the primacy of rural development in panchayat functions has remained, while regulatory functions such as law and order and revenue administration, as well as judicial functions, have been kept outside the sphere of panchayats. In fact, as E.M.S. Namboodiripad argued in his dissenting note in the Asoka Mehta Committee report, the very terms of reference of the various committees that have looked into panchayati raj have been such that PRIs have been viewed in the context of socio-economic development.

As the Asoka Mehta Committee considered the role and functions of PRIs, it recommended keeping law and order and regulatory functions outside their purview, arguing that PRIs themselves were sites where social tensions, arising in a fast changing society, were enacted.[1] Namboodiripad in his dissenting note to the report argued that integrated powers and responsibilities be conferred on PRIs with no demarcation between regulatory and developmental functions, though even he was willing to admit that there could be reason for keeping law and order with the state government (GoI, 1978). The idea of entrusting judicial functions to PRIs was similarly marginalized. During the late-1950s and early-1960s, 'nyaya panchayats', i.e. popular bodies that could dispense speedy justice, were established in several states, such as Gujarat, but were not successful (Vakil, 1977). The Asoka Mehta Committee did not favour dispensation of justice by PRIs, arguing that judicial work was performed better by qualified persons, possibly with some local assistance. Though ideas such as elected district governments with the district bureaucracy squarely under them, responsible for the totality of district governance, have continued to exist and be debated (Mukharji, 1996), the role of panchayats in regulatory functions has not really been a focal point in policy. In Indian policy, PRIs have emerged as institutions that perform civic and developmental functions, with a separate judiciary and a centralized bureaucracy in charge of regulatory functions.

The 73rd Constitutional Amendment retains this focus on socio-economic development and Article 243G specifically mentions the devolution of powers for the preparation of plans and implementation of schemes with respect to economic development and social justices. However, it also mentions PRIs 'as institutions of self-government'. In general, the reading has been that the Constitution *allows* the state governments to devolve functions other than development to PRIs, and sets a floor rather than a ceiling (GoI, 2001; Venugopal, 2001). The 73rd Constitutional Amendment includes an Eleventh Schedule to the Constitution, which lists 29 functions that state governments may devolve to the panchayats. These include, subjects pertaining to rural development such as agriculture, minor irrigation, animal husbandry, small-scale industries, etc.; social infrastructure such as schools and hospitals; poverty alleviation programmes, welfare of weaker sections, the public distribution system; and civic functions such as drinking water, markets and fairs, maintenance of community assets.

This Eleventh Schedule list is a suggested rather than a mandatory one, and basically, it is up to the state governments to decide upon the functions to be devolved. The devolution of functions is however, a complex task. Merely allotting 'sectors' to PRIs, such as 'school education' does not result in role clarity, as governments at various levels continue to perform different roles in a sector. For instance, in school education, so far the national and state governments have prescribed curricula, textbooks and the examination pattern while in some states, the (partial) administration of schools has been transferred to PRIs. Precision in the devolution of functions is important if it is to be given concrete shape. In practice however, in many state panchayat acts passed after the constitutional amendment, the subjects transferred have been listed broadly. The precise activities to be taken up at various levels of PRIs have not been defined, with the result that there is a lack of clarity about the role of PRIs (GoI, 2001a). Moreover, in several state acts, even though functions devolved to PRIs are listed, they can be changed as per the executive orders of the state government (GoI, 2001; Oomen, 1999).

A much discussed question in Indian policy has been the extent to which panchayats 'plan' or select their own projects and activities, as against merely implementing centrally designed schemes. The idea of 'area planning', i.e. the optimal allocation of resources as per the specific needs of an area, has existed since the First Five Year Plan, and has been reiterated in policy documents since (Sambrani, 1979), and the 74th Constitutional Amendment[2] makes the setting up of a district planning board mandatory, to consolidate rural as well as urban local body plans. However, several state governments have either not constituted such boards, or placed ministers and officials as chairpersons (GoI, 2001a), and centralized planning with its sectoral earmarking and central and state government schemes dominates the scenario. There are as many as 300–400 schemes of various departments at the district level, some of which have overlapping activities and some very meagre funds (GoI, 2001a). For funds that devolve to panchayats, budgets are fixed quite tightly under various 'heads'. Where discretion to panchayats has been provided to plan, the quantum of funds made available has been small, as in the case of Maharashtra and Gujarat (GoI, 2001).

All the four successful states mentioned above, i.e. Gujarat, Maharashtra, West Bengal and Karnataka, have delegated substantial powers of *implementation* of central and state schemes to panchayats. Usually, development schemes as well as institutions have been 'handed over' to PRIs (Inamdar, 1977; Nair, 1987; Ray, 1987; Vakil, 1977). But methodologies for formulating decentralized plans have been incompletely developed, and the planning exercise at the district level has comprised largely of desegregation of state schemes. In Karnataka, 'bottom-up' planning was attempted initially, but was not very successful, and departmental budgets were subsequently devolved in the form of pre-determined schemes with very limited flexibility (Crook and Manor, 1998). In general, bottom-up, area-specific planning has been much discussed, but not been visible in practice. Here, the Kerala experience, described in the following chapters, marks a significant departure.

Though reducing PRIs to mere implementation agencies has often been seen as under-cutting their planning and decision-making roles (GoI, 2001a), experience shows that 'implementation' of projects and management of institutions through panchayats can be quite critical. The West Bengal case illustrates this most clearly. In West Bengal, village panchayats have been deployed in an extremely creative manner to push pro-poor government policies. Village panchayats played an important role in land reform, i.e. in identifying ceiling surplus lands, forcibly vesting land, identifying probable beneficiaries, and mobilizing tenants to register. They also played an important role in agricultural development, particularly in distributing mini-kits of improved seeds, fertilizers, etc.,[3] in the distribution of various types of pensions and in mobilizing people to send their children to *anganwadis* (government-run nutrition and health centres as well as pre-schools), and for health-related programmes (Bhattacharya, 2002; Webster, 1996). Panchayats in West Bengal have played a critical role in making state policy more effective. However, a criticism of the panchayats in West Bengal has been that in the absence of untied funding and the supportive services of the local bureaucracy, they have not been allowed to grow as institutions of self-government, though changes have now been initiated on this front (Ghatak and Ghatak, 2002; Ghosh and Kumar, 2003).

It is important to note here that the line between 'policy', and 'planning' on the one hand and 'implementation' on the other, is less sharp than often portrayed. In fact, 'implementation' involves critical choices, just as 'planning' does. For example, the setting up of a school may be 'planned', i.e. it may be decided that resources would be allocated to this activity, but where the school is set up and how, may be seen as implementation issues. These involve choices as significant as the ones regarding the allocation of resources.

THE THREE TIERS

The three tiers of local government: at the village or a group of up to five villages, sub-district (usually the block) and district levels, have emerged in India in the context of the particular administrative structure of the country. Village-level administration, as well as village-level caste-based decision-making bodies, have had a long history in India. The district has been a critical administrative unit during as well as after colonial rule. For regulatory administration, the district is split into sub-division or sub-district, *taluk* and smaller units. In keeping with this administrative structure, during the colonial period, local bodies were set up in the form of village panchayats, along with district and *taluk* level boards. The block, coterminus with the *taluk* in some cases and smaller in others, became an important unit of development administration during the late-1950s and early-1960s, when the CD programme was taken up. Across the country, in terms of population, districts vary, blocks are somewhat more uniform and village panchayats vary a great deal. To talk of a village panchayat therefore, can be somewhat confusing, as it can embrace a unit of population of 200–1,000 or 20,000–30,000 in different states.

How many tiers of local government should exist and which tier should be the most important, has been debated intensively in panchayati raj policy. As noted earlier, the Balwantray Mehta Committee recommended a three-tier PRI structure, at the village, block and district level, with the block as the most important tier. Beginning with Rajasthan and Andhra Pradesh, this structure was adopted in several states in the late-1950s and early-1960s. However, the pattern of panchayati raj across the states was not uniform, and two tiers[4] and even single tiers[5] of PRIs continued to exist in some states (Ram Reddy, 1977). At this time, district councils were marginal in several states and even ceased to exist in others (Chaudhri, 1969; Shiviah et al., 1976). But in the two most successful panchayati raj initiatives that followed, i.e. Maharashtra and Gujarat, the importance of the administrative capacity that existed at the district-level was recognized, and district level panchayats or zilla parishads and not the block panchayats became the most important local government tier. In Maharashtra other tiers remained weak, while in Gujarat there was some devolution at all the three tiers (Ghosh and Kumar, 2003; Inamdar, 1977; Vakil, 1977). The Asoka Mehta Committee, learning from this experience, suggested that 'the first point of decentralization below the state level should be the district' (GoI, 1978: 37) because of the 'administrative and technical competence of the requisite calibre is available only at this level and not, at a lower, say, sub-divisional and block level' (GoI, 1978: 37).

The Asoka Mehta Committee also argued that most of the villages in India were too small to tackle anything other than traditional, attenuated civic and welfare functions and recommended the creation of panchayats at the level of the 'mandal', with a population of 10,000 to 15,000 comprising a central village and a number of hinterland villages. The central or larger villages would be 'growth centres', where appropriate physical and social facilities would be located to accelerate technological adaptation. The Asoka Mehta Committee recommended a two-tier system of the mandal and district PRIs as the basic structure of the panchayati raj system (GoI, 1978). This was broadly the pattern followed in Karnataka in 1987. The district council was the most important tier, and below it was the mandal panchayat. There was a *taluk* panchayat, but it was merely an advisory body. The gram sabha comprised the fourth tier[6] (Crook and Manor, 1998; Ray, 1987).

In later central government reports, the importance of the district as a key level for planning for rural development was reiterated. However, the empowerment of district-level local bodies often presents a dilemma as the district level politicians are viewed as, and often are, competitors of their state-level colleagues. The strengthening of the district-level local bodies shifts this power balance in favour of the former, with the result that it is often resisted by state-level politicians. The other tier recommended by the Asoka Mehta Committee, i.e. the mandal did not become a key unit except in Karnataka and Andhra Pradesh. Instead, the block continued to be an important centre for the implementation of several rural development programmes, especially anti-poverty programmes (GoI, 1979; GoI, 1984; GoI, 1985; GoI, 2001a). Both the district and the block derive their importance from the fact that they are critical administrative units where the field offices of various departments are located. To a large extent, the 'which tier' question has revolved around the creation of democratic structures at levels where administrative and technical capacity for socio-economic development exists.

The West Bengal experience, wherein greater attention was paid to the possibilities of people's participation through the village panchayat, added a new dimension to this question. The village panchayat, which has a population of around 10,000 in West Bengal (and is actually closer to the mandal panchayat envisaged by the Asoka Mehta Committee), became an important site for organizing people to implement land reform and poverty alleviation programmes (Webster, 1996). The importance of the village panchayat, and with it the gram sabha, was subsequently recognized in central policy too, especially in the context of anti-poverty programmes, as a consequence of the increased emphasis on people's participation (CAARD, 1985). Moreover, the fact that the village panchayat could be made directly accountable to the people was often seen as a solution to the problems of corruption and poor implementation. There is evidence that in West Bengal, the implementation of anti-poverty programmes through the village panchayats helped contain corruption (Ghatak and Ghatak, 2002; Swaminathan, 1990).

With the constitutional amendment, all states except those with vary small populations (below 20 lakh/2 million) have to put in place three tiers of panchayats. While panchayats at the village or a group of villages and district level are mandatory, the 'intermediate tier' can be either the block or the mandal. The imposition of a uniform three-tier structure across the country, which demanded changes in the existing panchayati raj systems in several states, was protested when the 64th Constitutional Amendment Bill was discussed. However, by the time the 73rd Constitutional Amendment was passed, political parties agreed to this provision.

At first sight, the 'which and how many tiers' question appears to have been decided. But in fact, while three tiers may be elected in all states, there is still considerable choice with the states as to the tier at which most functions and finances are devolved. It is possible to have three tiers of local government with a particular tier that is specially vibrant, as in the case of zilla parishads in Maharashtra, and another that is more or less inert, as in the case of the block level panchayat samitis in the same state. Even if the 'how many tiers' question is decided, the 'which tier' story is still unfolding. While the district continues to be recognized as an important tier, there is an increasing focus on the lowest tier, i.e. the village panchayat, as it provides a forum for participation. The principle of 'subsidiarity', which requires the assignment of functions to the *lowest* level of local government capable of delivering the service or performing the function more efficiently, has been stressed (GoI, 2001a; GoI, 2004).

POLITICAL STRUCTURE AND PROCESSES

The question of the political structure and processes of PRIs, as the later parts of this book will show more clearly, is of central importance. In post-independent Indian policy, the discussion in this area may be seen as having revolved around four topics, i.e. the role of political parties, direct or indirect elections to PRIs, the committee structure and reservation of seats. These are summarized below.

The Role of Political Parties

As shown in the previous chapter, in the 1950s and 1960s, participation of political parties in panchayats was feared. Instead, attempts were made to promote 'consensual' panchayats and several state legislations contained incentives for forming panchayats by consensus. But though political parties did not participate formally in panchayat elections, in practice, they took a great deal of interest in the election process and PRI representatives were usually aligned to one or the other political party (Ram Reddy, 1977). For instance, in Gujarat, though the stated policy was to keep politics out of panchayats, and the district as well as block representatives were elected indirectly, in practice, state political leaders kept in close touch with the panchayat leaders and allocation of funds to a particular panchayat too was affected by political considerations (Vakil, 1977). In the late-1970s, the Asoka Mehta Committee argued that political party participation would lead to clearer programme orientation, provide a constructive outlet for opposition parties and offer greater scope for weaker sections to avail opportunities offered by the political process (GoI, 1978: 52). West Bengal was the first state to hold panchayat elections with active participation of political parities. Subsequently, the presence of political parties has come to be an accepted feature of panchayat elections in most states, though some state acts still attempt to keep village panchayat elections non-political.

Direct *versus* Indirect Elections

The question of direct *versus* indirect elections has occupied considerable space in the panchayati raj debate. Initially, the suspicion of grassroots politics led to policy recommendations for direct elections to one tier only and indirect elections to the others, i.e. the village panchayat representatives being elected by the people, and in turn electing the block panchayat representatives, and the latter electing district representatives (GoI, 1958). However, experience during the 1960s and 1970s showed that indirect elections provided greater opportunity for manipulation of various kinds, including the use of bribery and force (Chaudhri, 1969; Gray, 1969; Shiviah et al., 1976). The Asoka Mehta Committee, given its view of competitive politics as the solution, rather than the problem, recommended direct elections to the mandal and district PRIs (GoI, 1978).

This issue was also debated considerably as the 73rd Constitutional

Amendment was discussed. In September 1991, when the 73rd Constitutional Amendment Bill was introduced in the Parliament, it had contained a provision for direct election at the village and intermediate tier, for panchayat representatives as well as panchayat presidents, and indirect elections at the district level. The Joint Parliamentary Committee (JPC), as it examined the bill, recommended direct elections of panchayat representatives at all levels, and this provision was retained in the bill that was finally approved by parliament. The JPC had recommended direct election of the village panchayat president by the people, and election by panchayat representatives of block and district panchayat presidents (Lok Sabha, 1992). The bill that was finally passed mandated the election of PRI presidents at the district and sub-district level by the PRI representatives, but left the election of the village panchayats president for the state governments to decide. After the conformity legislations following the constitutional amendment, some states, including Gujarat, have opted for the direct election of village panchayat presidents, while in several others, e.g., Maharashtra, Karnataka and West Bengal, village panchayat presidents are elected by panchayat representatives (GoI, 2001).

Direct election of the panchayat president by the people is sometimes interpreted as a move towards the type of local government that exists in some parts of the United States (and corresponds to its political system based on direct election of the president), whereby the directly elected mayor of a local body enjoys considerable power and autonomy (Smith, 1985). However, in policy discussions in India, strong reservations have been expressed regarding 'all-powerful' panchayat presidents, and the fact that such presidents may not enjoy the support of the majority of panchayat representatives, while the idea of the joint responsibility of the panchayat representatives has been quite consistently advocated (GoI, 1978; GoI, 2001). In fact, direct elections of the panchayat president have not been promoted with the intention of creating a powerful leader. This idea has arisen rather, in the context of the centralized character of political parties in India on the one hand, and the constant play of patronage and rent-seeking in Indian politics, on the other. Since the mid-1980s, as panchayati raj has been seen as a solution to the problems within the government, direct elections of panchayat presidents have been seen as a modality of escaping the problematic nature of Indian politics, undercutting its patronage-based and rent-seeking tendencies, by ensuring that meritorious rather than sponsored candidates hold office.

The Committee System

In India, wherever there has been substantial decentralization, the 'committee system' (a characteristic of the British local government system [Smith, 1985]), whereby a few councillors are appointed to a particular committee, such as on finance, agriculture or education,[7] which then takes on several functions in the allotted area, has been favoured (GoI, 2001a). Such committees were recommended by the Asoka Mehta Committee and created in Maharashtra, Gujarat and West Bengal (Bhattacharya, 2002; Inamdar, 1977; Vakil, 1977). In case of Maharashtra, Inamdar (1977) notes that the committees allowed all councillors to participate in the executive functions of the panchayat and prevented the monopolization of power (Inamdar, 1977). That the committee system is favoured is not surprising, given the constant fear of misuse of power by individuals, politicians as well as bureaucrats. It is expected to foster a decision-making process in which several persons are involved, thereby curtailing arbitrariness. At the district panchayat, district departmental heads are usually made secretaries to the committees pertaining to their departments, thus allowing a working relationship between the elected panchayat representatives and the bureaucracy to be forged.

Co-option and Reservation

In the initial days of panchayati raj, there were several 'co-opted' members to panchayats, i.e. individuals who did not fight elections, but were simply appointed as panchayat representatives. The co-options were of three types. The first was the co-option of 'weaker sections', i.e. members from SCs and STs and women. Such co-option allowed elites to select people who were friendly to them, or whom they could dominate. Realizing this, the Asoka Mehta Committee suggested reservations of seats for SCs and STs, whereby there would be elections to such seats but only persons from these social categories would be allowed to contest, in proportion to their share in the population.

In the constitutional amendment, not only has reservation for SCs and STs been ensured for PRI representatives as well as presidents, but a third of the seats have been reserved for women (something that has not been possible in national and state legislatures), as well. While no reservations are mandated for Other Backward Classes (OBCs), the constitutional amendment does not bar state governments from making such reservations. And in fact, a large number of states have opted for such reservations including Gujarat, Maharashtra and Karnataka (West Bengal has not). However, it has been difficult to devise a transparent and rational procedure for determining the population size of OBCs in different constituencies, and this has led to a great deal of litigation and delays in elections (GoI, 2001).

The second type of 'co-option' included powerful rather than powerless individuals, such as MPs, MLAs, chairpersons of cooperatives and persons with 'administrative experience'. The experience with members co-opted on grounds such as 'administrative experience' was not happy, as they were often not interested in becoming members of the lower tier PRIs, but wanted power and prestige at the higher tiers and several town-dwellers were thus co-opted (Chaudhri, 1969; Gray 1969). There is no provision for this type of co-option in the constitutional amendment. The inclusion of MPs and MLAs in PRIs, however, has been, and remains, a contested issue. One argument is that MPs and MLAs, if made members of PRIs tend to dominate or have not time for meetings. The contrasting argument is that they have valuable experience, and their membership in the PRI is therefore desirable (GoI, 1978). In the original constitutional amendment bill, it was proposed that MPs and MLAs would not have voting rights, but this provision was subsequently abandoned. The 73rd Amendment allows state governments to legislate to include MPs and MLAs as members of sub-district- and district-level PRIs, and such membership has been provided for in several state legislations. An exception here is Maharashtra, which has a long tradition of not having such representation in PRIs (GoI, 2001). Notably, the membership of MPs and MLAs can sometimes have important repercussions. For instance, in Karnataka, in the 1987 elections, the Congress had a majority in four districts, but because of the nomination of MPs and MLAs, two zilla parishads were dominated by the Janata Party (Ray, 1987).

The third type of co-option in PRIs is relatively unproblematic, and is concerned with creating inter-linkages among the various PRI tiers, whereby chairpersons of the lower tier PRIs can be co-opted to the higher tier PRIs (for instance, village panchayat chairpersons can be made members of the block panchayat). This provision has been considered important for securing an 'organic link' among the various tiers of PRIs, the logic being that such membership would help different tiers of PRIs in taking up activities that are mutually supportive, and enable higher tier PRIs to respond to the needs expressed by lower tier

PRIs. The 73rd Constitutional Amendment does not make such co-option mandatory, but enables states to incorporate it in their legislations.

THE BUREAUCRACY

As indicated at the beginning of this chapter, policy *vis-à-vis* panchayati raj has developed in the context of a perceived permanence of the bureaucracy, while panchayats have appeared as new, experimental or merely token institutions. The panchayati raj 'system' has consequently been influenced a great deal by the administrative structure, sometimes in the sense of fitting in with it, and at other times in terms of grappling with its problems. Consequently, it is important to understand some key characteristics of Indian administration in order to follow how panchayati raj policy has approached it.

Indian administration is organized along highly fragmented lines with numerous departments, so that the field administration is characterized by the presence of a plethora of agencies. For example, at the district level, the CAARD committee identified more than 20 major developmental agencies and departments (GoI, 1985) and another study identified 25 (Dayal, Mathur and Bhattacharya, 1974). The departmental system has been critiqued as having no locus of accountability, as various departments deal with highly fragmented aspects of the same issues. People have to contact officials of different departments for a single problem, and long delays are caused because the departmental tasks are interdependent, while the departmental activity is uncoordinated. Two specialist agencies that deal with rural development and poverty alleviation are the Block Development Offices at the block level and District Rural Development Agencies (DRDAs) at the district level, and these are controlled by the departments of rural development in the states.

Each field office of a government department maintains a distinct identity of its own and is closely linked to and controlled by its parent office at the state level, which allocates budgets and manages the departmental personnel. The state governments recruit the departmental officials and also 'post' them to field-level offices, so that an official can be shifted easily from one place to another. Such an arrangement makes way for the execution of top-down orders rather than the formulation of area-specific strategies for issues that emerge from the ground.

Field administration, with which PRIs are concerned most directly, is concentrated at the district-level (and hence the successful district level PRIs of Maharashtra, Gujarat and Karnataka). This means that at the block and village panchayat level, the implementation capacities are small. While the need to move the bureaucracy downwards from the district level is recognized (GoI, 2001a), such steps have not yet been taken in practice. The District Collector or District Magistrate (DM) has the responsibility of overall supervision at the district level. The DM belongs to the Indian Administrative Service (IAS), whose members are generalists recruited at the all-India level and allotted to the states. Though often perceived as all-powerful, the DM actually exercises fairly limited legal authority over the departments. The weakness of horizontal linkages across departments can be gleaned from the fact that at the district level coordinated personnel management, budget allocation and even an integrated report of all the activities of the district do not exist (Chaturvedi, 1989; Dayal et al., 1974).

In the context of an administrative system organized around a plethora of vertically integrated departments on the one hand, and the key role in socio-economic development envisaged for PRIs on the other, an important question in panchayati raj policy has been that of enabling PRIs, in terms of administrative and technical capacities, to undertake and coordinate development programmes as per area specific needs. The answer, as it emerged in the first phase panchayats of Gujarat and Maharashtra, has been to place district-level departmental heads under the day-to-day control of the zilla parishad and provide it with a chief executive officer (CEO), envisaged as the administrative head of all the officials of the zilla parishad (GoI, 1978; GoI, 1985). For instance, in Maharashtra, a CEO, an IAS officer, headed the zilla parishad and various departmental heads functioned as heads of departments of the zilla parishad (Inamdar, 1977).

The role of the DM *vis-à-vis* the district panchayat and the relative seniority of CEO *vis-à-vis* the DM are two issues that have been discussed a great deal in panchayati raj policy. The prestige enjoyed by the DM, and the overall coordinating role assigned to him, has sometimes led to the suggestions that the DM function as the CEO of the zilla panchayat. For example, in West Bengal, the DM functions as the executive officer of the zilla parishad (Ghosh and Kumar, 2003). However, the DM performs important regulatory and quasi-judicial roles, not the domain of PRIs, and is rarely able to devote adequate time to the zilla parishad. At the same time, to be able to coordinate several departments, an officer whose authority is accepted, is necessary.

Consequently, several policy documents contain the suggestion that an officer senior to the DM be made the CEO of the zilla parishad, while the role of the DM be made minimal (GoI, 1978; GoI, 1985; GoI 2001a). This model was attempted in Karnataka.

At the block level, the BDO is usually the CEO of the panchayat samiti. During the CD programme when Block Development Offices were established, technical personnel in these offices were officials on deputation from various line departments, and functioned under the dual control of the BDO as well as the departmental head. However, as the funds for CD projects dried up and sectoral plan schemes were implemented, the line departments gained importance and the position and status of the BDO were diminished, and even when anti-poverty programmes were conducted through the BDO, he could not regain his pre-eminent position (GOI, 1985). The BDO, consequently, is even less capable of coordinating the multiplicity of agencies than the district panchayat CEO (Dayal et al., 1974; Ray, 1985; Yugandhar and Raju, 1992). At the level of the village panchayat, there has in general been little attention to the development of a coherent administrative structure. The village panchayats have part-time or full-time 'panchayat secretaries', who are very junior employees.

The CEO model has not replaced vertical departmental control. Where PRIs are not empowered, the departmental system continues fairly untouched, and even where attempts have been made to empower the zilla parishad and provide it with a senior CEO, departmental officials have functioned under the 'dual control' of the state offices of their departments and the zilla parishad. This means that the officials remain employees of the state government, and their salaries, promotions, etc., as well as postings continue to be managed by the department, and only the monitoring of their day-to-day functioning shifts to the PRIs. Allowing PRIs to hire their own personnel, and have complete control over them, has by and large not been endorsed in policy documents (GoI, 1958; GoI, 1985) and there are no examples of PRIs hiring their own long-term technical staff. At best, PRIs have recruited clerks and helpers (Inamdar, 1977; Vakil, 1977).[8] Important here is the fact that conflict between the elected representatives and the bureaucracy is a prevalent feature of Indian governance, as the former tend to promote political and partisan interests over organizational ones, and the latter do not recognize adequately the legitimate role of the political representatives (Chaturvedi 1989; Dayal et al., 1974; Hargopal and Balaramulu, 1981). This in an important context in which complete control of PRIs over the bureaucracy has not been considered seriously in policy or practice.

Two other characteristics of the field bureaucracy, which have important repercussions for PRIs, need to be noted. First, as policies as well as schemes and programmes are formulated at the national and state levels, and are separated from 'implementation', which is the domain of the field offices, the usual task of the field bureaucracy is to implement pre-decided programmes in a fairly mechanical manner. In other words, the formulation of intelligent strategies to address particular problems and contexts, as envisaged in panchayati raj, has never been in the repertoire of the field bureaucracy. (In fact, in the 'regulatory' sectors such as law and order, problem solving at the field level is encouraged much more.) Consequently, the administrative personnel transferred to the PRIs have few of the skills needed for independent strategy and project formulation. Second, as noted in the previous chapter, patronage-based functioning and rent-seeking are common practices within the bureaucracy. In other word, the field bureaucracy, with whom the PRIs deal, lacks a professional character.

PARTICIPATION

The revival of panchayati raj in central policy began in the late-1950s as the Balwantray Mehta Committee noted the lack of popular initiative in CD projects. At this time, the creation of an organized democratic institutional structure, i.e. the three-tier PRIs, was seen as key. In contrast, the Gandhians pressed for a more direct role of the people. The Central Council for Local Self-Government, of which Jayaprakash Narayan was the chairperson, pressed for the statutory recognition of the gram sabha and for assigning it a role in formulating programmes and reviewing progress made by the village panchayat. However, the Diwakar Committee, which went into this issue in detail, though recommending the statutory recognition of the gram sabha, argued that 'the task of bringing the gram sabha to an effective position could be best achieved by strengthening the institution of the panchayat' (GoI, 1963: 20). The Diwakar Committee doubted if an all-village institution, i.e the gram sabha could be developed easily (at least in the short-term) in a community that was essentially divided. While it considered such an all-village institution to be desirable, it argued that 'To make its previous consent necessary for all decisions and actions of the panchayat . . . appears unnecessary and may act as a fetter . . .' (GoI,

1963: 46). This focus on representative institutions, i.e. the PRIs, rather than direct participation of the people, was visible in the Asoka Mehta Committee report too, which did not address the gram sabha in any significant way, apart from stating that it 'deserved encouragement' (GoI, 1978: 44), and that the village panchayat members meet the gram sabha at least twice in a year.

Since the mid-1980s, however, the emphasis on direct participation of the people was revived. In the context of anti-poverty programmes in the CAARD committee report, people's participation was seen as empowering the poor and leading to the formulation of more relevant and meaningful projects (GoI, 1985). The emphasis on participation has increased during the 1990s, and is in consonance with the growing stress on people's participation in development programmes, expected to improve project performance and counter the self-interest of bureaucrats and professionals, among international funding agencies, as well as the non-government sector[9] (2002). It also 'fits' as a solution to the problem of ensuring the accountability of the elected representatives and the bureaucracy (GoI, 2001a).

The constitutional amendment recognizes the gram sabha but leaves it to the state government to determine its role.[10] In state legislations that have followed, three broad, largely advisory, roles of the gram sabha have been envisaged. First, the gram sabha has been seen as a forum for the accountability of the village panchayat to the people, where accounts, reports, plans, etc., may be placed. Second, the gram sabha is expected to make suggestions regarding appropriate development activities. Finally, it is also expected to aid implementation of village panchayat activities by selecting beneficiaries for programmes and eliciting voluntary contribution for the activities of the village panchayat (Jain, 1997). These roles of the gram sabha are very similar to the ones that have been discussed in Indian policy in the past. However, in the state of Madhya Pradesh, the role of the gram sabha was expanded substantially in the late-1990s and 2000, by introducing a provision for 'recall' of panchayat representatives if initiated by the gram sabha, and making gram sabhas directly responsible for planning and taking decisions through their committees (Jafri and Singh, 2006; Manor, 2001).

Apart from the stress on the gram sabha, the emphasis on people's participation has influenced panchayati raj policy in several other ways too. In recent years, PRIs have been viewed as forums of participation, and consequently, the focus on the village panchayat, rather than higher tier PRIs has increased, as direct participation is possible only at the lowest tier. For example, the CAARD committee report states that 'It is . . . necessary to consider methods of improving local level participation in planning. . . . The Village Panchayats must be invigorated for this purpose in the first instance' (p. 29). The success of West Bengal during the late-1970s and early-1980s in making village panchayats forums through which people could participate to implement land reform policies and subsequently, anti-poverty programmes, has been an important concrete example. At the same time, the development of participatory processes within the village panchayat has received some attention, such as the development of a 'Village Planning Forum' suggested in the CAARD committee report. Intensive efforts in this direction in Kerala are outlined in the following chapters.

A significant development here has been the attempt to institutionalize participation through user-groups or self-help groups (SHGs) such as water users' associations, joint forest management committees, thrift and saving groups, etc., in several programmes and projects, especially those funded by international agencies, though the outreach of such organizations is as yet limited and not comparable to that of PRIs (Mathew, 1999; Narayan, 2003). Such associations are a heterogeneous lot, with varying goals and criteria for membership, such as being users of a common service, nomination by some administrative authority and in some cases, elections by those engaged in a particular activity. The relationship of such community-based associations to PRIs has been the subject of some debate. One argument has been that by establishing a system through which user-groups or SHGs and PRIs interface efficiently, it is possible to usher in people-centred development and empower the marginalized (Bandhopadhyaya et al., 2002). On the other hand, it has been argued that such groups, when created in parallel to the panchayati raj structure, can be used to promote various agendas and marginalize the PRIs (Powis, 2003). For instance, in several states PRIs have few funds, while such parallel organizations, because they are created as part of well-funded projects, are resource rich, and this effectively diminishes the role of the local village panchayat (Behar, 1999). Moreover, creating their own parallel community-based organizations, government departments can remain in charge, while at the same time involving the 'community'.

Yet another context in which the relationship of PRIs to civil society is situated is the non-government sector, which has grown rapidly in recent years. Since the mid-1980s, the involvement of the voluntary sector came to be viewed as a crucial part of the development process (Sheth and Sethi, 1996), and there are an estimated 1.2 million or 12 lakh NGOs in the country today (Srivastava and Tandon, 2005). In some cases, agencies that have established bases in particular areas see PRIs as competitors, while others see them as opportunities for new types of engagement with a more accessible state (Mathew, 1999). At the same time, several voluntary agencies are engaged in developing and supporting the PRIs.

FINANCE

In the federal public finance structure in India, local governments are very marginal players. For instance, in 2002–3, the total expenditure of local governments as a percentage of the combined expenditure of union, states and local bodies was a mere 4.7 per cent, and the tax revenue of local governments as a percentage of the combined tax revenue of state and local governments was as low as 1.6 per cent (Oommen, 2005). A mismatch between the functions devolved to the PRIs and the resources at their disposal has been, and remains, a persistent feature of panchayati raj in India. This means that the functional devolution to PRIs remains a devolution on paper, as they simply do not have the funds to carry out the tasks assigned.

This picture stands in sharp contrast to the recommendations of the Balwantray Mehta and Asoka Mehta Committees of routing a large proportion of development funds through the PRIs. The Asoka Mehta Committee had recommended increased financial independence of PRIs by the assignment of more taxes, recovery of fees for services such as lighting, sanitation, water supply, etc., by these bodies, as well as the creation of profitable assets such as shops and nurseries. The constitutional amendment provides for the constitution of a State Finance Commission (SFC) every five years to review and make recommendations on panchayat finances, and has also broadened the scope of the Central Finance Commission (CFC), so that it can recommend measures to augment the Consolidated Fund of the states and supplement resources to local bodies. At least two rounds of SFC reports and three CFC reports that concern themselves with panchayat finances have now become available.

The income of PRIs comprises the resources raised by them and financial transfers from the state government. The various sources of

PRI income include: taxes, tolls, fees, and so on, assessed and collected by the PRIs; taxes and cess collected by the state government and shared with the PRIs; income from assets owned by the panchayats such as ponds and markets; grants by state governments that could be for establishment or development works; and institutional finance and public contribution. The own revenues of panchayats tend to be quite small, usually less than 10 per cent of their requirements and grants from the state government remain the major source of panchayat income (GoI, 2001; Oommen, 1999). Traditionally, village panchayats have levied several types of taxes including house tax, professional tax, vehicle tax, etc., and they remain the strongest tier in terms of 'own revenue'. Higher-tier PRIs in most states have received funds for development schemes from the state governments, though in a few states they have also had the power to raise funds through taxes and other means (GoI, 1978; GoI, 2001a).

So far, the financial empowerment of PRIs has been attempted largely through the devolution of funds from the state level to the PRIs, rather than the strengthening of their own resources. The four successfully decentralizing states considered in this chapter, have transferred a larger share of state government grants for development to PRIs. In the post-constitutional amendment scenario, the tenth, eleventh and twelfth CFCs have recommended grants-in-aid to local governments from central government funds, to be spent on development works.[11] However, the amounts transferred in this way from the central government to the PRIs remain small. For instance, the amount recommended to be transferred to PRIs by the Twelfth Finance Commission was only 1.24 per cent of the shareable revenues and 0.9 per cent of the estimated gross revenue receipts of the centre (GoI, 2000; GoI, 2005; Oommen, 2005). Parallelly, SFCs have generally recommended more transfer of funds from the state government to PRIs, rather than ways of augmenting PRI resources. However, the reports have often not been taken seriously by state governments (Bandopadhyay, 2003; GoI, 2001a; GoI, 2000; GoI, 2005). By and large, with some exceptions, the devolution of funds continues to be meagre in the post constitutional amendment scenario too (Palharya, 2003).

The dependence of PRIs on state government grants is problematic in several ways. State government grants vary from year to year, and also with changes in state government policy (GoI, 2001a). Another argument has been that the provision of grants is detrimental to efficiency, which is possible only when fiscal resources for locally provided goods are raised from within the beneficiary space. It has been argued that assigning PRIs the responsibility for raising their own revenues will augment fiscal responsibility, giving them a stake in the cost effectiveness of expenditure, while the transfer of state government grants exacerbates low tax efforts by PRIs (Rajaraman, 2000; Rajaraman and Vashishtha, 2000).

However, the question of fiscal autonomy of PRIs is a complex one. Firstly, at present the majority of the taxes assigned to PRIs are not very productive of revenue and the tax-base is weak as well as narrow, though a reassignment of taxes to local government has often been recommended in policy. Secondly, several village panchayats are extremely small, and there is a high degree of poverty and unemployment in many areas. This limits the capacity to raise revenue locally. Finally, a critical issue here is that of 'horizontal imbalance', i.e. the fact that as villages, blocks and districts vary widely in terms of resource endowments, economic growth and revenue capacities, the fiscal autonomy of territorial sub-units exacerbates uneven development between richer and poorer areas. At the same time, a basic standard of minimum services needs to be provided uniformly, even in the poorest areas. Fiscal autonomy, consequently, needs to be matched with equalization grants to ensure that it does not increase inequity (Rani, 1999).

Added to the issues outlined above are serious problems of 'do-ability' regarding the question of PRIs raising their own resources. Though the case for PRIs raising their own revenue is often made, in fact, through the PRI literature and policy documents runs the theme that PRIs simply do not pay much attention to raising resources. Tax collection by PRIs has in general been meagre, and PRIs have often been content to see arrears accumulate (Chaudhri, 1969; Crook and Manor, 1998; GoI, 1978; Jha, 2002; Oommen, 1999). Two problems with respect to revenue raising efforts of PRIs are mentioned frequently. One, PRIs do not have the administrative wherewithal to raise revenue (GoI, 1978). In this context, it must be recalled that administrative functions, and consequently, the administrative personnel who collect land and other types of revenue have been kept separate from the PRIs. Second, the closeness of PRIs to the people does not make them appropriate agencies to collect taxes, especially where powerful actors are involved. For instance, in Karnataka, the mandal panchayats could not collect taxes from large-scale industrial units in their jurisdiction

(Oommen, 1999). Not surprisingly, most SFCs have left unchanged the existing tax powers of PRIs (Jha, 2002). Where wide powers have been given to PRIs, such as the power to collect 'any tax', it has rarely been used. PRIs perform better when the assignment of taxes to be collected is more specific (GoI, 1978).

Not only have the PRIs had very limited funds, but even for the funds that have been available to them, these bodies have had very limited decision-making powers regarding expenditure, as funds available through state government are tied to specific schemes (GoI, 2001a; Jha, 2002; Oommen, 1999). Where untied funds have been provided to PRIs, the quantum has been small. This has been the case even when the devolution of funds has been substantial. For instance, in 1988–9, the best year for Karnataka's decentralization, the share of the district sector out of the state plan was only 26 per cent and even out of this only 14 per cent was available to the district panchayats for their own planning (Oommen, 1999).

If the financial disbursements through the PRIs are to be increased, the question of an appropriate financial system acquires urgency. At present, most state government themselves often do not have accurate information about PRI finances, and PRIs lack trained accounts staff. Consequently, the Eleventh Finance Commission set apart separate funds to create a data base, and the Comptroller and Auditor General of India was given the responsibility of giving technical guidance for the proper maintenance of accounts in PRIs (GoI, 2000; GoI, 2001a; GoI, 2005). Some of the important problems that bog the panchayats include poor accounting procedures, delays and unpredictability of state grants, dishonouring of PRI cheques because of liquidity crises at the state level, and cumbersome procedures for disbursement (World Bank, 2004).

ACCOUNTABILITY

In panchayati raj policy, accountability has largely been seen as flowing upwards, with PRIs being accountable to the state government. This was a corollary of the system of centrally designed schemes, in which PRIs were seen as implementation agencies. In the 1950s and 1960s, a more general, institutional control of the state government over PRIs was also seen as essential for preventing malpractices. Even though such control led to the disempowerment of PRIs during the decades that followed, state governments have continued to retain the powers of audit, inspection, appeal, suspension of unlawful resolutions and in some circumstances, the removal and suspension of office-bearers (Inamdar, 1977; Vakil, 1977; Ram Reddy, 1977; Nair, 1987).

A crucial feature of this upward accountability is that it has not been mediated through independent or quasi-independent institutions, such as an independent ombudsman, insulated from state level political pressures. Instead, such powers have often been exercised by the bureaucracy, which in turn is controlled by the state governments. To some extent, the practice of higher-tier PRIs exercising control over lower-tier PRIs has also been in existence. For instance, in Karnataka in 1987, the district councils could approve annual budget estimates of the mandal panchayats, investigate their annual accounts and administration reports, intervene in the event of irregularities, and appoint and control their administrative staff (Crook and Manor, 1998).

At the same time, the idea of 'downward accountability' to the gram sabha has been in existence, though in practice, the gram sabha has rarely exercised its powers. In recent years, in line with the fact that PRIs are increasingly seen as a way of countering the problems of centralized government, accountability to the people rather than supervision by the state level has been stressed (GoI, 2001a). Notable in this direction have been the efforts of the Mazdoor Kisan Shakti Sangathan, an NGO working in Rajasthan, which initiated public hearings (*jan sunwais*), in which village residents demanded documents related to public works, many of which upon scrutiny were found to be fictitious or incomplete. This led to some village panchayat presidents paying up recoveries, complaints by the people to the district administration and institution of criminal cases (UNDP, 2000). In the same vein, a resolution made at a conference of panchayati raj ministers states '. . . . Social Audit Policies may be targeted at facilitation of popular participation in fighting corruption' (GoI, 2004: 34).

Such efforts notwithstanding, provisions to ensure accountability in PRIs remain sketchy. Gram sabhas do not generally hold panchayat representatives to account. There have been recommendations for setting up quasi-judicial bodies independent of state governments, such as the ombudsman to enquire into citizen complaints (GoI, 2001a), but these have not yet been implemented rigorously. Auditing of panchayat accounts, in spite of the initiatives of the CFCs in recent years, is variable across states and usually quite patchy.

INSTITUTIONAL DESIGN AND THE SOCIO-POLITICAL CONTEXT

In this chapter, we have examined ideas regarding institutional design in policy discussions and debates. As mentioned above, these ideas are rooted partly in the reasons for promoting panchayati raj, and partly in the perception of success achieved in various states. However, policies rarely play out exactly as planned, for the context in which they take shape has a powerful influence on the ultimate outcome. This is especially true of panchayati raj policy, which are concerned with creating and strengthening institutions at the grassroots.

In the following chapters, which comprise the second part of this book, we shall examine this dynamic in detail, in the specific context of Kerala. This scrutiny will encompass the socio-political context of the state, panchayati raj policies as well as the 'outcomes' as visible on the field. This analysis will help in grasping institutional and organizational dynamics *vis-à-vis* PRIs. Also, this analysis takes our investigation of institutional dynamics further in one more sense. Kerala's decentralization, promoted vigorously in the mid-1990s has been admired nationally as well as internationally, and has been wide in scope, entailing a substantial devolution of funds, matched by intensive attempts to develop meaningful processes. Consequently, it raises new questions about institutional design, and also provides new answers to old questions.

NOTES

1. The Asoka Mehta Committee did however suggest that regulatory functions related to development such as school inspection and enforcement of fishing or fodder rights be entrusted to the PRIs, and also suggested that the issue be reviewed after such time as when the PRIs had become established institutions.
2. The 74th Constitutional Amendment pertains mainly to urban local government.
3. Since the mid-1980s land reform activities in West Bengal have lost their vibrancy and the supply of mini-kits is small (Bhattacharya, 2002).
4. Karnataka, Himachal Pradesh, Orissa.
5. Jammu & Kashmir and Kerala.
6. This pattern was subsequently changed.
7. The committee system is a feature of the British local government. In the United States the chief executives of municipalities are directly elected and enjoy considerable executive powers (Smith, 1985).

8. Across the world, countries vary in the amount of leeway available to local government in changing local staff with a change of political regime. In many parts of UK staff is permanent, in France and Germany (and parts of UK and the USA), a small senior staff changes with the political party in power. In Latin America such changes are allowed for a larger number of posts. In African countries there is a fusion of the party and the state, i.e. the staff needs to belong to the political party in power (Cameron, 2003). In India, this question does not arise for rural local governments, as they simply do not hire their own staff.
9. Important influences here have been, Robert Putnam's work on 'social capital', that emphasizes the value of civic associations for socioeconomic development and Robert Chambers' work on Participatory Rural Appraisals about the use of local knowledge by indigenous people for the self-management of projects
10. In areas listed in the Fifth Schedule of the Constitution (where Scheduled Tribes live), Panchayats Extension to the Scheduled Areas Act 1996 makes the gram sabha far more central, giving it the power to approve plans and select beneficiaries for various programmes (Singh, 1999).
11. The eleventh CFC included a criteria of the extent of decentralization undertaken by a state government in determining the size of this grant, but the twelfth CFC did not use it.

PART 2

CHAPTER 4

Policies and Practices in Kerala

AN INTRODUCTION TO KERALA

The long, narrow coastline to the west has exposed Kerala to maritime influences from the earliest times, which has impacted its society and economy. Historically, the Hindu community in Kerala formed one of the most elaborate caste systems in India, but there are also substantial Christian and Muslim minorities in the state. Conversion to Christianity is reported to have begun as early as the fourth century. The Muslims of Kerala originated in the eighth and ninth centuries through the settlement of Arab converts trading with the Malabar. Among the Hindu community, traditionally, Namboodiri Brahmins have stood on the top of the hierarchy and Nairs have formed the land-owning caste. Ezhavas comprise a large proportion of agricultural labourers and small landowners. Syrian Christians, concentrated in central and northern Travancore and southern Cochin, make up about three quarters of the Christian population. A prosperous community, they are well represented in business, banking, government service and plantation agriculture. The Muslims are spread across the state, though in southern Malabar there is a high concentration of a poor Muslim community (Nossiter, 1982).

Kerala saw significant economic and social changes in the nineteenth and early twentieth centuries. Contact with the Arab and European world in search of pepper and spices had led to commercialization of agriculture and extensive cultivation of cash crops. The importance of the cash crops was boosted in the nineteenth century by a dramatic rise in agricultural prices, the improvement in transport facilities, and the investment of British capital on a significant scale, in plantations and in coir.[1] Subsequently, substantial changes came about in the traditional Kerala society in the early twentieth century, and these paved the way for significant political developments. Caste associations among the Nairs and Ezhavas promoted education, self-help and attempted to liberate the communities from superstition and taboo. The collapse of the traditional structure of rural society facilitated the growth of communist and socialist movements, and as the state of Kerala was formed in independent India, it saw the first communist party in the world to come to power through democratic elections in 1957 (Nossiter, 1982).

Post-Independence, successive governments have followed re-distributive and social welfare policies, which have culminated in the world famous 'Kerala model' of development, i.e. high human development indicators (HDIs) in a low economic growth context. In the beginning of the 1990s Kerala had the lowest population growth rate, highest life expectancy rate, lowest infant mortality rate and the highest female literacy rate in India and these indicators were comparable to those of middle and high-income countries. The ready availability of infrastructure and facilities has narrowed down the rural-urban divide, giving the state a 'rurban' character. Rural poverty began to decline from the early 1970s onwards as in rest of India, but the decline was sharper for Kerala. These gains in human development were matched by the existence of a vibrant civil society. Nearly a third of Kerala's adult population is affiliated to mass organizations such as trade unions, peasant associations and student, youth and women's organizations, and these are supplemented by a wide variety of sports clubs, theatre and art groups, science movements and voluntary organizations (CDS, 1975; Dreze and Sen, 1996; Franke, 1989; Kannan, 1995; Ramachandran, 2000; Thomas Isaac, 2000).

EVOLUTION OF PANCHAYAT POLICIES

PRE-INDEPENDENCE PANCHAYATS

Historically, Kerala comprised three separate regions, which were socially, politically and economically varied,[2] and the pre-Independence history of decentralization in Kerala is a history of these three separate regions. Two of these regions, i.e. Travancore and Cochin, were princely states, whose rulers followed progressive policies of land reform,[3] education and social legislation. Malabar was a neglected outpost of the Madras province of British India, on which the British spent little beyond requirements of law and order.

In the early twentieth century, in Travancore and Cochin, the space for popular voice in government was increased. Travancore was the earliest among Indian states to establish a legislative council in 1880, reconstituted subsequently from time to time with widening powers. In 1900, an elected 'popular assembly' met once a year to enable representations to be made to government on local needs and matters of general interest. In Cochin, a legislative council was established in 1924. In 1938, the post of a minister responsible to the legislature was created and he was entrusted with the departments of rural development, making Cochin the first Indian state to inaugurate ministerial government. In 1946, more departments were placed under popular ministers, and a council of ministers responsible to the legislature was established. In contrast, in Malabar, from 1801 onwards the District Collector was the local government representative. Unrest in the region necessitated the appointment of senior and experienced officers to this post, and the District Collector enjoyed a high status and played an important decision-making role in the administration of Malabar. Below the district, tahsildars (officers responsible for collection of revenue and general administration) for each *taluk* and revenue inspectors for each *firka* supervised the work of village officers (GoK, 1958; Nossiter, 1982).

In all the three regions, the village was the basic unit of administration, and the village headman enjoyed various types of authority. In Travancore, the earliest legislation relating to local self-government in 1894 concerned urban areas, while village panchayats, based on adult suffrage, were established in 1925 and 'village unions' in 1939 (GoK, 1958). In Cochin, nominated advisory bodies were established in important towns in 1902. These took on a stronger elective character in the 1920s and the 1930s. Panchayats for specified areas were constituted in 1913, and over time, nominated members in these bodies were replaced by elected ones. Modern self-government began in 1871 in Malabar, when the Local Funds Act of Madras was passed. Local boards were established at three levels, i.e. a group of villages, the *taluk* and the district, with official as well as nominated non-official members, to raise funds for and execute public works. The powers of local boards and the participation of non-officials were increased subsequently. In 1920, the Madras Village Panchayat Act was passed, though this was abolished a decade later, while panchayats were included in the scope of the Madras Local Boards Act. *Taluk* boards, found to be redundant, were abolished. Subsequently, seats were filled up by election and cadres of officials such as those of engineers and health officers were provincialized. However, in Malabar, unlike in Travancore and Cochin, where panchayats existed throughout, there remained several areas where panchayats did not exist. The panchayats in Travancore and Cochin were large, with a population of 10,000–40,000 or so, while those of the Malabar were much smaller, with a population of 500 or so (GoK, 1958).

Travancore and Cochin were integrated in July 1949 and subsequently, the Travancore-Cochin Panchayat Act 1950 was enacted. Parallelly, in Malabar, village panchayats were reconstituted in 1950 under the Madras Village Panchayats Act and invested with larger powers. A provision for the appointment of a full-time government employee to manage the day-to-day functioning of the panchayats was made in the Travancore-Cochin as well as the Madras Acts and panchayat officers were appointed subsequently in all the panchayats. Elections to panchayats were held in 1953, and panchayats were classified into three grades on the basis of their annual income (Biju 1998). When Kerala was formed in 1956, the Madras Village Panchayats Act 1950 was in force in Malabar, and the Travancore-Cochin Act 1950 was applicable to the Travancore and Cochin areas (GoK, 1956).

The Initial Vision

In the new state of Kerala, formed as the Balwantray Mehta Committee submitted its report at the centre, the first vision of panchayati raj was articulated in the report of the Administrative Reforms Committee 1958 set up when the communists were in government, and chaired by the then chief minister, E.M.S. Namboodiripad. The report of this Committee is an important landmark for decentralization in Kerala, as it put forth several important ideas that persisted. The Administrative Reforms Committee, though it followed at the heels of the Balwantray Mehta Committee, differed from it in many crucial ways, and illustrates the vision of panchayati raj of the communist government in the state, as against the Congress government in the centre. The communists had begun to win elections to local bodies during the early 1950s, and saw these as institutions which could be used to provide direct benefit to the people, because of their proximity to the people who elected them, and because of their day-to-day contact with the executive machinery. In its election manifesto, the Communist Party of India (CPI) had promised to restore honesty and economy to government by a substantial degree of decentralization. However, the Administrative Reforms Committee was not just a CPI affair, and its members included a serving and a retired chief secretary, the founder of the Indian Institute of Public Administration, a former Travancore-Cochin minister and a left-wing Congressman (Nossiter, 1982).

Importantly, while the Balwantray Mehta Committee had looked at the idea of panchayats in the context of the CD projects, the Administrative Reforms Committee scrutinized panchayats in the context of overall administrative reforms. The Administrative Reforms Committee noted that the objectives of government had altered fundamentally after Independence, i.e. to promote people's welfare as against mere tax collection and maintenance of peace in the pre-Independence phase, and the method was democratic, with the administrative machinery accountable to people's representatives. For this new role, it found the administration to be over-centralized, and consequently saw decentralization as necessary. Moreover, it emphasized the importance of people's participation, noting that:

> We have, no doubt, adopted the democratic system of Government, but this system, as it exists in India today, (it is not different in Kerala), has a major defect that the general participation of people does not extend below the Central and State levels. Democracy has not reached down to the village. (GoK, 1958: 22)

As is evident, the Administrative Reforms Committee's emphasis on people's participation differed from that of the Balwantray Mehta Committee. While the latter saw PRIs as institutions where people would collaborate in socio-economic development programmes, the former, while acknowledging the need for such collaboration, saw the need for participation in overall administration. The Administrative Reforms Committee did not place the same faith in centralized bureaucracy as the Balwantray Mehta Committee. Instead, it considered that 'democratization is a necessary corollary to decentralization, because it constitutes an effective check on the proper exercise of delegated authority by the executive' (GoK, 1958: 23). Unlike the Balwantray Mehta Committee, it did not envisage that party politics could be kept out of panchayati raj elections, and nor did it view village-level politics and disagreements with the apprehension that the Balwantray Mehta Committee did. Here, it anticipated the Asoka Mehta Committee.

With these concerns, the Administrative Reforms Committee saw 'the need for democratic bodies at the lowest level in the scheme of administration' (GoK, 1958: 23). Consequently, the village panchayats, and not the block panchayats, were envisaged as the key tier. The Administrative Reforms Committee saw a wide, coordinating role of the village panchayats, recommending that 'they should be the only organization at the village level between the government and the people' (GoK, 1958: 27). The Committee envisaged an institution with not only civic functions and developmental duties, but also with significant responsibilities in revenue and regulatory administration, to which all the village-level staff would be accountable, while also supporting village courts. At the same time, the Committee accepted that the village panchayat would implement a number of state government programmes and schemes, and did not perceive that this role would 'detract from the democratic character of Panchayats' (GoK, 1958: 34). The village panchayat would be assigned taxes adequate to cover salaries for its staff and carry on municipal functions, while funds for various development programmes would be made available by the state government. The Administrative Reforms Committee recommended direct elections to the village panchayat, reservation of seats for SCs and STs, co-option of women, but no reservations or co-option of other individuals. By creating 'functional committees' for subjects such as health, education, sanitation, etc., the panchayat would seek participation from people interested in public welfare, and by creating ward committees with local inhabitants as members, it would assess the needs of different wards.

It is important to keep in view the fact that the 'village panchayat' of the Balwantray Mehta Committee and the Administrative Reforms Committee were very different entities. Kerala lacks the nucleated village that marks the settlement pattern in large parts of India. In Kerala, the village is more an administrative concept than a physical fact,[4] as people live in individual homesteads in more or less one continuous habitation (Nossiter, 1982; Sreekumar, 1990). The Administrative Reforms Committee recommended the minimum size of a village panchayat to be a population of 5,000, which given subsequent population growth, was closer to the mandal panchayats recommended by the Asoka Mehta Committee. Advisory committees for the CD projects were in existence in Kerala at this time at the block and district levels. The Administrative Reforms Committee, as it recommended strengthening the village panchayat as the basic unit of administration, did not recommend a strong block panchayat as the Balwantray Mehta Committee had. Even though under the NES and CD projects the block-level development administration had already been set up, it envisaged a *taluk*-level office which would be responsible for regulatory and developmental administration, and a council at the *taluk* (and not the block) level, constituted through indirect elected elections and confined to an advisory role.

The Administrative Reforms Committee was divided about the need to have a strong democratic body at the district level. One view was that along with the strengthening of the relatively large-sized village panchayats, district councils, which played an advisory role, were adequate. The other view was in favour of the creation of directly elected district councils with executive functions. In the end, the Administrative Reforms Committee did not recommend a directly elected district-level institution, but rather an 'advisory and coordinating agency to begin with' (GoK, 1958: 62), with membership of MLAs and representatives of the block advisory committee and municipalities, observing that:

> The creation of an elected body at the district level almost parallel to a similar body at the state level (though without legislative powers) in which Government will vest all their functions including executive responsibility in the field of development activity within its jurisdiction, will not be conducive to efficient administration and might lead to perpetual conflicts between the State Government and the District Body. (GoK, 1958: 61)

Moreover, though the Committee saw the village panchayat as the basic unit of administration, it did not favour political intervention in administration at the district level, as the civil service was already working on the directions of the state ministers. The recommendation ultimately was to strengthen district councils in three stages, beginning with an advisory and coordinating role, with administrative responsibilities *vis-à-vis* social welfare and developmental functions increasing over time.

Competing Ideas and Politics of Centralization

The story of local government in Kerala, from the time it was formed till 1987, is one in which important ideas were developed regarding panchayats, but little action was taken. Policies regarding panchayats were formulated in a context of stiff political party competition. Unlike many Indian states, where the Congress party formed the government for long periods after independence, in Kerala the CPI won the state elections and formed the government in 1957. Intense competition among the two major political parties, i.e. the CPI and the Congress followed and neither could really become dominant in state politics. In fact, until 1970, no ministry lasted for more than three years. Additionally, there were splits within both the major political parties and increasingly, ministries were based on multi-party coalitions, and the interests of the constituents were not always in line with each other (Nossiter, 1982, 1979). For such governments, it was sometimes not possible, and at other times not expedient, to focus on panchayati raj. The picture was further complicated by changes in policy that followed the formation of new governments. The progress of panchayati raj, consequently, was halting and wavering, with several reversals.

Following the recommendations of the Administrative Reforms Committee, the Kerala Panchayati Raj Bill 1958 and the Kerala District Councils Bill 1959 were introduced, but the Kerala government was dismissed in 1959, and the bills lapsed. In the subsequent elections, the Congress and it allies formed the government and piloted the Kerala Panchayat Act 1960, bringing the entire state under the Act, unifying existing laws in Malabar and Travancore-Cochin regions. Subsequently, the first gram panchayat elections in Kerala state were held in 1963, and panchayats came into existence on 1 January 1964. The Act also saw the village or gram panchayat (GP) as the nodal, integrated unit of administration. It assigned an impressive list of duties and functions to the gram panchayats, and provided that the government could authorize the panchayats to exercise other functions such as collection of land revenue, maintenance of survey and village records, etc. One seat was reserved for SC and ST representatives in every panchayat, and one for women. There was provision for the appointment of a government servant[5] as a full-time executive officer to supervise all other personnel working in the panchayats. However, in practice, gram panchayats performed largely civic duties, and very few developmental functions were assigned to them, and establishment charges were a major claimant of the income of gram panchayats. In 1964, the government formed by the Congress introduced legislations for a three-tier panchayati raj structure along the lines recommended by the Balwantray Mehta Committee, but this bill too could not make progress as the government fell and there was a prolonged spell of President's rule (Biju, 1998; GoK, 2000; Nossiter, 1982; Ramachandran, 2000 and 1988; Thomas Isaac, 2000; Ramachandran, 1988).

In the meanwhile, there were important political changes in the state. In 1964, there was a split in the CPI, the party breaking into

CPI and the CPI (Marxist) in India. In Kerala, the Congress had also split. Subsequently, in the 1965 elections, the CPM emerged as an important political force in the state. However, the fragmentation of parties and electoral support was such that neither the communists nor the Congress could gain a working majority. A United Front ministry of the left, headed by E.M.S. Namboodiripad was formed in 1967 and it introduced the Panchayati Raj Bill 1967. The significance of this bill lies in the fact that it addressed the question of the zilla parishad, and contemplated a two-tier system of elected local government at the village and district level. In the original bill, the functions envisaged for the zilla parishad were developmental. But subsequently, the bill was considered by a select committee of the legislature, which held wide consultations within the state, and also conducted a study tour of Maharashtra, Rajasthan and Andhra Pradesh. This committee suggested that the district councils be given wider powers regarding regulatory administration, including a provision to enable the state government to delegate powers related to the collection of taxes, police administration, civil defense, prisons and revenue records to the district councils. In other words, the suggestion here was of an integrated administration, combining regulatory and developmental functions, through an elected body at the district level. This idea was contentious, and the report of this committee contained several dissenting notes, the most important being that police administration, civil defense, prisons and revenue records be kept out of the purview of district councils. While these important ideas emerged, little changed in practice as the ministry fell, and the bill lapsed as the legislative assembly was dissolved. In 1969, a new coalition government with a CPI chief minister, which relied on Congress support, was formed for a brief period and introduced a Kerala District Administration Bill in 1971, the general structure of which was based on the recommendations of the select committee. But this too lapsed because of political instability (GoK, 1971 and 1968; Nossiter, 1982; Ramachandran, 2000 and 1988).

A measure of ministerial stability was obtained in Kerala between 1971 and 1977, as the CPI collaborated with the Congress to form the government with Achuta Menon as chief minister (Nossiter, 1982). But while the ministry was stable, the political scenario was not. The CPM, in opposition, endeavoured to orchestrate all forms of struggles and continued to hold on to a large mass base. There were also intense struggles among the political parties within the ruling coalition. Given these circumstances, it is not surprising that panchayati raj was sidelined. There were repeated postponements of panchayat elections after 1963 and the panchayat representatives elected in 1964 remained in office till 1979 (Biju, 1998). Rather, centralized action gained in importance. Popular extra-Parliamentary pressure was applied through peasant movements and unions, guided by centralized parties (Nossiter, 1982; Tornquist and Tharakan, 1996).

The Congress government with A.K. Anthony as chief minister, formed after the 1977 assembly elections, introduced the Kerala District Administration Bill 1978. The structure of this bill was similar to the 1971 bill, but provisions that enabled the state government to delegate the control to district councils over police administration, prisons, etc., were removed and other regulatory functions were also limited. This bill received the President's assent in 1980. But quick regime changes followed. Subsequent developments showed that opinion within political parties about decentralization was divided. Neither the brief CPM-led coalition (1980–2) nor the Congress-led coalitions (1982–7), which followed implemented the legislation.[6] A committee was set up in 1984 to reconsider the Kerala District Administration Bill but could not give its report. In fact, even the elections to gram panchayats, due in 1984, were not held until 1987 (EPW, 1991).

But it is important to note here that though at this time Kerala shared with the rest of the country the proclivity for centralization, it differed substantially in being able to implement policies that positively impacted the lives of people. During this period, Kerala carried out important land reforms, which abolished tenancy and conferred homestead land to hutment dwellers by enabling them to acquire a tenth of an acre occupied by them at a nominal price. The Agricultural Workers Bill 1972 that came into effect in 1975 provided for some measure of security of employment, and also created a welfare fund for agricultural labourers. From time to time, the government also declared 'prescribed' wages. The increasing unionization of agricultural and other workers strengthened the position of labour in the state, and resulted in a rise in real wage rates. Starting from this period, the state government in Kerala continued to plan and implement several social welfare programmes, investing in health and education and developing a robust public distribution system. The achievements of the state in terms of HDI indicators have been noted at the beginning of this chapter. While Marxist-led ministries excelled in such basic welfare programmes, these also became an all-party affair (CDS, 1975; Nossiter, 1982; Kannan, 1995; Ramachandran, 2000). These interventions were implemented by the bureaucracy, and the expansion of various state programmes and institutions added to centralization (Nossiter, 1982; Tornquist and Tharakan, 1996). This period may be characterized as one in which people's empowerment took place in the context of centralized rather than decentralized government.

Forces for Decentralization

From the late-1980s onwards, various forces for decentralization became stronger. As against the previous scenario of policy without much practice, there were significant concrete developments in panchayati raj from 1987 to 1996, which took strong roots. Briefly, in the 1987 elections, the Left Democratic Front (LDF) coalition led by the CPM had stated in its election manifesto that the District Administration Bill would be implemented. Subsequently, elections to district councils were held in 1991. In 1994, the Kerala Panchayat Act was passed by the United Democratic Front (UDF) government led by the Congress as conformity legislation to the 73rd Amendment, ensuring a three-tier PRI structure and regular elections. But it was in 1996, as the LDF came to power in Kerala, that the unique decentralization initiative of Kerala unfolded. It included among other things, a detailed process of local-level planning through the People's Plan Campaign (PPC) and a very substantial devolution of funds to PRIs (GoK, 2000; Thomas Isaac and Franke 2000).

The reasons for this dramatic shift are located in not one, but several contexts, i.e. the problems of governance, problems of the economy, political considerations of the ruling party, influence of the non-government organization Kerala Shastra Sahitya Parishad (KSSP), and the background of the constitutional amendment. An attempt is now made to sketch this context.

The success story of Kerala, i.e. the positive impact on HDIs through re-distributive and welfare measures has been noted. However, these achievements were not matched by a parallel growth of the economy.[7] Agriculture had begun to stagnate from the mid-1970s, showing a declining trend in area and yield. Agrarian unemployment grew as farmers shifted from paddy cultivation to more lucrative commercial crops such as rubber, as the latter are less labour absorbing. Additionally, in the early 1990s, a steep fall in the prices of commercial crops further affected Kerala's agriculture adversely. Environmental degradation became more acute, resulting in a rapid decline in the area under forests as well as declining rainfall and agricultural productivity (Bhattacharya and Sakthivel, 2004; GoK, 2002; Joseph, 2003; Kannan and Pushpangan, 1990 and 1988). The industrial sector was equally disappointing. Among the south Indian states, Kerala remained the least industrialized, with predominantly medium and small industries concentrated on a narrow range of products (food, textile, wood, chemicals and rubber products). Moreover, the working of state enterprises remained poor, with a large number of enterprises continuously incurring losses (Pillai, 1990; Subrahmaniam, 1990). The service sector had begun growing,[8] but the important point is that by the 1990s, the low production base of the economy was viewed with concern by sympathizers as well as critics (Franke and Chasin, 1998; George, 1998; Gulati, 1994; Herring, 1989; Kannan, 1998; Raj, 1994; Tharamangalam, 1998; Thomas Isaac and Kumar, 1991).[9] These problems of the economy lent support to critics of the LDF, who argued that the political climate in the state, unionization, extensive welfare and higher wages had become the bane of Kerala society. Additionally, the post-liberalization scenario provided a particularly slippery terrain for conventional left politics, as state governments competed with each other to attract investment.

In this economic scenario, unemployment was a major issue, and had very direct political repercussions. In the early 1990s, Kerala had the highest rate of unemployment in India (21 per cent against a national average of 7.3 per cent and in 1999–2000) (Joseph, 2003). Unemployment grew with the increase in educational opportunities, which led to a sharp increase in the proportion of workers seeking white-collar jobs. The wage rate for agricultural workers was pushed up through unionization, which, combined with a shift from paddy to less labour-intensive cash crop cultivation, led to an increase in rural unemployment also (Oommen, 1992). In the above scenario, migration from Kerala to other parts of the world became an important facet of economic and social life in the state.[10] Zachariah et al. (2002) estimate that in 1998 the state had 60 migrants per 100 households, of which 32 per household resided outside Kerala (27 per 100 households had returned). Towards the end of the 1990s, Keralites working abroad constituted 10 per cent of the workforce in Kerala, equal to the workforce in the public and private organized sector in the state.

Significantly, Kerala faced a crisis of state finances. The government had faced a budgetary deficit since the mid-1970s, which deepened in the late-1980s and the government began to carve out surpluses on its capital account in order to finance its recurring revenue deficits (George, 1990; Joseph, 2003). The fiscal crisis put into question, the ability of the state government to sustain its much acclaimed social welfare programmes, much less expand them. This made new policy initiatives necessary for the left parties. Importantly, these new policy thrusts would be mediated through institutions and organizations of government, which in turn had several problems of internal functioning. Though several political leaders in Kerala are distinguished by their personal integrity, and the level of corruption may possibly have been less in Kerala than in other parts of the country, the state was by no means free of the patronage-based, rent-seeking proclivities, which were a feature of government functioning across India. For instance, dispensation of patronage and corruption were identified as critical problems in the International Congress of Kerala Studies in 1994 (Saradamoni, 1994). The scope and scale of corruption had been enlarged by the influx of Gulf money (Nossiter, 1988). Moreover, support to union activities by political parties had not helped the cause of efficiency and effectiveness in government. Commenting on the functioning of government servants in West Bengal, Tripura and Kerala (where communist governments have been formed), Nossiter says that:

> To the extent that they (government employees) are predominantly unionized by the communists in the three states, the parties face very real difficulties in persuading or coercing supporters to abandon their customary inertia and petty corruption. Half-educated, under-paid, short on commitment at work and long on transport at work, it is hardly surprising that they perform their tedious tasks with little enthusiasm. Politicians who need votes are inclined to back employees against disciplinary officers. (Nossiter, 1988: 183)

To these problems of governance, must be added the special dilemmas of the left parties in Kerala, as it was the LDF that took the decision to devolve substantial funds to panchayats. As argued by Tornquist and Tharakan (1996), these dilemmas necessitated new thrusts. In Kerala, the political base of the left had begun to deteriorate. Many former tenants who had become landowners had begun to hire agricultural workers, and were at odds with them over better wages and working conditions, and had ceased to support the left. A new agenda to address productivity and unemployment was necessary. At the same time, the crisis of state socialism in Europe in the 1990s generated much reflection,[11] and further strengthened the perceived need for new strategies (Thomas Isaac and Tharakan, 1995; Tornquist and Tharakan, 1996).

While the problems of the economy and governance demanded redressal, and the left needed to evolve a new strategy, ideas about local participatory planning for optimal use of resources had been gaining ground. Significant here is the work of a non-government organization, the Kerala Shastra Sahitya Parishad (KSSP), many of whose member were LDF supporters. It had developed its own vision for local economic development which involved local planning through people's participation, and decentralization. The KSSP began primarily as a movement for popularizing science and creating a scientific temper among the people in the 1960s. In the 1970s, it extended its activities to include optimal utilization of local resources and became active in building an environmental critique of developmental projects. In this context, decentralized planning came to be seen as key, and by 1989, KSSP had begun to demand genuine decentralization and strengthening of village-level capabilities for self-reliant growth (Thomas Isaac et al., 1995).

From 1989, KSSP began a People's Resource Mapping Programme (PRMP) in collaboration with the Centre for Earth Science Studies and the Land Use Board. The goal of PRMP was to mobilize rural resources and manpower and use these optimally, shifting away from energy exhausting inputs. This entailed a significant upgradation of expertise and use of scientific methods on the one hand and mass participation as well as development of local institutions on the other. In Kalliasseri panchayat, a CPM stronghold with a long tradition of mass movements, the KSSP moved ahead to develop an intensive methodology for local area development planning based on people's participation (Thomas Isaac and Franke, 2000; Thomas Isaac et al. 1995; Tornquist and Tharakan, 1996). This model had significant influence on panchayati raj in Kerala.

The Journey to the PPC

After the 1987 assembly elections, as the LDF formed the government, aggressive developmental measures to address productivity and unemployment were high on the agenda. Within the left in Kerala, there were two major schools of thought about how this could be brought about and these have been characterized as, 'state modernists' and 'popular developmentalists' (PDs) by Tornquist and Tharakan (1996). State modernists argued for state intervention to promote economic growth to ensure that people got their fair share of the cake in a globalized regime. For this, the state had to measure up on the markets, and public administration had to be streamlined.[12] The other school, i.e. the PDs, chiefly activists of the KSSP, argued for better management of natural and human resources, creation of a better work culture within state institutions and decisions and actions based on collective productive interests rather than party or union interests (Tornquist and Tharakan, 1996).

In the late-1980s, KSSP had some influence on the LDF government. In 1989 'group farming', a KSSP idea, was promoted with vigour by the agriculture ministry and Krishi Bhawans were established at the GP level across Kerala. In the group farming initiative, farmers were encouraged to undertake agricultural operations as a group in order to collectively utilize economies of scale while retaining private ownership of land. KSSP also led the statewide Total Literacy Campaign (TLC) supported by the state as well as the central government (Kumar, 1993; Tornquist and Tharakan, 1996; Thomas Isaac and Franke, 2000). However, the decision to decentralize was not an easy one. Though the LDF had promised to implement the District Administration Bill in its election manifesto, it took an year after forming the government to appoint an advisor, and then more than two years to carry out elections to the district councils (*EPW*, 1991).[13] Tornquist and Tharakan write:

> All the parties (of the LDF coalition) . . . had to get influential positions and access to some ministries and state agencies. Many ministers and politicians . . . would have to give up much of their power. . . . Privileged bureaucrats and most public servants and their unions . . . were also afraid of losing out. There were also many traditional leftist arguments in favour of central leadership, to guide the most deprived, to uphold party discipline and to thus prevent corruption. (Tornquist and Tharakan, 1996: 1966)

As in the other successful cases of decentralization in India, electoral calculations appear to have provided an important impetus. District council elections were held in 1990, just before the state government decided to go in for early elections, and the LDF gained control of all but one district council. Subsequently, offices and officers as well as funds were transferred to the newly formed councils (*EPW*, 1991; Ramachandran, 2000). However, as the government changed again in 1991, the plan allocation to district councils was reduced, the composition of the councils was changed to include MPs and MLAs, District Collectors ceased to serve as secretaries of the councils, and the councils lost control of their staff (*EPW*, 1991; Tornquist and Tharakan, 1996; Thomas Isaac and Franke, 2000). Political party competition seemed to triumph over panchayati raj again.

But, by 1993, the overall situation regarding decentralization had changed substantially. With the 73rd Constitutional Amendment, the state was obliged to pass conformity legislation. The Kerala Panchayati Raj Bill was introduced in March 1994 by the UDF government, modified after criticism from the CPI(M), and then passed by the legislature (Thomas Isaac and Franke, 2000). As per the constitutional amendment a three-tier structure of panchayats at the village, block and district level, rather than the two-tier structure that had evolved in state policy was put in place. The first elections for the three-tier panchayati raj were held in September 1995 and the panchayats came into being on 2 October 1995. A government order was issued in September 1995 transferring various institutions and staff to the three-tier panchayats.

At the same time, the PD advocacy for decentralization was gaining ground, and got special support from E.M.S. Namboodiripad, CPI(M)'s widely respected leader. Democratic decentralization forged a new agenda, in which people would come together for local economic development. In August 1994, at the International Congress on Kerala Studies (organized by the AKG Centre for Research and Studies of which E.M.S. Namboodiripad was the director), in his inaugural address he was to say that:

> the one big question that we face is whether the organized strength and political consciousness of our people can be used to increase production and productivity . . . the government and the ruling classes must change their attitude to the organizations of people and their demands. . . . Further, institutions and social mechanisms have to be developed to ensure that the toilers get due share of from increased production. I must emphasize the importance of democratic decentralization in this context. (Namboodiripad, 1994: 5)

In 1996, as the LDF came to power in Kerala, panchayat elections had been held and the LDF had won in 585 of 966 gram panchayats (Das, 2000). The stage was now set for a decentralization that was the most extensive in India in terms of powers and funds devolved (Jha, 2002; World Bank 2000). Moreover, once the step to devolve substantial funds to PRIs had been taken, it was not easily undone. With some changes, the initiative continued as the UDF came to power in 2000.[14] There is a good case here for the argument that the constitutional amendment enabled Kerala's decentralization efforts to survive *across* political regimes. As has been noted above, *within* the two major political coalitions of Kerala, the UDF and the LDF, there were considerable differences of opinion about decentralization. In both the political parties, decentralization was supported by some important top-level leaders, but not by all (Kannan, 1994: International Congress on Kerala Studies). With the constitutional amendment, those in favour of decentralization were strengthened in both the political parties.

DEFINING FEATURES OF PANCHAYATI RAJ IN KERALA

Panchayati raj in Kerala as it developed after 1996, has several features, which are unique in India. In this section, the attempt is to capture its important elements. To do so, it is necessary to understand panchayati raj in Kerala at three levels. First, in addition to what has been learned about panchayati raj in Kerala so far, it is important to understand the new influential ideas about local economic development and participatory planning. The Kalliasseri experience, described briefly below, provides a good glimpse. Second, it is important to understand the People's Plan Campaign, through which these ideas and initiatives, tried out on a small scale in Kalliasseri, were translated on to a large scale with PRIs. Finally, it is important to comprehend the basis of a more solid and permanent status of the whole project through legal mechanisms, financial devolution, and so on. Below, all these three aspects are described, to bring out the core elements of the panchayati raj 'policy' or 'pattern' which developed.

THE KALLIASSERI EXPERIENCE

In Kalliasseri, the idea of socio-economic development was based on the premise that even though economic self-sufficiency was not possible, the village panchayat could aspire for the fullest utilization of its internal growth potential by better management of its natural and human resources, as against a one-sided emphasis on advanced productive forces. The economy was sought to be strengthened, not by relying on large industrial capital, but by relying on local resources, both human and material. The attempt was to make the local economy strong enough to withstand onslaughts of the global economy. And the very methods of public action that had led to Kerala's successes in the redistributive and social sectors were to be used, in a modified form, to also create a solid economic base (Parayil, 1998; Parameswaran, 1998; Tornquist and Tharakan, 1996).

At Kalliasseri, an exhaustive planning exercise was undertaken with people's participation, which entailed a detailed understanding of the socio-economic situation through the development of an environmental appraisal map and a socio-economic survey; an analysis of problems and issues; discussion with people, officials and experts; and the formulation of plans and schemes. Planning in Kalliasseri had two important features. One, it accessed a fair degree of technical expertise and was based on resource assessments, surveys and technical studies, with a significant contribution by experts within and outside Kerala. Two, it was participatory and the plan relied heavily on voluntary labour, of which the panchayat had a history. Most of the volunteers were members of mass organizations such as trade unions and various wings of political parties. The village panchayat president was enthusiastic about the exercise (Thomas Isaac et al., 1995).

Given the very limited financial and other powers of the GP at that time (in 1991–2), a new development institution, the Kalliasseri Development Society (KDS), with the panchayat president as its ex-officio chairman, was formed. It had a general body of 200 persons comprising an elected representative for every 25 households, elected panchayat representatives and government officials. Elections to the KDS were usually based on consensus, and voting rarely became necessary. KDS was headed by a working committee, which was responsible for the day-to-day functions and also set the agenda, as discussions of the general body normally took place around a document presented by the working committee. The working committee comprised panchayat elected representatives, technical experts, a representative from KSSP and government officials. There were also eight sub-committees dealing with agriculture, fisheries, animal husbandry, irrigation, energy, education, health and communication (Thomas Isaac et al., 1995).

There were some important successes in Kalliasseri, but several limitations were also visible. A planning methodology that married expertise and participation had been worked out, but it was a very long-drawn out process. Some projects, such as the construction of a new canal, the repair of an old one, and the construction of a road, were highly successful, and were implemented with great speed with the help of voluntary labour. Government support was also forthcoming. However, projects in the productive sector posed a special challenge. For instance, to encourage self-employment, unemployed youth were organized for vegetable cultivation on fallow land, while seeds were supplied at subsidized rates. Problems arose in providing irrigation facilities on time, and in obtaining high quality seeds. The issue of marketing was not addressed, and as a result, when the harvest came, prices plummeted to one-third of the level of the planting season, and the expected profits did not materialize. During the second year, many groups dropped out and the programme was re-oriented to promote vegetables for the self-consumption of homestead labour.

'Community participation' too was a complex process. In several projects people participated and worked voluntarily. But at other times, cooperation of landholders was a problem, especially if they themselves did not benefit. Owners were often reluctant to allow vegetable cultivation on their land, and to give relinquishment statements for construction of canals, etc. These difficulties were overcome by the intermediation of the sponsoring institutions and panchayat representatives, and by incorporating members of landholders' households into the vegetable cultivation group, and in some cases, work was even carried out in spite of their protest. Collaboration with government departments, though forthcoming in some projects, was not easy. The experience of schemes implemented in collaboration with government agencies in minor irrigation, rural energy, soil conservation, health awareness, floriculture and fisheries was mostly unsatisfactory. There were problems of flexibility, delays, and lack of interest among the departments (Thomas Isaac et al., 1995).

To sum up, the basic vision in Kalliasseri implied the development of local resources through public action. A methodology for participatory planning at the grassroots was developed and implemented to this end through an institution created at the grassroots, though there was plenty of support from external experts. In Kalliasseri, a CPI(M) stronghold, the level of participation was high, and some projects were highly successful. However, many questions were left unanswered. Productive sector projects were difficult as marketing and other tie-ups were hard to establish and modalities for working with the government set up had not been worked out.

People's Plan Campaign

The PPC attempted to adapt the planning processes of Kalliasseri on a much larger scale, and also learn from the work of other grassroots organizations.[15] The State Planning Board (SPB) steered the whole exercise, while creating mechanisms to collaborate with experts and KSSP activists. The PPC drew heavily on voluntary resource persons (RPs), mobilizing and training around 100,000 people, who conducted training camps, facilitated discussions among the community, and provided feedback to the SPB for mid-course corrections (GoK, 2000; Thomas Isaac and Franke, 2000).

The PPC was organized in six phases, spanning a range of activities from mobilization to plan preparation. The activities across these phases comprised a unique process to facilitate wide-ranging consultation and discussion with people, a massive exercise of decentralized planning whereby panchayats in Kerala began to access funds regularly on the basis of the plans that they made. The gram panchayat was the most critical institution in this exercise. While the processes developed in the PPC, described briefly below, can be called inspired in many ways and are instructive, the campaign was not without its problems. Many of its strengths as well as its limitations raise key issues related to democratic decentralization that go well beyond the campaign.

The first phase of PPC began with the mobilization of people all over Kerala, with the tone being set by theatrical processions on the theme of power to the people. Subsequently, gram sabhas met in each ward to discuss local developmental problems, their causes and solutions. A broad structure of these meetings was developed at the state level. Focus was provided through a model agenda and trained resource persons facilitated the discussions. In general, the gram sabhas were a huge success and generated a state-wide public debate on development, though in several GPs, group discussions were not satisfactory, and tended to lapse into a mere listing of local demands. During the second phase of the campaign, 'development seminars' were organized in every GP, and 'development reports', that contained a list of recommendations on the basis of an objective assessment of the resource potential and problems, were formulated. However, only some panchayats had completed the PRMP exercise, and a socio-economic survey, as undertaken in Kalliasseri, was thought to be too time-consuming. Consequently, an attempt was made to map the resources of panchayats through the method of a 'transect walk' by appraisal teams, consisting of experts in fields such as agricultural engineering, and to facilitate the use of secondary data. But though all local bodies collected data, and nearly all carried out the transect walk, only 50 per cent actually compiled the data or identified eco-zones. The actual utilization of findings was even less common. Consequently, development reports were based largely on discussions in the gram sabhas. The limitations of resource persons at the local level were a major hurdle, while the panchayat representatives, officials and the community were not clear about the concept of resource-based planning. Yet this phase did succeed in fostering discussion on development all over Kerala and for the first time in the state's (or the country's) history, the GPs prepared local development reports. But the resultant development reports proved to be of varying quality. The best analysis tended to be for agriculture, followed by education, for which many schoolteachers provided support. The chapters on industry, energy and resource mobilization were the weakest (Chattopadhyaya et al., 1999; GoK, 2000; Thomas Isaac and Franke, 2000).

The third phase involved preparation of detailed project proposals to carry out these recommendations. Support for this phase was provided at the state level through a handbook and the design of a project format. At the GP level, sector-wise task forces, each with an elected representative as chairperson and local official as convener, were constituted to prepare projects. At this stage, it was realized that greater participation from officials and experts within the government was necessary, and training camps were organized to orient them. But this training was not as successful as the previous ones. A review by SPB showed that the task forces did not function as effectively as expected. The projects tended to imitate model projects given in the handbook or to adopt ongoing schemes of the departments. Financial and technical analyses, especially of production-related projects, were weak. An attempt was then made to revitalize the task forces. Workshops were organized to examine project proposals and rectify mistakes, gram panchayats were encouraged to co-opt new members and that failing, a core team of active members could prepare projects. But the preparation of projects remained problematic: 34 per cent of the projects were written by a core group of members, and only in 12 per cent of the panchayats were all the task forces fully active (GoK, 2000; Thomas Isaac and Franke, 2000).

During the fourth phase projects were to be prioritized and incorporated into plans. Every GP was expected to have a shelf of projects ready, but because of the problems that cropped up in formulating projects, this was not the case. Subsequently, plan formulation ran concurrently with the preparation of projects. In spite of more large-scale orientation and training, drawing up the plan documents proved to be difficult and only a handful of GPs finalized their plans by the due date. The local activists found it difficult to prepare the statistical statements required in the plan documents, and there were much confusion about concepts. The fifth phase was concerned with preparation of block and district plans (GoK, 2000; Thomas Isaac and Franke, 2000).

When the plan campaign was launched, only five phases were visualized, but the experience with project preparation showed the technical soundness of projects to be a problem. Consequently, a new sixth phase for the technical and financial appraisal of projects was now added. Retired technical experts and professionals were encouraged to appraise the projects, and rectify the technical and financial mistakes. Later, teams of officials and non-officials worked together to scrutinize the projects and mechanisms were developed for approving plans. This completed the first round of planning by local bodies. The first release of funds to a grama panchayat took place after a year-and-a-half of discussion and planning, and much later for a majority of the panchayats (GoK, 2000; Thomas Isaac and Franke,2000).

As can be seen, in consonance with its goal of putting in place a process of participatory planning at the grassroots, the main focus of the PPC was the gram panchayat and not the other two tiers. The major successes of PPC lay in fostering public discussion about development, and providing a framework wherein plans could be articulated with people's participation. However, focusing the discussions on development was a difficult task and there was a tendency to make wish lists rather than plans to optimize existing resources. The PPC had limited success in enabling panchayats to carry out resource surveys, identify key strategies to achieve developmental goals, and convert them into viable projects (Sharma 2003). These elements, as we shall see, remain a key dynamic for decentralization in Kerala.

Institutionalization

The institutionalization, or the long-term significance and space for participatory planning fostered in the PPC through the village panchayat, has been attempted through the legal framework, financial devolution to local bodies as well as the transfer of personnel to PRIs, as described briefly below.

The Legal Framework

The Kerala Panchayat Act was brought into force in 1994 by the UDF government. In 1996, when the LDF came to power, it set up a Committee of Decentralization of Powers (Sen Committee) to review the

Act, and in 1999 modified the Act on the basis of its recommendations. The report of the Sen Committee as well as the Act give central importance to people's participation and planning for local development. The preamble of the Act states clearly that the three-tier PRI structure is established 'for securing a greater participation of people in planned development and local government affairs'.

The Act lists the functions of the three tiers of PRIs separately. In keeping with the importance of the GP in participatory planning, the largest number of functions is devolved to the GP. The village panchayat is the custodian of public property (though it cannot sell or transfer it), and is responsible for the maintenance of water tanks, streetlights, burial grounds, etc. The Act also gives the village panchayat a role that may loosely be described as 'activist'. It is expected to mobilize people for various activities and build awareness about social evils, the environment and economic offences. Finally, a large number of developmental functions covering 19 sectors have been devolved to it. At the block and district level, the PRIs are expected to mobilize technical support for the lower tiers and make plans after taking their schemes into consideration. Several developmental functions are also devolved to the block and district PRIs, but the range is less than that of the gram panchayat. All panchayats have to make annual development plans, five-year plans and fifteen-year perspective plans, and to submit these to the District Planning Committee (DPC). The DPC can suggest modifications only on a few counts, i.e. whether or not sectoral allocations are followed, whether adequate funds have been earmarked for SCs and STs, etc. In other words, each PRI is enabled to decide its own priorities, subject to very minimal guidelines.

The focus on participation is visible in a detailed articulation of the role of the gram sabha, though many of its activities are consultative and voluntary in nature. As per Section 3(7) of the Act, the panchayats have to give 'due recognition to the recommendations and suggestions of the gram sabha'. The gram sabha is expected to formulate proposals and make suggestions for various development projects, assist in various ways in implementation and also contribute in terms of voluntary labour. A gram sabha may also appoint sub-committees to study specific issues. It can pass resolutions on a majority basis, though decisions based on consensus are to be encouraged. However, there are also provisions that define specific functions and rights of the gram sabha. Beneficiary selection for schemes is clearly to be done by the gram sabha, and it has a *right* to know about the budgetary provisions, plan outlays, etc., and the officers of the village panchayat have to attend gram sabha meetings as required. Gram sabhas are to be convened at least once in three months and the required quorum is 10 per cent of the voters of the area.

In accordance with the constitutional amendment, all the three tiers of panchayats are constituted by direct election, and one-third seats are reserved for women and seats are reserved for Scheduled Castes and Scheduled Tribes in proportion to their population. Similar reservations exist for the panchayat presidents and vice-presidents, and seats are reserved by rotation in each district. The president and vice-president of all tiers are elected by the members of the panchayats, i.e. the Act does not provide for direct election of the GP president. The panchayat samiti, comprising the elected members of the panchayat, is the decision-making body and decisions are to be taken by a simple majority. The executive powers are vested in the panchayat president, but all the members of the panchayat have the right to move resolutions.

Three standing committees related to finance, development and welfare are provided in the Act at the GP and block levels, while five such committees related to finance, development, welfare, public works, and health and education are provided for at the district level. These committees can perform such functions as entrusted to them by the panchayats and all members of the panchayat are distributed across the standing committees. A steering committee comprising the president, vice-president and chairpersons of the standing committees is to coordinate and monitor the functions of the standing committees. The panchayats are empowered to constitute functional committees for different subjects, sub-committees to assist the standing and functional committees, and ward committees can be constituted by the GP to study and report on the needs of the panchayats. A panchayat may also constitute joint committees with other panchayats for any purpose.

The Act provides for an ombudsman to make inquiries regarding corruption, maladministration and irregularities. The ombudsman can make financial recoveries and impose penalties. It also provides for the constitution of a Tribunal for Local Self Government Institutions with judicial powers where appeals can be instituted against the decision of a local government. The Act also makes it clear that the state government can intervene in various ways if the functioning of a panchayat is not satisfactory, though it lays down the conditions of such intervention. The state government retains powers of scrutiny of panchayat records and departmental officers can inspect the various works of PRIs. The state government also retains the right to issue general guidelines to PRIs. It can call the explanation of a panchayat president or secretary in case he defaults in carrying out any order of the government. Resolutions of the panchayat that are illegal, endanger life, safety or communal harmony or violate directions with respect to government grants can be cancelled by the government, but only after consultation with the ombudsman and the tribunal. The government can dissolve a panchayat if it fails to pass the budget or if all its members resign. Such notifications, however, have to be laid subsequently before the legislative assembly, and the legislative assembly has the power to modify or cancel such resolutions.

An important feature of the legal framework for decentralization in Kerala is that amendments have also been made to 44 state legislations affecting departments such as education, health, drinking water, etc. These amendments are aimed at creating the necessary legal framework for ensuring the smooth functioning of local governments and to transform them into a third tier of governance. Thus, legitimate legal space for their activities has been created in all enactments.

Financial Devolution

In the pre-PPC period in Kerala, the village panchayats, the only tier of local government in the state, had a revenue base adequate for their civic functions (Oommen, 2004). A small untied grant was given to the GPs from 1990 onwards, but it was irregular and a great deal of discretion was exercised by the state government in allotment. In 1996, along with the PPC, a decision was taken to devolve 35–40 per cent plan funds to panchayats at the three tiers,[16] for the SC and ST as well as general category funds. Of the three tiers, the maximum financial devolution is to the GP, and funds are divided in the ratio of 60:20:20 at the village, block and district levels, respectively. Additionally, while GPs have their own sources of revenue, the block and district PRIs are totally dependent on grants. From 1998–9 onwards, the state government created a composite index of the entitlement of each PRI, taking into account the population, geographical area, area under paddy and an index of backwardness based on houses without latrines and electricity (GoK, 2002; Oommen, 2004; Thomas Isaac, 2000).

Each local body has to prepare a comprehensive area plan to claim this grant-in-aid, which is approved by a District Planning Committee.

The plan outlay of PRIs is not confined to the grant in aid, but includes all the funds available to the local body, including own revenue surpluses, state and central schemes, loans from financial institutions, beneficiary contribution, voluntary labour and donations. There are no scheme-specific allotments, but only broad guidelines (see Table 15 for details), to ensure adequate expenditure in the productive sector and for marginalized groups. Here, Kerala has made a sharp break from past practice in India.

Since the PPC, PRIs in Kerala have begun to receive and expend a large quantum of funds. For example, expenditures made by the GP rose from around Rs. 17 lakh per GP and Rs. 68 per capita in 1993–4 to over Rs. 101 lakh per GP and Rs. 421 per capita in 1997–8. This requires new and improved accounting and auditing systems. A new set of simplified financial rules was issued by the state government, but the budgeting and accounting systems of the PRIs have remained problematic, and there have also been frequent changes in the method of disbursement from the state. PRIs are audited by the Local Fund Audit, but the approach of this audit has been found to be too legalistic. A Performance Audit Authority has been created to assist panchayats in building their financial capacity and conducting their internal audit, but significant effects are not yet visible (Oommen, 2004).

Personnel

While the functions devolved to the PRIs are impressive, and financial devolution substantial, the Kerala government's success in providing PRIs with the appropriate personnel has been more limited. Each GP in Kerala has a panchayat secretary and a small staff, appointed at a time when the tasks of the GP were quite small. In spite of the enormous upgradation of the functions of the panchayat, this situation has remained unchanged. Government documents (GoK, 2002) comment on the lack of a central official position in the GP for efficient and effective coordination. But several attempts to recruit better-skilled people as GP secretaries have been stymied because of pressures from employee unions as well as narrow departmental interests. At the block panchayat, the situation is somewhat better, as the BDO and the block extension machinery stand transferred to the block panchayat. The position of the district panchayat is in between that of these two tiers.

Technically, a great deal of the staff and institutions of various government departments stand 'transferred' to panchayats, but this transfer is actually quite limited in scope. Local governments have operational control over the staff, i.e. they can assign duties, supervise, review and inspect performance, and enforce minor punishment. But the local governments cannot create new posts and have to go by the normative pattern of salary, promotion, etc., laid down by the state government. Recruitment as well as transfers remain the domain of the state government though local governments are allowed to fill interim vacancies. This problem of staffing is especially acute in the case of the GP, where substantial functions as well as funds have devolved.

Decentralization in Kerala began with a massive capacity building effort, that could not, however, be sustained. The precursor of the PPC, the Kalliasseri project, drew upon the enormous expertise available both within and outside Kerala. The PPC itself was a huge capacity building exercise wherein 600 Key Resource Persons, 10,000 District Resource Persons and 100,000 Local Resource Persons were trained to support the process of planning in the PRIs. A great deal of knowledge that was created in organizations such as KSSP and the Centre for Earth Science Studies about a host of issues such as planning and watershed development, formed the background to this campaign. The training in PPC focused on general propositions and the process of planning. Subsequently, the problems that arose during the PPC in the making of plans and projects showed the need for much greater capacity building and the need to institutionalize the process. The magnitude of the task can be gauged from the fact that there are an estimated 18,000-panchayat representatives, 15,000 panchayat staff and between 1.2–1.5 lakh transferred officials, to be trained. The Sen Committee suggested strengthening of the Kerala Institute of Local Administration (KILA) to this end. Subsequently, a project named Capacity Development for Decentralization in Kerala was commissioned in 1999 with financial support from the Swiss Development Agency. Several attempts were made to strengthen KILA, but these ran into problems with the change of the political regime. At the time of this study, KILA had a minimal faculty and training programmes were conducted with the help of external resource persons from across the state.

CONCLUSION

Post-Independence, panchayati raj has been the subject of a great deal of discussion and debate in Kerala. The village or gram panchayat has been the enduring tier of panchayati raj in Kerala, while the block and district PRIs are relatively new entrants. With the PPC, because of the strong focus on local development and participation, the village panchayat has strengthened further in importance. At the same time, the original vision of the village panchayat performing regulatory as well as developmental functions has been dormant, the emphasis shifting to optimal utilization of local resources.

Kerala has broken new territory in panchayati raj in the empowerment and autonomy of PRIs. The legal framework and financial devolution enable the PRIs to fix their own priorities. Unlike the rest of the country, PRIs in Kerala do not merely implement centrally designed schemes with rigid guidelines and norms, but prepare their own plans and projects based on local needs. At the same time, attempts have been made to institutionalize a process of public debate and participation by specifying the role of the gram sabha and making space for other community-based bodies such as functional committees.

We shall now, in the next three chapters, turn to the question of how this initiative has actually shaped up on the ground. In this scrutiny, the focus will be on the institutional structures created and strengthened, i.e. the PRIs, rather then the specific processes, such as those of planning or participation. Panchayati raj implies a long-term shift in the politico-governance structures, and the state itself, and it is from this point of view that the Kerala initiative has been analysed in terms of outcomes. To begin with, this analysis focuses on the village panchayat, as it has emerged as the critical tier, and then moves on to look at the three tiers holistically.

NOTES

1. By 1956, only 44 per cent of the cultivated area was under food crops (with a further 14 per cent under food-cum-cash crops). The area under cash crops continued to expand from the mid-1970s onwards and today, food crops, i.e. rice, pulses, minor millets and tapioca, occupy only 15 per cent of the cultivated area (Nossiter, 1982; GoK, 2002).
2. Natural divisions in Kerala run longitudinally, in contrast to the three pre-independence political divisions that run latitudinally. The coast, the most densely populated region, is low lying and fertile. The high plateau of the midland zone is unattractive for agriculture, while the valleys are cultivated intensely. The highland zone is naturally either forest or downland and here from 1877, the European entrepreneurs experimented with a variety of plantation crops (Nossiter, 1982).

3. Traditionally, most of the land of Kerala was in the hands of a numerically small class called *janmies.* However, the *janmies'* rights were not those of absolute ownership of land and were heavily qualified by custom. In Malabar, during British rule, the *janmies* became absolute proprietors with a contractual title and enforceable rights in a court of law and also gained the title of extensive uncultivated lands. The actual cultivator was gradually reduced to the status of a tenant-at-will. In contrast, in Travancore, the traditional interpretation of the rights of the *janmies* was upheld to the advantage of the tenants. Successive Maharajas concentrated land ownership in the hands of the government, until by 1812 only one-third of the cultivated area was in private corporate hands. In 1865, the tenant cultivators on government land were enfranchised and a free market in land developed. Cochin was in an intermediate position, where by 1812, some 40 per cent lands were held by the government. The *janmies* who owned the rest of the land were as unbridled as their counterparts in the Malabar. However, the situation was somewhat better than in Malabar because of the existence of government wasteland and the outlet afforded by the port and its industry. In 1951, tenants were about one-tenth of the agricultural population in Travancore, compared to more than one-fourth in Cochin and nearly two-fifths in the Malabar (CDS, 1975; Nossiter, 1982).
4. Only in the Muslim area of southern Malabar are nucleated settlements common (Nossiter, 1982; Sreekumar, 1990).
5. Recruitments were entrusted to the Kerala Public Service Commission.
6. In the mid-1980s, the Special Component Plan (SCP) and Tribal Sub-Plan (TSP) were decentralized to be prepared at the district level. However, this planning was undertaken mostly by officials, with very little popular participation (Thomas Isaac and Franke, 2000).
7. See a set of studies entitled 'Kerala Economy at the Crossroads' in *Economic and Political Weekly*, 1 September, 8 September and 15 September 1990.
8. Kerala presents an extreme picture of the shifting sectoral composition of the Indian economy: a rapid decline in the primary sector and a rapid growth in the tertiary sector, rather than the secondary sector. Kerala, along with Maharashtra, now has the highest share in the service sector in India (Shetty, 2003; Joseph, 2003). The predominance of the service sector in Kerala is expected to pick up further speed with emphasis on tourism, technical education and health services in the state (Joseph, 2003).
9. A debate on these issues may be seen in the *Journal of Concerned Asian Scholars*, vol. 30, nos. 1, 3 & 4 (1998) and in special issues of *Economic and Political Weekly*, vol. 25, nos. 26 and 27, 8 and 15 September 1990.
10. Kannan and Hari (2002) estimate that remittances constituted an average of 22 per cent of the SDP, 111 per cent of government expenditure and 179 per cent of value added in manufacturing in the second-half of the 1990s.

11. For instance, see Yadav (1993)'s argument that the collapse of the Soviet Union and the socialist world posed a serious threat to the socialist movement in India and that a new way needed to be forged.
12. In 1987 the LDF government actively courted private capital. An export processing zone was opened in the industrial area of Ernakulum in 1989 and a stock exchange was opened in Cochin in 1988. A techno-park was also commissioned in Thiruvananthapuram to attract investors in software and electronics. At the same time, there was an attempt to restrain the unions, and the CPM Secretariat specifically called upon the working class to develop a new 'work culture' (Heller, 1995).
13. In 1989–90, the state government provided every village panchayat with an untied grant (GoK, 2000).
14. After the new government was formed in Kerala in 2000, there was an agitation by tribal leaders, who protested against the lack of initiative by the panchayats with respect to the use of funds earmarked for tribals in the tribal sub-plan (TSP). This amount was then withdrawn from the PRIs and handed back to the tribal department to administer. Subsequently, after further protests, 50 per cent of the TSP funds were handed back to the PRIs to administer.
15. For a detailed account of the PPC, see Thomas Isaac and Franke, (2000).
16. During the Ninth Plan period (1997–2002), PRIs received 30.5 per cent of plan resources.

CHAPTER 5

The Institution of Village Panchayat (Kerala)

The GP, historically the only continuing tier of panchayati raj in Kerala, remains the most critical one. Since 1996, it has been envisaged as an institution for the people to participate in planning for their socio-economic development. The functions of the GP, as listed in the Kerala Panchayat Act 1994, are extensive. The GP has 'mandatory functions', which include the protection and maintenance of public assets, regulation of building construction, eating places, fairs and festivals, health and sanitation measures, etc.; 'general functions', which include collection of statistics, involvement of people in development, organization of voluntary workers, awareness building against social malpractices and inculcation of civic practices; and development-related functions, identified separately for 19 sectors. The GP is thus an institution expected to perform civic functions, foster participation of the people and promote socio-economic development.

An idea of the developmental role envisaged for the GP can be had from noting its functions in three sectors, i.e. agriculture, education and drinking water (see Annex 3). In agriculture, these include land management, i.e. cultivation of waste and marginal lands, ensuring optimal utilization of land and soil protection; agricultural development activities such as production of organic manure, seed protection, fodder development, etc.; organizing people, including support for co-operative farming and self-help groups (SHGs); and institutional responsibilities, i.e. the management of Krishi Bhawans. In education, the functions of the GP include management of government pre-primary and primary schools, implementation of literacy programmes and the management and promotion of reading rooms and libraries. In the field of drinking water, GPs are entrusted with the setting up and management of water supply schemes within their area.

The capacity and the likelihood of the GP to play these roles is dependent, to a large extent, on the type of institution or organization it is. Panchayati raj policy, i.e. the legal provisions, financial devolution and other processes highlighted in the previous chapter, are attempts, which may be more or less successful, to enable the GP to perform these roles. These are important, but so are several other dynamics. These include the political processes and ethos that develop, the administrative and technical capacities and processes, and the relationship of the organization with various social groups. These dynamic processes are often either not addressed in policy, or are dealt with only partially. Moreover, when attempts are made to address these, policy enters a slippery terrain, for the dynamics are complex and rooted in the larger sociopolitical context. The particular 'institutional character' of the GP in Kerala has emerged as panchayati raj policy has played out in its unique context. In this chapter, we shall attempt to analyse these institutional characteristics of the Kerala GP.

THE GP: A COMPLEX ORGANIZATION

The analysis of the GP is based on the idea that it is essentially a state institution. In a broad sense, the approach followed here is one suggested by Peter Evans (1995), of viewing state institutions and their capacity to carry out various agendas in terms of their internal structure and dynamics on the one hand, and their relation to society on the other. Evans argues that the success of the state government in Kerala in its project of social transformation was enabled by a relatively coherent and competent, or 'autonomous' state apparatus, along with an 'embeddedness' in society which was achieved through public action and mass mobilization campaigns organized by political parties. The GP as an organization is viewed through a similar lens, i.e. in terms of the internal structure and dynamic on the one hand, and the types of relations and networks forged in society on the other.

While this broad approach has been adopted, it is necessary to appreciate that the GP, while it is a part of the state apparatus, is different from apex state institutions, and also from the 'field offices' of such structures. On the one hand, the GP is situated in a larger political-governance structure. GP representatives are members of national and state political parties, its bureaucracy part of a state structure, and it is subject to overall macro-policy. In this sense, the internal dynamic of the GP partakes from the macro political and governance context in which it is situated. However, the GP is not simply an arm of this macro-structure. It differs significantly from the apex state-level institutions, not only in its mandate, but also because it is close to the grassroots, and its interface with people is far more direct. It is also different from the field offices at the grassroots as it has its own politics, which guides a fairly large part of the decision-making space.

In fact, the Kerala GP is an extremely complex organization. While the elected political representatives form its focal point, the GP extends into society through the gram sabha and various community-based associations, spreads into government departments through the departmental offices transferred to it, and is also linked to resource persons, experts and civil society organizations by their participation in its processes. The characteristics and modes of functioning of all these players, and the interaction among them on the one hand, and the manner in which they relate to various sections of society on the other, make up the institutional and organizational characteristics of the GP. The analysis of the GP in this chapter attempts to take into account this complexity, and is based on detailed fieldwork (described in Box 1 and Annex 1) across twelve GPs in three districts of Kerala, tapping into all these aspects (see Box 2 for details).

The GP may be understood in terms of four sub-systems, which vary in their structure, involve different actors and follow their own specific processes. First, there is the 'core' GP, which is quite small, comprising panchayat representatives and a small staff, where decisions are taken and the day-to-day business of the GP is transacted though panchayat meetings, committees and so on. The second sub-system of the GP comprises the gram sabha and various community-based associations. The gram sabha scrutinizes its activities and plays an advisory role and is integral to the GP. Community-based associations of various types are more loosely linked to the GP, and often play a role in implementing GP activities. The implementation of GP projects takes place mainly through the government departmental structure, the third sub system of the GP, functioning under the dual control of the state departments and the GP. Finally, resource persons and NGOs participate in several GP processes including planning, training, technical committees and in the case of NGOs, implementation of projects, and form a fourth sub-system.

Not only do these sub-systems perform different roles, but significantly, they also embody varied priorities, capabilities and modes of functioning, as each sub-system is rooted in its specific macro-structure. The panchayat samiti, with its political representatives who are members

Box 2: Studying the GP

The study of each village panchayat entailed:

(a) *Study of panchayat records* such as panchayat development reports, project reports, financial statements, minutes of meetings of the panchayat committee, standing committee, gram sabha, and other relevant documents.

(b) *Observation of panchayat buildings as well as of social infrastructure and socio-economic conditions in two wards.* In each village panchayat one ward with the highest SC/ST population (referred to as ward 1) and one with an average social composition (referred to as ward 2) was selected. The social infrastructure and socio-economic conditions of these wards were noted. In addition panchayat buildings, infrastructure, and so on were also observed.

(c) *Interviews with key actors* provided the bulk of the qualitative data. Interviewees included:

i. Panchayat secretary of each GP
ii. Panchayat representatives (PRs): 3-4 elected representatives including the panchayat president, leader of the opposition and at least one woman and one representative from SC/ST category.
iii. Resource persons: Two resource persons who had been involved in training, committees, working groups, plan appraisals and other activities.
iv. Departmental officials dealing with the three selected areas, i.e. agriculture, school education and drinking water.

(d) *Focus group discussions* (FGDs) with the residents were held in the two selected wards, i.e. ward 1 and ward 2, in each GP.

(e) *Short case studies* were conducted to provide detailed information regarding some aspects of the GP. These included:

i. Community-based association in the GP: In each GP, one community-based association such as self-help groups, parent teacher associations or farmers' groups were studied. This involved discussion with the organizers, participants and beneficiaries, as well as observation of the work done.
ii. Largest project: In Thrissur and Wayanad, one of the five largest projects of each GP was selected for detailed study. Preference was given to projects which were repeated over the years. Investigations included interviews with persons who planned, formulated, implemented and supervised the project and those who were affected by it as well as observation of the project site.
iii. Special project: Researchers were also asked to select another project that was considered 'special' in some way, in terms of being innovative, or especially important to some people, etc. One such project was studied in detail in each gram panchayat in Thrissur and Wayanad districts.

of various political parties, is linked to the ideologies and dynamics of these parties. The bureaucracy is linked to the larger governmental structure. The gram sabha and community-based associations link the GP closely to society. So do resource persons and NGOs, but in a different way. Notably, the network of the various GP sub-systems and the macro-systems is not simple and one to one. For example, political parties influence the GP not only through its panchayat representatives, but also impact the bureaucracy as a whole at the state level. However, each sub-system varies in the manner in which it internalizes various influences, and the emphasis it places on them.

To analyse the GP as an institution, it is important to understand the key features of each of its sub-systems, in terms of role, structure, capacity, processes and dynamics. At the same time, it is important to understand on the one hand, the relation of these sub-systems to each other, i.e. the extent to which each is central or peripheral, and on the other, the nature of interaction among them. Below, we shall attempt to comprehend the GP in all its complexity, in two steps. In the first step, we shall try to understand each sub-system of the GP, its internal structure and dynamic, and the manner in which it is linked to the larger political and governmental structures as well as society. In the second step, we shall examine how these various sub-systems stand in relation to each other. This analysis will enable an understanding of the GP as an institution, and the manner in which it relates to society.

THE CORE GP

The 'core GP' comprises panchayat representatives (PRs) and a small administrative staff.[1] PRs are by far its most important actors, as they comprise the panchayat samiti, which is the central decision-making body, and has the formal power to drive the agenda of the GP. Therefore, it is important to focus on the PRs, i.e. who they are, their priorities, style of functioning, etc., and also examine the panchayat samiti, in terms of its composition, processes and dynamics.

Social Composition and Dynamics

An important characteristic of the Kerala GP is that the GP PRs tend to be ordinary people, rather than elites. Representation of SCs, STs and women has been ensured through reservation, and across the sample GPs 37.3 per cent of all PRs were women and 22.5 per cent belonged to the SC or ST categories. Notably, in some GPs, the percentage of

SC and ST representatives was quite significant (Table 1). At the same time, the general-category PRs were not social elites either (Table 2). For instance, no PR reported a monthly income of more than Rs. 10,000; nearly 70 per cent of those interviewed owned neither cars nor motorcycles, while a mere 5 per cent owned a car; and half the PRs who were wage earners were blue-collar workers.[2] No GP was reported to be dominated by a socially powerful person or group of persons.

However, though SC/ST representatives, women, and less well-off persons had become members of the panchayat samiti, their social status affected the role that they played within the GP. First, representatives from reserved categories could not easily be leaders within the GP. In GPs where SC/ST or women representatives were panchayat presidents, some other PR was often reported to be influential. In 3 out of the 6 such GPs, the panchayat president admitted to relying a great deal on some other male representative of the general category. This was not the case in any of the 6 GPs with males of general category as presidents. Notably, such GP presidents were usually politically experienced, while those from reserved categories were not.[3] The equation between caste and gender on the one hand, and experience and perceived effectiveness on the other, was also evident in the three 'best GPs', all of which had general category, politically experienced men as presidents. Additionally, in the panchayat standing committees, where there were no reservations, women and SC/ST PRs were rarely chairpersons.[4] Moreover, women and SC members, if they were chairpersons at all, headed the less important committees, i.e. development and welfare committees, and not the more important finance committee.

Second, this marginality was reflected in the attitude of PRs to their SC/ST and women colleagues. Though the attitude was rarely one of outright hostility, and was in fact, often sympathetic, doubts about the ability and effectiveness of PRs from reserved categories were often expressed, and it was generally acknowledged that they had special problems.[5] Women were viewed by both men and women PRs as having difficulty in working late, in travelling and mingling with people, or paying less attention to work because of duties at home, and lacking training, experience and influence, while facing discrimination and harassment by male colleagues. Many PRs said that women had problems within political parties too. Similarly, several SC/ST as well as non-SC/ST PRs saw lack of clout, education and experience as well as financial difficulties as problems of the former. The fact that PRs of reserved as well as non-reserved categories mentioned common

TABLE 1: COMPOSITION OF PANCHAYAT SAMITIS OF VILLAGE PANCHAYATS

	Thrissur				Wayanad				Thiruvananthapuram			
	GP1	GP2	GP3	GP4	GP1	GP2	GP3	GP4	GP1	GP2	GP3	GP4
No of seats	11	15	12	14	15	13	16	18	14	14	13	14
% Women	36.4	33.3	41.7	35.7	33.3	46.2	37.5	33.3	35.7	NA*	46.2	34.7
% SC	36.4	33.3	41.7	7.1	0.0	7.7	0	5.6	7.1	NA*	7.7	7.1
%ST	–	–	–	–	20.0	46.2	18.8	16.7	–	–	–	–
% UDF	36.4	60.0	50.0	42.9	60.0	30.8	93.7	50.0	78.6	50.0	38.5	71.4
% LDF	63.6	33.3	50.0	57.1	40.0	61.5**	6.3	44.4**	21.4	50.0	61.5	28.6
Political control	LDF	UDF	EqualΔ	LDF	UDF	LDF	UDF	UDF	UDF	EqualΔ	LDF	UDF

Notes:

* Not Available

** One BJP member

Δ President LDF

TABLE 2: PROFILE OF PANCHAYAT REPRESENTATIVES INTERVIEWED

	No. of Panchayat Representatives		
	GP PR = 43	Block PR = 8	District PR = 8
Age			
35 years or below	12	1	2
36–49 years	24	4	2
50 years or above	7	2	4
NA	0	1	0
Education			
8th grade or below	3	0	2
9–12 grades	33	5	2
College education	7	0	1
NA	0	3	3
Occupation			
Non-wage earning	17	2	2
Blue collar	13	1	1
White collar	6	0	3
Farmer	7	5	2
Reported income (Rs. per month)			
0–1,000	8	0	0
1,001–3,000	15	3	0
3,001–5,000	12	2	2
5,001–7000	5	0	1
7,001–10,000	1	0	0
More than 10,000	0	0	1
NA	2	3	4
Land owned			
10 cents or less	21	2	2
11 cents-1 acre	9	1	0
1–2 acres	5	1	1
2–5 acres	4	0	1
More than 5 acres	4	1	1
NA	0	3	3
Vehicle owned			
None	27	5	3
Two-wheeler	9	1	1
Car/jeep	2	0	1
Two-wheeler and car/jeep	1	0	1

NA	4	2	2
Previous political experience			
Party or party association worker	10	3	2
Local elected body member	14	2	0
Students'/teachers'/workers' union	5	2	3
No political experience till election	13	0	1
NA	2	1	2
Years of experience in panchayat			
0–5 years	27	2	4
6–10 years	12	4	2
More than 10 years	4	0	0
NA	0	2	2

handicaps for the former, indicates that these were to some extent genuine problems and not only prejudices, though the latter may have been an ingredient too. Whatever the reason, the point is that PRs from reserved categories were perceived as weak within the panchayat. Moreover, a significant number of non-SC/ST PRs were lukewarm or negative about the performance of SC/ST representatives, though the assessment of women PRs' performance was more positive.[6] Importantly, such perceptions were visible among community members also. When FGDs were asked if some PRs lacked influence, they usually mentioned an SC/ST or woman PR, attributing it to their personal shortcomings, i.e. lack of seriousness or ability of the individual.

However, while the internal organization of the GP had some inegalitarian features, the manner in which the institution related to the larger society essentially showed a concern with the basic problems of the people: PRs of all categories showed a concern for human problems. For instance, when PRs were asked to describe their role, most (65 per cent) gave answers in terms of 'helping people', 'providing basic facilities', 'fulfilling people's basic needs', etc. and more than a quarter (28 per cent) said specifically that their role was to address the needs of the less privileged. A much smaller number (19 per cent) mentioned 'development' or 'strengthening of the productive sector' as an important role. Similarly, when PRs were asked to name the activities on which they spent their time, more than half (51 per cent) said that the largest proportion of their working time was spent on people-oriented activities and only a quarter (25 per cent) said that it was spent on more technical aspects of projects and development-oriented activities. Some PRs reported spending their time on Kudumbashree, a women's empowerment programme. The sensitivity to the community was visible in other ways too. FGD discussions revealed that GP representatives had frequent interactions with the community.[7] People reported that the topics of discussion with PRs revolved around issues such as drinking water, roads, housing, etc., and people also made personal petitions and requests. PRs were generally viewed (in 22 out of 24 FGDs) as being sincere and making an effort.

Politics in the GP

A very critical dynamic of the GPs was intense political competition along party lines. Two elections to PRIs had been held in Kerala up to the time of this study, and in these, the political party in power had changed in eight out of twelve of the GPs. Additionally, in two GPs there were equal representatives from both political parties (Table 1). GP PRs had strong allegiance to one party or the other, and most were experienced in political life, having been party workers or members of trade unions and other political associations (less than one-third reported having had no political experience at all). The standing committee chairpersons, except in one case, invariably belonged to the ruling party of the GP. Several PRs (of the LDF) also admitted that party supervision and direction in panchayat affairs was substantial.

Notably, disagreements in the panchayat samiti tended to be along political party lines (and not caste or other identities). Major conflicts tended to follow a change of political regime. For instance, from among four GPs where the political party, i.e. the LDF, had remained in power across two elections, serious differences had arisen in only one. However, out of six GPs where the party in power had changed from LDF to UDF, in five some sort of 'event' such as alleged scams, cancellation of beneficiary lists, and *gheraos* had taken place. Moreover, when discussing the interaction of the GP with higher tier PRIs, PRs were most likely to highlight arbitrariness or a negative relationship if they belonged to the opposite political party.

However, while political party divisions were key, they played out around local developmental issues and the functioning of the GP. When PRs and FGDs were asked to recall the major issues and promises of the previous election, in 11 out of 12 GPs, these concerned socio-economic development and basic facilities—the availability of drinking water, condition of roads, the development of tribal areas (in three GPs of Wayanad). Corruption and nepotism were election issues in five GPs, and in one GP, alleged corruption was perceived as the reason for the previous party losing out. After the GPs were formed, the allocation of resources for projects and corruption remained centre-stage. Thus competitive politics, though organized along (centralized) party lines, focused on local concerns.

Along with the political competition, there also existed shared perceptions and goals across political parties for the GP, indicated by the fact that there was often broad agreement about the overall needs and the development strategy. Conflicts arose, instead, regarding the distribution of funds across wards (in two GPs) and over the selection of projects and sites (in two GPs), corruption (in three GPs), and the selection of beneficiaries (in three GPs). These issues became contentious because of their potential impact on the popularity of PRs, and their chances at the next elections. PRs jockeyed to get good deals for their wards, and allegations of corruption, containing different degrees of truth, were used quite liberally by political opponents against incumbents. In other words, GP politics was organized around issues such as resource allocation and corruption, and not caste and religion.

This development needs to be viewed against the fact that Kerala has a long history of social mobilization and public action around redistributive and welfare issues, while the politics of caste and religion are much weaker than the rest of the country. Thus the centrality of developmental and welfare related concerns in GP politics is to a large degree a reflection of the space that these have occupied in centralized politics in the state. However, the centrality of socioeconomic development in GP politics has also been stimulated by the considerable efforts made by the state government since the PPC to generate a public discourse on these issues, by developing and facilitating processes such as development seminars, associating resource persons and building capacities.

With decentralization, important shifts were visible in the discourse too. First, the focus on rent-seeking was quite sharp in several GPs, facilitated by the fact that specific instances, and their impact, were highly visible, and could be used well by political opponents in election campaigns. One indication was that when FGDs were asked to compare corruption before and after decentralization, in a majority of the FGDs the opinion was that corruption had reduced, though in some FGDs, the opinion was favourable but qualified, i.e. that corruption still existed, but was less. However, this development was not uniform across the GPs. For example, in one GP in Wayanad, some panchayat members were reported to be involved in *benami*[8] works, and a contractor had considerable influence on the panchayat. Overall, there is reason to hope, that in the context of Kerala, institutional practices and overall governance might change for the better with democratic decentralization, but this is by no means certain.

The second point to be noted is that democratic decentralization did seem to strengthen the relationship between personal merit and political success. When people and PRs were asked to identify influential persons in the GP and the reason for their influence, the reasons given most often were that they were experienced, committed or capable, and not that they were politically or socially powerful. Though, as pointed out above, when the opposite attributes were ascribed, these were with reference to SC/ST and women representatives. The fact that positive assessments were made in terms of personal merit, rather than social or political power, is important. At the GP level, the personal contribution of individuals is visible, and considered important, even though these perceptions may remain tied to caste and gender to some degree.

Political conflict could sometimes be resolved within the GP framework, but at other times hindered the GP in moving towards its developmental agenda. In several instances, conflicts had been resolved through discussion and compromise, or through protest within the GP framework. For example, in one GP politically opposed groups disagreed on beneficiary selection but had reached a compromise. In another, the previous GP regime had been accused that the area of some acquired land was actually less than shown in documents, which the accused had refuted. This disagreement was recorded as a dissenting note in the minutes of the meeting. In several GPs however, there were more serious repercussions, and developmental projects had been stalled or adversely affected in some way. In one GP, one panchayat samiti had built a veterinary centre in one ward, but subsequently, the party in power had changed and the new panchayat samiti wanted it elsewhere. The dispute led to a *gherao*, petitions were sent to the state government, and the building that had been constructed lay unused. In this GP, because of disputes among ward members over projects, even the Special Component Plan (SCP) fund was distributed ward-wise and a drainage project had been sanctioned from SCP funds in a ward that had only one SC person. In a second GP, computer installation had been delayed as a court case had been instituted because of disagreements. In a third GP, women's groups formed during the previous regime were dismissed as the opposition came to power and work on a children's park was stopped as a court stay order was obtained. In a fourth GP, differences over distribution of project funds among wards resulted in the main roads being neglected, while small roads were developed as a compromise among various local pressure groups. Finally, in a fifth GP, there had been a no-confidence motion along with delay in implementation of projects and wastage of money. Thus in several instances, political competition did not just lead to highlighting of critical issues of socio-economic development, but also to an impasse, and poor use of resources.

Strong leadership could counter these problems. In all the three 'best GPs', the presidents were politically experienced, and were able to negotiate across political parties and evolve common agendas. In one such GP, decisions were often taken by consensus (though political parties were evenly matched). In this GP, all the members had got together and forced a private college to allow the construction of an overhead tank for a water supply project in its premises. In the other two GPs, there had been disagreements, but these had been dealt with effectively by the president. However, if the GP president was not capable of negotiating across political groups, there were no mechanisms to address the stalling of work.

Administrative and Technical Functioning of the Core GP

The political vibrancy of the core GP was not matched by a parallel administrative and technical capacity. Its two mechanisms for administrative and technical work, i.e. the administrative and technical staff, and its various committees, did not provide adequate support for its planning, decision-making, coordinating and supervisory roles. The staff of the core GPs was meagre, comprising a panchayat secretary, 1–2 extension officers (for rural development) and 1–3 overseers and engineers and some and clerical and ministerial staff. Here, it may be recalled that the GP is expected to plan and execute its projects through the departmental bureaucracy transferred to it, through various committees in which resource persons and other advisors participate, and in collaboration with people and NGOs. Such an exercise demands complex coordination and facilitation skills. However, the panchayat secretaries, the nodal government officials in the GP, had neither been recruited nor trained for this role (see Table 3). Additionally, transfers

TABLE 3: PROFILE OF PANCHAYAT SECRETARIES

	No. of Panchayat Secretaries		
	GP N = 12	Block N = 3	District N = 3
Gender			
Male	11	3	3
Female	1	0	0
Social category			
General	12	12	2
SC	0	0	0
ST	0	0	1
Education level			
Class 12	3	1	0
Graduate	6	2	2
Post graduate	3	0	1
Training status			
Received Induction training	4	3	3
Trained during PPC	11	2	2
Joined as			
Clerk	7	0	0
Executive officer	2	0	0
GP secretary	2	0	0
Not clear	1	0	0
BDO		1	2
Extension officer		2	0
Tehsildar		0	1
In current post for			
Less than 1 year	5	1	0
1–2 years	3	1	0
More than 2 years	0	0	1
NA	4	1	2

of panchayat secretaries were controlled by the state government, and their tenures tended to be brief.

Nor did the three standing committees related to finance, development and welfare fill in this gap. While some PRs noted that these committees increased transparency, and helped the GP by scrutinizing issues in advance,[9] these committees were not particularly effective, as their role was not clearly articulated, and nor had any processes been developed to enable them to function effectively. Additionally, the recommendations of these committees were often overturned by the panchayat samitis. The finance committee functioned well in some GPs, as it had the clearest role and contributed to financial accountability, but others did not.[10] The GP also has another committee, i.e. the steering committee comprising the president of the GP and chairpersons of the standing committees, which is supposed to coordinate the GP's activities. However, the steering committee was not effective in any GP and had, in fact, ceased to exist in three GPs.

Instead, a great deal of administrative decision-making, usually done by administrators and managers in government, was done by the panchayat samiti itself. During the course of fieldwork, minutes of samiti meetings were examined,[11] which showed that a great deal of meeting time was taken up with administrative activities, rather then more substantial discussions about the problems that confronted the panchayats. In fact, out of 34 meetings reviewed, in only 4 were there such discussions (these included topics such as the increasing antisocial activities in the panchayat, the drinking water problem, drought relief activities and schemes for the aged, children and the handicapped. Instead, a very large chunk of samiti time was devoted to discussions and decisions related to project implementation such as approval of beneficiary lists, tenders and sanctions, as well as routine tasks such as approval for travel bills and arrangements for functions. Plans and budgets were also discussed, but less often. This development is of some significance, as it implies a particular type of politicization of implementation. Implementation in India is politicized at the state and central levels too, but the influence is covert rather than overt. Here, implementation was thrown into the open as it were, and debated and contested. As implementation-related decisions are often a source of corruption, the fact that these were taken by a group of persons belonging to competing political parties, rather than an individual official, who could be corrupt himself, or be subject to pressures from powerful people, signalled an important shift. We have already noted above that corruption had become a contentious political issue in the GPs, and GPs were perceived as less corrupt than centralized agencies.

Notably, the panchayat samiti functioned in an organized fashion in the sample GPs. Samiti meetings were held frequently,[12] the attendance of PRs in the samiti meetings was good,[13] and the processes orderly. This development may be seen against the background that, not only were GP PRs reasonably well educated (usually with high school education), but they had often had experience of working, or at least membership in some public institution. Additionally, around one-third PRs of the sample had been GP representatives earlier, while several others had been involved in GP activities as members of task forces. Several PRs had been members of farmers' associations and cooperative societies. Thus GP PRs had usually had some organizational experience, which was reflected in the acceptance of organizational rules and procedures.

FINANCES

In this study, limited information was obtained about GP finances, as a detailed analysis of the same is already available.[14] However, in order to give the reader an idea of GP finances, the receipts and expenditure of four GPs of Thrissur for 1998–9 and 2001–2 are presented in Tables 4A and 4B. As can be seen, GPs receive and expend a substantial amount of funds. The GPs had received between Rs. 69 lakh to 101 lakh in these two years, and expended Rs. 41 lakh to 84 lakh. GP funds comprised their own funds, untied plan grants received from the state government, funds received for specific central and state govern-ment schemes, funds of institutions transferred to the GP and pensions disbursed by them.

The own funds of the GP are derived from tax and non-tax sources and are used to fund salaries and establishment expenditures, and some civic functions. In 1998–9 and 2001–2, receipts in the own fund across the four GPs of Thrissur varied between Rs. 13 lakh and 33 lakh. Ordinarily, these comprised less than 20 per cent of total GP funds, but in one particular GP (the best GP), these were 33 per cent and 43 per cent of total receipts in the two years, respectively. Untied grants from the state government comprised the largest share of GP receipts. The plan grant receipts of the Thrissur GPs varied from Rs. 32 lakh to 72 lakh and expenditure from Rs. 12 lakh to 53 lakh in the two years. In all the GPs, the plan grant expenditure was substantially less then the receipts in both the years, suggesting a high carry-over from year to year. Funds for specific state and central schemes (much smaller amounts compared to the state plan grant) and for transferred institutions have not been included in the table presented, as information regarding them was not available evenly. There were either no beneficiary or voluntary contributions or these comprised very small amounts.

There were some important shortcomings of the financial system of the GP. First, inspite of the fact that GPs received and spent large

TABLE 4A: RECEIPTS OF FOUR GPs OF THRISSUR DISTRICT

Receipts	1998–9				2001–2			
	GP1	GP2	GP3	GP4	GP1	GP2	GP3	GP4
Total (Rs. in lakhs)	79.11	92.81	100.46	95.58	98.10	71.56	88.61	69.11
Own fund (Rs. in lakhs)	18.55	18.34	15.88	31.86	14.88	13.11	32.30	29.48
% Own fund of total receipts	23.45	19.76	15.81	33.33	15.17	18.32	36.45	42.66
Composition of own funds								
% Tax	26.95	17.99	33.75	33.99	59.50	50.34	29.84	50.20
% Non-tax	20.59	1.91	9.70	9.29	25.40	8.78	64.09	3.70
% State grant	52.43	80.10	56.55	56.71	15.05	40.89	6.07	46.1
Plan grant (Rs. in lakhs)	36.45	71.63	69.57	47.15	39.10	48.40	47.02	32.24
% Plan grant of total receipts	46.08	77.18	69.25	49.33	39.86	67.64	53.06	46.65
State sponsored schemes (Rs. in lakhs)	8.45	2.57	10.26	9.02	31.03	2.96	0	0
% State sponsored schemes	10.68	2.77	10.21	9.44	31.63	4.14	0	0
Centrally sponsored schemes (Rs. in lakhs)	4.27	0	2.34	5.79	7.38	6.90	6.37	3.76
% Centrally sponsored schemes	5.40	0	2.33	6.06	7.52	9.64	7.19	5.44
Others (Rs. in lakhs)	11.39	0.27	2.41	1.76	5.71	0.17	2.92	3.63
% Others	14.40	0.29	2.40	1.84	5.82	0.24	3.30	5.25

TABLE 4B: EXPENDITURE OF FOUR GPs IN THRISSUR DISTRICT

Expenditure	1998–9				2001–2			
	GP1	GP2	GP3	GP4	GP1	GP2	GP3	GP4
Total (Rs. in lakhs)	42.46	79.87	83.96	83.46	41.91	42.32	64.26	55.80
Own fund (Rs. in lakhs)	20.52	24.25	24.54	31.90	17.64	12.37	29.55	31.20
% Own fund of total expenditure	48.33	30.36	29.23	38.22	42.09	29.23	45.99	55.91
Plan grant (Rs. in lakhs)	18.69	52.65	52.66	36.54	12.59	23.17	23.17	15.41
% Plan grant of total expenditure	44.02	65.92	62.72	43.78	30.04	54.75	36.06	27.62
State sponsored schemes (Rs. in lakhs)	3.06	2.70	4.97	7.64	8.28	2.80	0	1.80
% State sponsored schemes of total expenditure	7.21	3.38	5.92	9.15	19.76	6.62	0	3.23
Centrally sponsored schemes (Rs. in lakhs)	0.19	0	1.37	5.62	3.40	3.98	3.69	3.76
% Centrally sponsored schemes of total expenditure	0.45	0	1.63	6.73	8.11	9.40	5.74	6.74
Others (Rs. in lakhs)	0	0.27	0.42	1.76	0	0	7.85	3.63
% Others of total expenditure	0	0.34	0.50	2.11	0	0	12.22	6.51

Note: Funds related to transferred institutions and pension schemes are not included, as the data with respect to these was not reliable.

amounts of funds, they had no trained manpower to keep accounts and manage finances. In all the sample GPs, clerks (and not trained accountants) handled accounts as well as taxation. Additionally, the accounting system of the GPs was quite complicated, and PRs as well as GP secretaries complained about the difficulty in obtaining correct figures. Second, the mechanisms of financial accountability were not rigorous. Before the PPC, the 'local fund audit' was the mechanism for auditing PRI accounts in Kerala. After the PPC, the government introduced a 'performance audit' to improve the accounting system of the GPs. However, in the sample GPs, these audits had usually highlighted minor financial problems. Third, revenue generation was not an activity that was taken up with any enthusiasm in the GPs. In the sample GPs, the methods used to deal with defaulters consisted of launching revenue collection drives and 'persuasion', and stronger action was rare. Their weakness as financial institutions can be assumed to add to this characteristic, as there was no qualified financial manager in the GP who could assist and advise in resource mobilization activities. Finally, the GP was also affected by the overall state-level financial system. The tight fiscal situation of the state government at the time of this study had impacted the GP. Several PRs complained of inadequacy of funds, frequent treasury bans as well as late transfer of funds.

PARTICIPATORY STRUCTURES AND PROCESSES

There are two important types of community-based sub-systems of the GP, i.e. the gram sabha, and various community-based associations such as self-help groups (SHGs), parent teacher associations (PTAs), farmers' groups, and so on. Both these are examined briefly below.

Gram Sabha

The gram sabha, made up of all adults of the village, has been envisaged as an integral part of the GP in Kerala. It is a structure to facilitate people's participation in the activities of the GP, with an advisory role in planning, assistance in implementation, and is envisaged to contribute in terms of voluntary labour. Gram sabhas have to be convened at least once in three months and the required quorum is 10 per cent of the voters of the area. Gram sabha meetings are held separately in each ward to facilitate maximum participation of people. Along with facilitating participation, the sabha is expected to increase the transparency of GP processes, and make the GP accountable to the people. Budgetary provisions and plan outlays have to be placed before the gram sabha, and it is responsible for beneficiary selection.

In practice, the pattern of participation in the gram sabha did not correspond to the romanticized ideas of the 'whole community' that are often associated with it, but revealed the importance of self-interest on the one hand, and the potential of organizing less powerful groups of society on the other. Against the notion of the 'whole community' was the fact that gram sabha meetings were thinly attended, and attendees comprised specific sections of society. In the sample GPs, though gram sabha meetings were held regularly,[15] a scrutiny of meeting records[16] showed that in more than half the meetings, the quorum could not be completed (Table 5). Rather surprisingly, attendance of women was high, and in some meetings even exceeded 70 per cent (this was the case in 10 out of 70 meetings for which information was available). Interviews revealed that the main participants in the gram sabha were of two types: potential beneficiaries and women from self-help groups of the Kudumbashree programme. The attendance of the potential beneficiaries was often based on simple self-interest. In the FGDs, people admitted that gram sabha meetings were seen chiefly as an opportunity for getting benefits in various schemes, and often, families classified above the poverty line did not participate in the gram sabha, as they did not stand to benefit in any way. However, as potential beneficiaries were people identified as being below the poverty line and from marginalized groups, the participation of the less powerful, rather than dominant groups was facilitated. At the same time, women from Kudumbashree groups, i.e. associations of the poorest and most marginalized people of the ward, attended gram sabha meetings because their organized groups could be accessed easily by ward members and persuaded to attend. As illustrated below in greater detail, Kudumbashree groups were able to influence the GP.

While the gram sabha did not function as an integrated community with one voice, some community feeling was also visible. For example, there was some participation to create common assets. In 2002–3, such contributions were made in seven out of twelve GPs. Mostly (in five GPs), this was in the form of voluntary labour, e.g., for road construction, cleaning of a school, clearing of a water stream, provision of free services as health volunteers or in socio-economic surveys. In two GPs, people had contributed money. In one GP, people had collected

TABLE 5: ATTENDANCE IN THE GRAM SABHAS

Total attendance				
% of person attending	Number of meetings			
	Thrissur	Wayanad	Thiruvanantha-puram	Total
0–5%	5	0	0	5
5–10%	19	8	9	36
10–25%	0	16	13	29
More than 25%	0	0	1	1
NA			1	1
Total	24	24	24	72

Percentage of women attending				
% of person attending	Number of meetings			
	Thrissur	Wayanad	Thiruvanantha-puram	Total
0–30%	0	4	0	4
30–40%	5	3	2	10
40–50%	12	5	3	20
50–60%	6	7	5	18
60–70%	1	4	5	10
More than 70%		3	7	10
NA			2	2
Total	24	24	24	72

Rs. 80,000 to buy land for a drinking water project from the business community, using the influence of the panchayat. In another GP, they had contributed to buy streetlights and computers for the school.

In parallel, gram sabhas meetings, though thinly attended, served to demystify the processes of the GP and induce greater transparency and accountability. In the gram sabhas, people made suggestions for new projects, discussed proposals, and panchayat representatives explained the projects to the people. Beneficiary selection through gram sabhas, though not perfect, was transparent. Beneficiaries were identified as per norms, lists were announced in the gram sabhas and disputes were settled. However, in spite of the transparency of the process, the PRs and the community groups were only partly satisfied. There was dissatisfaction about the criteria for selection, and potential beneficiaries were reported to provide wrong information, leading to wrong selection. In the latter case, other people did not protest because they did not want to make long-term enemies.

Community-Based Associations

Along with the gram sabha, the GP fanned out into the community through various community-based associations, such as self-help groups (SHGs), parent teachers' associations (PTA), farmers' associations, and so on. In the sample GPs, several types of such associations, usually facilitated by government departments, were in existence (Table 6). Although such associations were not strictly a part of the GP, in Kerala, they were closely linked to it. GP members were often chairpersons of these associations and the GP supported them in various ways. The associations, in turn, implemented GP projects and managed funds provided by the GP. In several associations conscious attempts had been made to establish clear linkages with the GP.

The interaction of such community-based associations with the GP needs to be seen against the fact that the associations themselves varied a great deal, in terms of goals, criteria for membership, organizational strength, etc. Women's self-help or Kudumbashree groups, engaged in livelihood enhancement activities, and farmers' associations, benefited the association members. On the other hand, PTAs and other school-related committees, as well as health and hospital development committees, supported a village institution, and their members did not benefit personally in any way. The same was true of beneficiary committees and ward development committees, formed specifically in the

TABLE 6: COMMUNITY-BASED ASSOCIATIONS IN THE GPs

Name/function of association	No. of GPs in which in existence N = 12
1. Kudumbashree	11
2. (a) Agriculture Development Committee/Agriculture Advisory Committee	4
(b) Paddy Growers' Association	7
(c) Coconut Development Committee	4
(d) Vanilla Development Committee	1
(e) Pepper Development Committee	3
(f) Irrigation Committee	1
(g) Veterinary Development Committee	1
(h) Watershed Development Committee	2
3. Hospital Development/Health and Drinking Water Committee	7
4. School Development Committee/Education Development Committee/Village Education Committee/Parent Teacher Association	7
5. Beneficiary Committee	4
6. Ward Development Committee	3

context of decentralization, the former to replace contractors with participatory structures for the execution of public works, and the latter to enable participation at the ward level. Except for Kudumbashree groups, which comprised a specific social group, i.e. poor women, the membership criteria for these committees was loose. Similarly, only Kudumbashree had a well-defined organizational structure, which included federations as well as technical support from the state level.

These associations varied a great deal in terms of vibrancy and level of activity, depending on the extent to which the members of the associations actually benefited from its activities, the clarity of goals of the association, the specificity of membership criteria, organizational processes, and technical support available to the association. The most vibrant of the associations were Kudumbashree SHGs, comprising a particular social group, i.e. poor women, around thrift and livelihood activities that benefited them directly, with a strong network of associations, supported by the state government.[17] Kudumbashree groups existed in all the sample GPs and were reported to be active (see Box 3). While in some SHGs activities remained limited to thrift and savings, in others, self-employment activities like brick manufacturing, vanilla cultivation, and kitchen garden had been taken up.[18] There

Box 3: Kudumbashree Succeeds in a Wayanad GP

There are 489 Kudumbashree SHGs in the GP, of which 104 are ST SHGs. The SHGs include all below poverty line (BPL) families of the area, though there are also some SHGs with combined Above Poverty Line (APL)-BPL membership, as well as APL-only SHGs. Area Development Societies (ADSs) are formed at the ward level from members elected by the SHGs. At the level of the GP, there is the Community Development Society (CDS) elected from among the ADSs. The panchayat president, the chairperson of the welfare standing committee and the junior superintendent of the GP are also members of the CDS committee. SHGs meet every week, the ADS and CDS every month and a monthly district-level review meeting of all the CDSs is also held.

All respondents and FGDs agree that Kudumbashree is the best functioning association in the panchayat. Nearly all SHGs are engaged in thrift collection and some are also engaged in income-generating activities. At present, 88 micro-enterprises are working under Kudumbashree. Their activities include mushroom cultivation, stone crushing, running of provision stores and restaurants, manufacture of paper bags, soaps and readymade garments, vermi-composting, etc. Their products are marketed through door-to-door selling. The unit members get a chance to introduce their products during CDS, ADS and SHG meetings. Additionally, Kudumbashree units cultivate land, run *bala sabhas* (children's assemblies) to develop children's cultural and other talents, and the CDS has also collected money to provide medical assistance to its members. Some ADS's have also constructed houses under the 'Ashraya' scheme of the panchayat very efficiently.

The panchayat committee takes a great deal of interest in the activities of CDS and also provides leadership. Women representatives are especially actively involved. The panchayat committee has put in tremendous effort to develop this association, and got the best panchayat award in the district for Kudumbashree activities.

were also instances of Kudumbashree groups supporting cultural and other activities for children.

While Kudumbashree members stood to gain directly from membership of the association, some community-based associations with public interest goals, rather than personal advancement, were also active. This was true of associations linked to village institutions, which were part of the daily life of citizens. Associations related to schools, such as village education committees, PTAs and school development committees were active in many GPs, and had taken up activities such as improvement of infrastructure and midday meals, and in some cases organizing study tours and cultural programmes. And, as in the case of Kudumbashree, state-level support had played a role. As one headmaster commented, in the education sector, decentralization had fortunately coincided with a centrally sponsored programme[19] in which there had been considerable state-level support for PTAs in terms of training and development of processes. Similarly, in one GP the hospital committee was extremely active and had taken up construction work in the hospital, held health talks in early childhood care centres and organized medical camps. In another GP, the committee had distributed medicines to prevent the outbreak of dengue fever.

Where community-based associations were successful, they did not come into conflict with the GP, but collaborated with it. Importantly, in Kerala, unlike several other states, such associations were not promoted along with the marginalization of GPs, but instead, existed in a scenario where the GP was empowered and had substantial financial resources at its disposal. Consequently, when successful, community-based associations acted as important links between their constituencies and the GP, and a mutually supportive cycle between the association and the GP had been established. Several GPs had collaborated actively with Kudumbashree groups and some PRs, especially women, reported spending a large part of their time on their activities. Some PRs said that because of such groups, women had become more active in public life, participating in gram sabhas and taking on small leadership roles. Similarly, active PTAs had collaborated with the GPs. In one GP, where the high school was managed by the GP, the PTA had raised funds for the school and had been instrumental in providing computer labs. A Kudumbashree group had also pitched in with six computers. A similar dynamic was visible in the case of a water management committee (see Box 4).

However, many associations themselves were inactive. This happened when the structure of the association itself was problematic, i.e. the activities of the association were not directly useful to the members, the goals were very general and unfocused, or membership criteria loose. For instance, during the PPC, the state government had suggested that 'ward committees' be formed in each ward to give recommendations about projects to the GP as well as help in their implementation (this type of committee had played an important role in Kalliasseri). In

Box 4: Drinking Water Project in a Wayanad GP

In 1988, a drinking water project was started in a government lower primary school in the village at the request of the PTA. A well was dug, a tank was constructed and a diesel motor and pump were purchased. At that time, the people of the GP were not very interested in the project. But subsequently, because of drinking water scarcity, some families residing near the school started taking water from this project. Then, after some time, a small sum of money was collected from them, and the project was made a public drinking water project. A committee was also formed to manage the project. In 1990, the school dug another well and bought a motor for its own use, and this project was then converted into a public one, and the number of beneficiaries increased.

In 1997–8, after the PPC had begun, the gram panchayat bought an electric motor and pipes to extend the water supply as recommended by the gram sabha. Parallelly, the beneficiary committee collected a small sum and bought another new diesel motor from its own funds, and voluntarily did the entire work of laying the pipes. Now 85 families benefit from this project and a committee of 11 members from these families manages it. Charges for the water consumed, as well as an additional amount to pay the salaries of the secretary, pump worker, and meter-reader and repairs, are collected each month from the users.

several of the sample GPs, such ward committees had been formed, but were no longer active. Notably, the role of the ward committee envisaged was a very general one, i.e. to represent the interests of the ward and assist the GP in planning, and the membership criteria were unclear. Such associations lent themselves easily to political manipulation. In one GP, where the members of the ward committee were nominated by the ward representative, the ward committee members were changed when the political party in power changed, and the ward committee subsequently became inactive. Similarly, beneficiary committees, envisaged as implementing public works taken up by the GP, faced considerable problems because lack of technical know how. As the government changed, they ceased to play an important role, and projects began to be implemented through contractors.

Associations also became inactive if they had been set up without adequate attention to organizational strength and technical know-how.

A few associations, as in the case of farmers' groups, e.g., paddy growers' associations formed to promote group farming, as well as societies for promoting a particular crop such as pepper or coconut, simply comprised beneficiaries of departmental and GP activities. A few were moderately active and performed a useful role as they formed a link between farmers, the agriculture department and the GP. Seeds, saplings and subsidies were distributed through such bodies. However, such associations did not play an agenda-setting role, as they lacked organizational strength and technical skills. Several such associations were also defunct.[20]

New lessons about 'people's participation' are clearly visible here. Self-interest is always an important ingredient of participation, and the extent to which participation is successful in enabling the marginalized to promote their own interests, it promotes social equity. However, this demands a fairly high degree of organization and resource support.

Interaction and Influence

While the gram sabha and the links with people's associations were the more structured forums of participation, other types of interactions among the community and PRs too formed a means of influence. As noted above, PRs interacted frequently with the community, especially people of their wards, to discuss projects and hear petitions. In addition, the community could exercise influence over the core GP by making complaints. Though complaints about the GP were not made often, when they were, they carried some weight. In the case of one GP, when there were complaints about a check dam, the problem was attended to and solved. In two GPs in Wayanad, there were many complaints with regard to the beneficiary selection for housing. In both the cases, the GPs had appointed committees to inquire into these complaints. Arguably, since the GP is far more accessible for direct interaction than centralized government, people are also able to influence it far more through direct interaction with decision-makers.

DEPARTMENTAL OFFICIALS TRANSFERRED TO THE GPs

The core GP has only skeletal administrative staff, and the Kerala government has sought to provide it with administrative and technical wherewithal by transferring to it government offices and officials from the development and welfare departments, which comprise its departmental arm or sub-system. This sub-system has its own characteristics and organization, which are in a sense 'inherited' by the GP. The transition of this sub-system to panchayati raj is partial, as officials function under the dual control of the GP and the departments. Their relationship with the GP is consequently not simple. Below, the bureaucratic or departmental sub-system of the GP is examined in detail in the context of three sectors, i.e. agriculture, school education and drinking water.

AGRICULTURE

Each GP in Kerala has access to an agriculture office (Krishi Bhawan). These were established at the GP level in the late 1980s, along with state government initiatives to promote group farming and have been transferred to the GPs. In the sample GPs, the staff comprised an agriculture officer (AO) assisted by 1–3 agricultural assistants. Most AOs had good professional qualifications, and the department had made some efforts to train them (Table 7). Thus, in agriculture, a GP-level structure with qualified personnel to enable the GP to carry forward its developmental agenda existed.

There was evidence that with decentralization the practices and ethos of the institution had also changed somewhat. In general, AOs accepted the dual control of the GP as well as the department, and most did not report any problems with the PRs.[21] There was also indication that a more consultative mode of functioning than had existed previously had been established in the case of panchayat projects. When AOs compared GP projects and departmental schemes, they pointed out that many people, i.e. farmers, PRs and other experts were consulted during the formulation of GP projects, whereas only officials were involved in the preparation of departmental schemes. Moreover, in three GPs, AOs also reported support from the community, i.e. Kudumbashree groups or local clubs, in the implementation of GP projects.

However, these changes, though valuable, were not adequate to enable the Krishi Bhawan to address its new role. For example, while AOs had earlier largely implemented pre-designed departmental schemes with set norms, as GP officials, they were involved in planning and project formulation. But AOs did not seem prepared for this change in role. When asked what their 'main' role was, a majority of the AOs saw themselves primarily as *implementers* of departmental as well as GP

TABLE 7: PROFILE OF AGRICULTURE OFFICERS INTERVIEWED

	No. of Agriculture Officers		
	GP Agriculture Officers = 11	Block Agriculture Officers = 3	District Agriculture Officers = 3
Personal characteristics			
Male	5	2	2
Female	6	1	1
General	11	2	3
SC	0	1	0
ST	0	0	0
Education			
Less than graduate	1	0	0
Graduate	6	2	3
Postgraduate	4	1	0
Joined as			
AO	9	3	3
Assistant officer/demonstrator	2	0	0
Induction training			
Nil	7	2	3
Short-term	4	1	0
In-service training			
Departmental	6	3	1
PPC	7	0	1
None	1	0	1

Note: Agriculture Officers were interviewed in eleven GPs. In one GP, an Agriculture Assistant was interviewed as the AO was new, and not aware of issues related to the GP. (Data with respect to the Agricultural Assistant is not included.)

projects, and only a few pointed to their role as planners, or saw it as encompassing development of the agriculture sector. Moreover, in the case of departmental schemes, AOs were used to following numerous specifications and instructions and regular review by senior officials, who also gave instructions and advice. In GP projects, in contrast, specifications and instructions were not available, and nor were GP projects reviewed by senior officials. At the same time, there was no evidence that the technical know-how of the AOs or their access to such support had increased adequately to enable them to function more independently.

Though the PPC had envisaged that resource persons and various technical committees would provide additional technical support, this was not the case in a majority of the GPs. In only two GPs out of 12 did the AOs report getting additional support from task force members and block-level experts. Moreover, except in one case, AOs themselves had not made any effort to access technical expertise from other sources. Not surprisingly, without the directions and supervision that they were used to, and without any substitute in terms of the development of their own skills or accessibility to other experts, several AOs were not comfortable in the new role, and felt that GP projects were 'risky', i.e. they could end up making a mistake. Similarly, the interaction of the AOs with the PRs, though not problematic, was not structured to ensure regular and speedy implementation. Only two AOs reported that they interacted with PRs through regular monthly review meetings, while the rest interacted with PRs sporadically.

School Education

In school education, government lower primary schools (LPSs) stood transferred to the GPs, but unlike the agriculture sector, there was no single nodal institution for education at the GP level. There were, instead, a number of LPSs in each GP. In terms of management, LPSs were of three types, i.e. government schools fully managed by the government; government-aided schools supported financially by the government but managed privately; and private unaided schools, privately funded and managed. In three GPs of Thrissur, there were no government LPSs but only government-aided and unaided schools.[22] Consequently, these GPs had neither an institution that they could work with, nor government teachers who could assist them, and were often unable to intervene in education in any way. In other GPs, the education department personnel available at the GP level were headmasters and teachers of the government schools.

There was some evidence that with decentralization, the government schools had become better rooted in the community. Across the GPs, the nine LPS headmasters (HMs) interviewed—generally high school graduates with teacher training diplomas[23]—were engaged mainly in teaching and managing their school. However, since the PPC, most had also begun to address local issues and engage with GP projects. In half the sample GPs, HMs had become involved in GP initiatives such as provision of better infrastructure for the school, additional inputs in the midday meal programme, starting of pre-primary classes, etc. In a third of the GPs, HMs reported that PTAs had become more active after decentralization, and they were able to access better support for their school. But two HMs also reported problems with the GP. One said that the there was political interference and conflict, while the other said that the GP was not interested in education.

Drinking Water

In the case of drinking water, the Kerala Water Authority (KWA) is the state-level nodal agency, and no officials of this agency have been transferred to the GPs. In any case, KWA engineers function at the 'circle' level (this comprises two–three GPs) and not at the GP level. This means that in many GPs, the GP secretary or a village extension officer is assigned the task of coordinating the work related to drinking water. GPs access support of KWA engineers through working groups and in different projects, but the link is a very loose one, inspite of the fact that in terms of their functions, GPs have an important role to play in this sector.

Across the Three Sectors

The important point that emerges from the above discussion is that the structure of the development and social welfare departments of government left wide gaps in the needed technical capacities of the GP. For drinking water, departmental presence itself was inadequate, and the GP simply lacked appropriate personnel. These gaps were heightened by vacant posts and frequent transfers of officials. In the case of agriculture and school education, where some institutional support was available to the GP, government employees had engaged with GP projects to a fair extent. Thus restructuring of the bureaucracy to facilitate GP-level initiatives emerged as an important area of concern.

At the same time, the capacities of the bureaucracy left much to be desired. For socio-economic development, there was no indication that the technical capacity of officials to perform their new role was adequate. Employees at the GP level were trained in implementing directions and used to supervision. Neither of these applied to GP projects. Significantly, GPs were not structured to tap the expertise available at more senior levels in government. GPs in Kerala have been envisaged as autonomous institutions, and consequently, intervention from senior officials as well as higher tier PRIs has been minimized. Consequently, departmental processes of technical support and monitoring did not operate for GP projects. At the same time, very little support was available from various technical committees or by other means to the officials. In other words while interference in GP decisions by senior officials had been minimized, a parallel technical support for such decision-making at the GP level had not been created within the departments.

Discussions with officials as well as in FGDs indicated that after decentralization departmental officials functioned in a more consultative manner and their responsiveness to the people had increased.[24] However, the ethos of the bureaucracy continued to be problematic. For instance, one GP was unable to control the mining mafia, which was reported to be supported by the police. The opinions of PRs about officials were mixed, and only half were satisfied with the performance of departmental employees. Some PRs made negative comments, e.g. officials were disinterested, uncooperative or arbitrary. Significantly, however, PRs reported that support from officials had improved over time.

RESOURCE PERSONS AND NGOs

The Kerala GP has been envisaged as being dependent not only on the bureaucracy for technical support, but also accessing it from the public domain. In the PPC, resource persons (RPs), many of who were activists and were trained specially by the Kerala government, provided enormous support, and many have continued to support GP activities subsequently, and GPs also collaborate with NGOs. The evidence from the field showed that while RPs and NGOs had provided support to the GPs, this support was neither comprehensive nor continuous.

In each sample GP, two RPs were interviewed, and their profiles (Table 8) show them to be well-educated men from the general category,[25] who had been associated with numerous voluntary organizations[26] (only one of 23 was not associated with any such organization). Fourteen RPs (61 per cent) were associated with NGOs (8 with KSSP and 6 with others), and others were also associated with science, sports and arts clubs, the local library or the PTA. In the sample, nearly 62 per cent RPs were LDF sympathizers, while 38 per cent were UDF sympathizers, and only one RP was neutral. Their motivation for becoming resource persons arose from their involvement with social issues, membership of the KSSP or other NGOs, instructions of the

TABLE 8: PROFILE OF RESOURCE PERSONS INTERVIEWED

	No. of RPs	
	GP N = 23	District N = 6
Personal characteristics		
Gender		
Male	22	6
Female	1	0
Social category		
General	21	6
SC	2	0
ST	0	0
Age		
35 or below	4	0
36–50	14	4
51 and above	3	0
NA	2	2
Educational level		
Below class 12	3	0
Class 12	7	0
College education	11	6
NA	2	
Profession		
Job in office	6	3
Retired official/ teacher	4	1
Farmer	5	
Insurance agent	1	0
Driver	1	0
Social worker	2	0
Gulf returnee	1	0
Teacher/professor	0	2
NA	3	0

	No. of RPs	
	GP N = 23	District N = 6
Political and social background		
Political party		
LDF	13	5
UDF	8	1
Other	0	0
No party	1	0
NA	2	0
*Other organizations associated with**		
Trade or other union	6	1
KSSP	8	5
NGO (other than KSSP)	6	0
Women's organization	1	0
Farmers' organization	1	0
Cooperative bank	2	0
Art/sports/film/science club	5	0
Local library/PTA	3	0
Caste organization	2	0
None	1	1
Interest in becoming RP		
General interest in social and developmental issues	7	1
Party decision/political activity	3	0
KSSP member	4	5
Member of other NGO	1	0
Participated in TLC	2	0
Wife is panchayat president	1	0
Request of panchayat	5	0

Note: *One RP could be associated with more than one organization political party, previous experience in the Total Literacy Campaign, or as a consequence of a request from the GP.[27]

RP support had been significant in the earlier stages of decentralization, but had declined subsequently. During and immediately after the PPC, RPs had participated in the preparation of development reports and plans, formulation and implementation of projects, training programmes, facilitation of gram sabhas and technical committees. But when the political party in power changed at the state level and subsequently in several GPs, their role declined. From among those interviewed, a third had ceased to play any role, while others remained involved in various sub-committees of the GP, in facilitating gram sabhas and SHGs. However, PRs were divided about the help provided by RPs. Several held that it was not much use, though many said that the GP or the RPs ought to make more effort at collaboration. An interesting development was that three of the RPs interviewed had fought elections and become PRs. The possible political competition that an RP could provide in the future may have made some PRs wary of them.

Expertise from NGOs was available to the GPs in a very sporadic way, in contrast to the wide range of tasks that the GPs were expected to address. In five out of twelve GPs, there was no NGO involvement at all. In other GPs, NGOs were involved in a small number activities, i.e. housing construction, watershed development, women's welfare, training, collection of statistics, etc. Several PRs made negative comments about NGOs, saying that they did not work, or were merely interested in making money.

THE GP

The above analysis of the sub-systems of the GP provides important information about the organization. The characteristics of each subsystem contribute to the institutional characteristics of the GP, several features of which have already been sketched out above. But this picture needs to be complemented on two fronts. Firstly, the relative importance of each sub-system, and their interrelationship need to be understood. Below, this dynamic has been examined through the window of the planning process of the GP, which engages all the actors, and is critical in setting the GP agenda. Secondly, the relationship of the GP to the macro-governance structure needs to be looked at in greater detail, though several features of this relationship have already emerged in the previous analysis.

Apart from the two types of analysis mentioned above, in this section, the GP has also been compared to the Kalliasseri Development Society, on which it has been broadly modelled. This comparison enables a still clearer appreciation of GP characteristics. Finally, the main institutional characteristics of the GP, and the shift that they imply in comparison to centralized government, are summed up.

Planning: An Illustrative Process

The planning exercise of the GPs in 2002–3 for the Tenth Plan was based on guidelines provided by the state government (GoK, 2002). As per the guidelines, GPs were to form at least eight working groups for different sectors. Each working group was expected to generate a vision and action plan for its sector by evaluating previous performance and identifying existing needs, and also prepare draft projects. The reports of the working groups were to be discussed in the gram sabhas, held separately for each ward. Subsequently, on the basis of the working group reports and discussions of the gram sabhas, panchayat committees were to prepare draft plans. These were to be discussed in a development seminar and then finalized. And finally, projects were to be scrutinized by the block-level Technical Advisory Committees (TACs), plans submitted to the DPC and approval obtained. These steps had been broadly followed in the sample GPs.

The planning process showed clearly that the panchayat samiti was the most powerful of all actors of the GP. In the planning exercise, the panchayat samiti played a pivotal role in all the GPs. In fact, in 11 GPs, it overshot its role, and identified priority projects and earmarked funds *before* the working groups began their deliberations. Only in one GP were projects first suggested by the working groups and then selected by the panchayat committee. The central dynamic of the planning exercise was competition over the allocation of resources across different wards. In all the GPs, ward-wise allocation of funds was negotiated fiercely and in at least three, funds were simply allocated equally among the wards. Thus competitive politics were central to the planning process.

Technical know-how was inadequate and appeared to be a secondary concern to politics. To begin with, technical expertise available for planning was inadequate. Skills within the core GP were very insufficient, and panchayat samitis did not involve many other professionals, in an attempt to keep control over the whole process. In only one GP had an RP been involved in the writing of the plan document. Moreover, though the GPs were free to select any GP-level official as the plan coordinator, most panchayat samitis stuck to the staff available in the core GP, i.e. the GP secretary or a GP clerk,[28] over whom the samiti had full control. Technical inputs were not provided during the appraisal of the projects either. The TACs and the DPCs focused mainly on issues such as whether financial guidelines had been followed. There was no scrutiny of appropriateness of the projects, conceptualization or suggestions regarding other possibilities. Some GP representatives and members of TACs admitted that because of time constraints, the appraisal had been casual. At the same time, PRs mentioned delay in getting technical sanctions as one of the problems faced by the GP.

The functioning of the working groups varied across the sectors, depending on the institutional structure at the GP level. Among the three sectors considered so far, i.e. agriculture, school education and drinking water, working groups were most efficient for agriculture, because a GP-level institution with qualified personnel was in existence, and AOs acted as conveners of the working groups. Other members of these groups were usually farmers, but in eight GPs, retired agriculture officers had been included. Working group reports related to education had been prepared fairly casually, mainly because the sector itself was not given much importance. For example, in one GP in Wayanad, no funds were allocated to education. Education-related groups were convened by a clerk of the GP, though some attempts were made to involve teachers. These functioned in a desultory manner. In one GP, no working group meeting was convened or report prepared. The convener submitted some suggestions to the panchayat committee, but these were not considered by the latter. Joint working groups had been formed for health and drinking water (with officials from the health sector as conveners), but limited information about these could be obtained during the fieldwork.

People's participation in the planning process was inadequate. Only a small number of people attended the planning discussions in the gram sabhas (Table 9). Out of the 22 sample wards for which information was available, in 5 attendance was less than the prescribed quorum, and in none did it go beyond 30 per cent.[29] Women comprised a large share of those attending, and the role of Kudumbashree groups in this context has already been noted. Attendance of SCs was higher than their share in the population, but that of STs was not.[30] Thus, the truly marginalized in Kerala, the STs, did not participate

TABLE 9: ATTENDANCE IN GRAM SABHAS TO IDENTITY PLAN PRIORITIES

Total attendance	No. of wards N = 24	% women attending	No. of wards N = 24	% SC attending	No. of wards N = 24	% ST attending in Wayanad	No. of wards N = 8
0–5%	0	0–30%	2	More than % SC Population in ward	10	More than % ST population in ward	1
5–10%	5	30–40%	2	Less than % SC population in ward	6	Less than % ST population in ward	7
10–20%	13	40–50%	6	NA	8		
20–30%	4	50–60%	7				
30% or more	0	60–70%	3				
NA	2	More than 70%	4				
Total	24	Total	24	Total	24	Total	8

adequately. Discussions on the reports of the working groups were either peripheral and ineffective, or dominated by ward-specific conflicts, particularly in the case of drinking water. But in one GP in Wayanad, a new suggestion came for the gram sabha during the discussion on the agriculture report—new water sources were identified and a new report was subsequently prepared.

The above conclusions were verified by the perceptions of those who had been engaged in the planning process. When PRs and officials were asked their opinion of the planning process, around half were satisfied. The main reason for satisfaction indicated was people's participation. The other half who were dissatisfied, commented mainly on the quality of the planning exercise, i.e. desultory discussion at the development seminars, equal distribution of funds among wards, the lack of capacity to make five year plans, vested political interests, the inability to impact agriculture and the problems caused by inadequacy of funds. Some officials were dissatisfied because they had not been involved and others with the priorities of the GP. For instance, one AO was dissatisfied because only irrigation projects were taken up in the agriculture sector and one HM because no attention was paid to the education sector. Poor participation by people was also mentioned as a cause of dissatisfaction in some GPs.

The GP and the Macro-Governance Structure

The Kerala government has sought to make the GP autonomous by devolving functions and untied funds to it, instituting a detailed process of local planning, and giving it some powers over the departmental bureaucracy. However, as is indicated by the discussion on different sub-systems of the GP, the macro-governance structure forms a critical context in which the GP is situated, and the GP reflects several of its characteristics. Political competition along party lines was a strong dynamic within the GPs, and could result in obstruction of work and non-rational allocation of resources. At the same time, the existing departmental structure as well as capacities and ethos were carried into the GP. This led to a particularly weak technical support structure, as GP-level government servants were trained to follow orders rather than take initiative.

But though the GP reflected the macro-governance structure in these ways, some of its characteristics also marked a significant shift from this larger structure. Three of the most critical shifts need to be highlighted. First, the GP existed in a far greater day-to-day contact with people than any centralized structure. In Kerala, this had meant that the non-elitist political leadership at the GP-level engaged closely with ordinary people, and the GP emerged as an organization responsive to the needs of the people. Second, in the GP, competitive democratic politics were extended to new arenas such as project implementation and day-to-day functioning, which had led to corruption becoming an important and contested issue. In this sense, the GP had moved towards greater accountability, though these gains stood to be diminished because of poor financial processes. Finally, for all the influence of centralized politics, local issues were central to GP politics. An interesting feature here was that some GPs had petitioned officials at the district level on various issues. For instance, GPs had requested the district authorities for funds for immunization programmes, provisions of drinking water through tanker lorries and had also made petitions regarding the posting of officials. Thus some panchayat samitis had acted as local pressure groups and had lobbied to get local needs addressed.

KDS and the GP

Some more clarity on the Kerala GP can be gained from glancing back briefly, and comparing it to the Kalliasseri Development Society, which had steered the planning process in Kalliasseri panchayat. KDS differed from the GPs that have been described in several significant ways. First, KDS, a society formed in the CPM dominated Kalliasseri panchayat, was characterized by a high degree of consensus. In contrast, the GPs were usually politically competitive. This meant that the decisions of the GPs were often contentious, and were arrived at by bargaining. This shift from consensus-based politics to tough competition meant that the logic of taking decisions changed. At its best, it rested on the idea of fair distribution (such as equal distribution of funds across wards). This could go against the selection of the most productive and effective strategies, as witnessed by the development of less useful small roads as compared to more useful larger roads in some panchayats. At its worst, the decision-making could also result in deadlock, as had happened in some GPs. On the other hand, the strength of the competitive bargaining process was that malpractices such as rent seeking stood the risk of being opposed.

Second, the technical resource support available to the GPs was nowhere near what was available in Kalliasseri. A high degree of technical resource support was built into the KDS though resource persons, and also accessed from various external experts. The PPC attempted to create this type of resource support for the GP, but this could not be sustained in the volatile politics of the GP. In KDS, the question of functioning through government departments had never been resolved. Yet the government officials transferred to the GP formed its major technical arm. Given the structure of the bureaucracy, the GP was left with crucial gaps in terms of technical support, and such GP-level officials as existed, were trained to follow directions rather than plan and implement projects independently.

Finally, the KDS and the GPs differed in the manner in which they related to people. The GPs were sensitive to the people, but this dynamic worked through the pressure that people could exert on their representatives, rather than direct participation. In neither case was their participation spontaneous, which sometimes seems to be envisaged various policy and other documents. In Kalliasseri, people's participation was sustained through the efforts of political and other activists who shared KDS goals and were an integral part of the whole project. In the GPs, such sustained efforts to mobilize people could not, in general, be made. Consequently, attendance in gram sabhas tended to flag. On the other hand, where in some way, as in the case of Kudumbashree, people could be organized, they could become important participants.

CONCLUSION

The GP was, first and foremost, a space for political contest. The panchayat samiti was the most important and powerful aspect of the GP, and set the GP agenda, often preempting the role of other actors. With the centrality of the panchayat samiti, competitive politics became the central dynamic for the GP. This made political party divisions and contests (along centralized lines) an integral, and critical, aspect of the GP. But at the same time, space was created for local issues too. This space was not inhabited by consensus, or by confrontations between local and centralized agencies. Instead, centralized political party divisions were organized around local issues. Allocation of resources and corruption emerged as core areas of contest, and this contributed to the transparency and accountability of the GP.

People's participation was not a very important dynamic of the GP. The gram sabha played a minor role, and only in some special cases did community-based associations become important. But this did not mean that the GP was cut-off from people. Rather, people's influence was mediated through pressure exerted upon elected representatives, in- stead of direct participation. The GP PRs themselves were non-elitist, and the long tradition of discourse and action in social welfare in the state predisposed them to addressing these issues. Their greater accessibility and people's ability to petition them served to enhance their responsiveness to the people.

The technical and administrative capacities of the GP remained small. Support from departmental officials was available to some extent, but was uneven, and weak and tenuous in some departments. Departmental functioning was not suited to the planning and strategizing tasks of the GP. At the same time, very limited support from other experts had been accessed, who played a marginal role.

To sum up, the GP in Kerala is an institution with greater responsiveness and accountability than the macro-governance structures, but also one with poor technical and administrative capabilities. These institutional characteristics of the GP form an important background to the plans and projects it undertakes, which we shall discuss in the next chapter.

NOTES

1. In terms of infrastructure and facilities, the sample GPs were well equipped. They were housed in buildings with five to nine rooms, some also had conference halls or auditoriums, all had telephones and four out of 12 GPs had jeeps. This infrastructure had existed at the GP level before the PPC. Only in two GPs extra money had been spent on infrastructure after 1995 and the amount, available for one GP, was a modest Rs. 2 lakh.
2. The high degree of unemployment in Kerala was also reflected in the occupational pattern reported. A little less than half the PRs (46 per cent) were not wage earners. Around a quarter reported being political or social workers, one-tenth said that they were unemployed and one-tenth were housewives.
3. Four out of six male general category presidents had had previous experience in PRIs, while the other two had had some experience in political organization. In contrast, out of six SC/ST and women presidents, five were politically inexperienced.
4. From among 36 GP standing committee chairpersons in the 12 GPs, only five were women (i.e. 13.9 per cent, of standing committee chairpersons were women, though 37.3 per cent PRs were women) and four were from

the SC category and none from ST category (i.e. 11.1 per cent standing committee chairpersons were from SC/ST category, while 22.5 per cent PRs were from these categories).

5. Only 7 per cent PRs (all men) were against reservations for women. But when PRs gave reasons for favouring reservations for women, these were in terms of empowering women and bringing them into the public sphere, rather than their positive contribution to the GP.
6. Women PRs' performance was seen as 'good' by 70 per cent PRs who commented on it. While a large proportion of PRs (63 per cent) did not see women PRs as having made a special contribution, some did say that women made a special contribution in women's programmes or issues, or increased women's access to the GP, or improved the GP by making it more peaceful or friendly.
7. In only three wards out of 24 did the community complain that they saw the panchayat and ward members rarely, while in others the interaction was reported to be frequent.
8. Where the work was actually contracted and executed by an individual other than as stated in officials records.
9. More than half the PRs (55 per cent) said that these committees were effective, but a substantial number (39 per cent) said that they were not effective, and others rated their performance as average or mixed.
10. In one GP the opposition leader was active in reviewing the revenue and expenditure situation through the finance committee.
11. Minutes of three meetings in each GP, i.e. a total of 34 meetings (in one GP data was available for only one meeting) were examined. One of these meetings was the last meeting held before the fieldwork while two were selected at random from among the meetings held in 2002–3.
12. There were as many as 16–31 meetings during 2002–3 across the twelve sample GPs.
13. In eight GPs, there were few (one or two) or no absentees in all three meetings. Only in two meetings in two GPs were there a large number of absentees (6–7).
14. See Oommen (2004).
15. During 2002–3, out of the 12 sample GPs, in 11 GPs, three gram sabha meetings were held and in one GP, two such meetings were held. The time, place and agenda of gram sabha meetings were fixed by the panchayat samiti in all the GPs. Ward members played an active role in distributing notices and making the dates and venues known and in four GPs; women's groups (Kudumbashree units, i.e. SHGs of women formed through a state government programme) were involved in this exercise.
16. Gram sabha meeting records of the two sample wards were examined. These included records of the last meeting of the gram sabha and two meetings held in 2002–3, selected at random. A total of 72 meeting records were scrutinized.

17. Kudumbashree is actually a government-sponsored programme, aimed at empowerment of women at the grassroots and eradication of poverty, which operates through a network of organized groups at various levels. SHGs of women are formed at the grassroots, a federation of these SHGs, an Area Development Society (ADS) is formed at the ward level and a larger federation, i.e. the Community Development Society (CDS) is formed at the GP level. Local groups are free to set their own agenda but the programme is monitored and supported at the district and state levels.
18. One Kudumbashree group had purchased land for paddy cultivation and another had started a small canteen. However, marketing remained a problem for these groups.
19. The District Primary Education Programme.
20. An important example here is the case of the beneficiary committee. During the PPC, beneficiary committees were formed as people's organizations to cut out middlemen and contractors, so that people could implement GP projects directly. While these beneficiary committees faced the challenging task of cutting out middlemen, rooting out corruption and fighting vested interests, they lacked organizational and technical capacity. Not surprisingly, a majority of beneficiary committees were not able to implement projects successfully (Thomas Isaac and Franke, 2000).
21. Only one AO reported problems with the PRs and another said that the dual control became problematic as departmental superiors and the GP made conflicting demands on his time.
22. There are many private aided schools in Kerala, where government provides financial assistance but the management is private.
23. Information about the qualifications of eight headmasters was available. Five HMs had studied up to class 12 and three were graduates. All had teacher training certificates.
24. When people were asked to compare the attitude of officials before and after decentralization, from among the 16 FGDs from which this information was available, in 12 the opinion was that the attitude and approach of officials had become more responsive.
25. Among 23 RPs, only one was a woman and only two belonged to the SC category. No RP belonged to the ST category. Nearly half the RPs had had college education and only 11 per cent had not completed high school (all these were form Wayanad). Only one RP reported being a blue-collar worker.
26. Two RPs reported being members of caste organizations (one of these was an organization of *Dalits* (SC) and another of Nairs, a dominant upper caste).
27. Only one RP indicated a personal reason, that of his wife having been a panchayat president (in the previous regime).
28. In eight out of 11 GPs, the plan coordinator was the GP secretary or a GP

clerk, and not a person who had any experience in the development sector. In other GPs, AOs and extension officers were plan coordinators.

29. In 13 wards, attendance was between 10–20 per cent of the voting population, only in four was it more than 20 per cent.
30. In the sixteen wards for which information regarding participation of SC/ST groups was available, the number of people from the SCs was more than their share in the population in ten wards and less in six. In seven out of eight wards of the Wayanad GPs, people from among the STs in the gram sabha comprised a far smaller proportion than their population in the ward.

CHAPTER 6

Plans and Projects of the Village Panchayat (Kerala)

The GP in Kerala has a fairly broad mandate of 'planning for local development', whereby it can select locally relevant projects after following a detailed planning exercise. The state government has devolved an impressive list of developmental functions as well as substantial finances to it. This level of autonomy of the GP is a new and unusual development in panchayati raj in India. This chapter focuses on the manner in which GPs have used this autonomy, i.e. the priorities that they have set, the kinds of activities and projects that they have undertaken, and the extent to which they have successfully grappled with local problems of development.

In Kerala, GPs are expected to address local problems and facilitate local economic development by formulating plans and projects, and it is in this context that the GP activities and projects need to be understood. In parallel, the GP approaches these issues with its particular institutional and organizational characteristics, i.e. its responsiveness, as well as its limited technical capacities. In this chapter, the plans and projects of the GP have been analysed against the socio-economic context and problems confronted by it, and this analysis shows that the manner in which the GP approaches these is related to its institutional characteristics. The analysis is undertaken in two steps. In the first step, the overall priorities of the GP are analysed. In the second step, the activities of the GP are examined in greater detail across three sectors, i.e. agriculture, school education and drinking water.

OVERALL PLANS AND PRIORITIES

The process of planning followed by the GPs in Kerala includes an analysis of the socio-economic situation of their area, setting of appropriate goals, and identification of relevant and technically sound projects, which are then implemented. At each stage, the success with which the GP performs its role can vary. Below, the various steps followed by the GPs, i.e. the socio-economic problems identified, the goals set, the actual projects selected and implemented are scrutinized.

Brief Socio-economic Picture of the GPs

An idea about the socio-economic situation in each sample GP can be obtained from Annex 4. As can be seen, agriculture was an important occupation across the GPs in all three districts, and in the Wayanad GPs, it was almost the sole occupation. Paddy and coconut were grown in all the sample GPs, and in the Wayanad GPs there were also coffee and pepper plantations. Other important crops included areca nut, banana, tapioca, ginger as well as rubber and tea. GPs in Thrissur had the most industries, including textiles, steel, tire and granite, and people also worked in quarries, brick units, tile factories, wood packing industries, textile mills and small spinning units. In the Wayanad GPs, other than agriculture, there were no major economic activities.[1] There were only some small scale and tiny enterprises, i.e. a printing press, a milk-chilling unit, a cattle feed unit, a spice powder unit, a chemical unit, hollow brick units, furniture, rice and flour mills. In the Thiruvananthapuram GPs there was traditional industry like coir and handloom, a cashew factory, a cocoa and areca nut processing plant and graphite and rubber industries. In these GPs people were engaged in activities such as rubber tapping as well as bamboo and reed work and some small industries such as cashew factories.

The poorest people across the GPs lacked adequate basic amenities such as pukka houses. In the Thrissur and Thiruvananthapuram GPs, SCs, whose share in population ranged from 6.6 per cent to 16.9 per cent across the eight GPs, were among the poorest people. In Thiruvananthapuram, the poorest people were engaged in traditional industries based on coir, cane and reed, collected forest produce, worked as agricultural labourers and domestic helpers, and were also engaged in illicit liquor brewing. In the Thrissur GPs the poorest people were engaged in casual labour in agriculture and industry. In Wayanad, the poorest people were usually STs, though there were also some very poor agricultural labourers of general category, while some STs were landowners. The population of STs in the four GPs hovered around 50 per cent. In the Wayanad GPs, the number of families below the poverty line was high (more than 60 per cent in two GPs), even allowing for the fact that the numbers may be somewhat exaggerated. The poor were engaged in agricultural labour. Settler farmers and estate owners were the better-off groups.

There was substantial in- as well as out-migration in the sample GPs. In Thrissur, people from Tamil Nadu, Orissa and Karnataka come to work in tile factories and as construction workers, and people from Bengal and Bihar come for gold ornament making. In recent years, people from Nepal had also started coming to work in brick-making units. The educated and professionally qualified people migrated to the United States and Europe and the unskilled workers to the Gulf countries. In Wayanad, in all GPs, there was in-migration from Karnataka and Tamil Nadu for construction work and agriculture. But from three GPs of Wayanad people had also migrated to Tamil Nadu and Karnataka as agricultural labourers during the season. In one GP in Thiruvananthapuram there was in-migration of casual labourers from Tamil Nadu. In three GPs there was out-migration to other parts of the country and in two GPs, there was migration to the Gulf, including that of women as housemaids. Thus the GPs showed a fair amount of movement of labour and the paradoxical situation of Kerala: high unemployment coupled with in-migration of labour from elsewhere.

Socio-economic Problems Identified

The main socio-economic problems identified across the GPs in development reports,[2] and confirmed by PRs and FGDs are summed up in Table 10.

As can be seen, the socio-economic problems identified in the GPs echo the issues highlighted by many scholars, described in Chapter 4. An important problem was unemployment, reported in nearly all the GPs. In two GPs of Thrissur the unemployment was identified as industrial, in three GPs of Wayanad as agricultural and in two GPs of Thiruvananthapuram, pertaining to 'loss of traditional occupation', e.g. reed work. Table 7 also shows that the crisis of production that underlies the unemployment problem is understood at the GP level. For instance, 'decline of agriculture' was reported in all four GPs of Wayanad and two GPs of Thiruvananthapuram. Development reports as well as various interviewees confirmed a fall in employment as a result of a shift from paddy to cash crop cultivation. In two GPs of Thrissur, the area under paddy had been further reduced because of large-scale clay mining. At the same time, at the time of this study, there had been a

TABLE 10: SOCIO-ECONOMIC PROBLEMS IDENTIFIED BY GPs

Socio-economic problems identified	No. of GPs in which the problem was identified		
	Thrissur	Wayanad	Thiruvananthapuram
1. Unemployment	3	3	4
No cause stated	1		2
Agricultural		3	
Industrial	2		
Loss of traditional occupation			2
2. Decline in agriculture production and prices		4	2
3. Decline of industry		4	2
4. Basic needs and infrastructure	4	4	3
Water scarcity	4	3	3
Lack of health facilities	1		
Lack of educational infrastructure		1	
Inadequate transportation		1	1
Housing problem		1	
5. Poverty and social equity		3	2
Alienation of Adivasi land		2	
Poverty		2	2
Social backwardness of SC people			2
6. Social problems	2	2	1
Illicit liquor production and consumption, increasing alcoholism		2	2
Migration			2
Sand Mining	2	1	
Industrial pollution	1		
7. Natural		1	
Drought		1	
Attack by wild animals		1	

decline in the prices of cash crops, causing landowners to employ less labour, and this exacerbated the unemployment problem. The latter impact was most acute in Wayanad. In Thrissur, 'decline in industry' was reported as a problem in three GPs, as several tile industries had closed down, leading to more unemployment. This picture was confirmed in FGD discussions. Additionally, in one ward in a Thrissur

GP, the in-migration of cheaper labour was identified as another contributor to unemployment.

The second important problem that emerged, in nine out of twelve GPs, was that of scarcity of drinking water, which was most acute in SC and ST colonies. In contrast, problems related to basic infrastructure such as lack of roads, health facilities, schools or housing were reported in a very small number of GPs, though in some SC and ST colonies such infrastructure was inadequate. This is in consonance with the fact that such infrastructure is in fact quite well developed in the state, barring some tribal pockets. Poverty and social equity related problems were identified most often in the GPs of Wayanad, i.e. in three GPs, where these mainly concerned STs. In two GPs of Thiruvanathapuram, 'social backwardness' of SCs was identified as an issue. Other problems identified in the GPs included illicit liquor consumption and production (in two GPs of Wayanad), illegal sand mining (in two GPs of Thrissur), industrial pollution (in one GP of Thrissur) and migration (in one GP in Thiruvananthapuram).

To sum up, at the GP level the perceived 'socio-economic problems' were: unemployment, with underlying agricultural and industrial stagnation and decline, problems pertaining to drinking water, the poverty of SCs and STs, especially the latter, and social problems, such as illicit liquor and drug production and consumption, and in Thrissur, the sand mafia and industrial pollution.

Goals in the Ninth Plan

Against the above problems, let us examine the goals of the GPs during the Ninth Plan period (1997–2002) as stated in development reports and plans. For convenience, in Table 11, these goals have been divided into four broad categories, i.e. production and productivity, employment, basic minimum needs and strategies concerned with inequities.

In two sectors, i.e. agriculture and drinking water, the problems identified within the GP matched the goals spelt out in the plans. In development reports of all the GPs, agricultural development and increasing agricultural productivity was a stated goal, i.e. GPs saw the importance of addressing agricultural stagnation that underlay unemployment. Additionally, in two GPs of Wayanad, the stated goals included development of animal husbandry and fishing. Similarly, provision of drinking water was a goal in nine GPs out of eleven, matching its identification as a 'problem' in ten out of twelve GPs.

TABLE 11: GP GOALS IN THE NINTH PLAN

Goals	No. of GPs in which these goals are stated		
	Thrissur	Wayanad	Thiruvanantha-puram*
Productivity			
Increasing agricultural productivity, development of agriculture	4	4	3
Irrigation	0	1	
Animal husbandry, fishing	0	2	
Start small scale industries	0	3	
Employment and income			
Increase employment	0	2	0
Income generation for women, SC/ST/unemployed youth	0		2
Basic needs			
Solve drinking water problem	4	3	2
Improve housing	0	3	2
Roads and transport	0	4	1
Electrification	0	2	0
Education: infrastructure and quality	0	2	2
Sanitation/latrines	1		2
Reduce morbidity, improve health	0	2	0
Infrastructure for health	0	1	0
Nutrition through Anganwadi and infrastructure	0	1	0
Equity			0
Upliftment of SC/ST	0	2	0

Note: * For one GP in Thiruvananthapuram clear information was not available; data from three GPs is reported.

In other sectors, the goals set had diverged from the problems identified. For instance, unemployment in the non-farm sector had emerged as a problem, along with unemployment in the farm sector. As per the functions assigned to them, GPs are expected to undertake self and group employment schemes for the poor. But employment and income generation were goals only in three GPs. Similarly, though the functions of GPs include the promotion of cottage and village industries as well as traditional and mini-industries, only three GPs in Wayanad had put promotion of small-scale industries as their goal. That GPs had not attempted to tackle unemployment in the non-farm sector needs to be seen against the fact that this requires extremely complex strategizing, and GPs did not have personnel with such skills.

There were also problems that the GPs could not address because relevant functions were not assigned to them. The problem of alienation of land among tribal people, identified in two GPs, could not be addressed at the GP level. Similalry, the loss of jobs in Thrissur that had resulted from the closure of industries was not in the ambit of the GP, either in terms of functions assigned, or in terms of availability of technical manpower. This is not to suggest that these functions ought to, or could have been, assigned to the GPs. However, it is important to note that though the more fundamental problems such as the closure of industry and alienation of tribal land could not be addressed at the GP level, the GPs were expected to address the manifestations of these problems, i.e. unemployment and poverty.

The goals of the GPs reflected a great deal of engagement with issues pertaining to basic needs and infrastructure, though except in the case of drinking water, these were not perceived as the most pressing problems. Housing and roads figured far more prominently as goals than they did as problems. For instance, the lack of housing was identified as a problem in only one GP, but provision of housing was a goal in six. Similarly, while lack of road and transport came out as a problem of only one GP, provision of the same was a goal in five. In two GPs of Wayanad, a somewhat ill-defined 'upliftment of SC/STs' was stated as a goal, though equity-related goals were implied in the goals related to basic needs and infrastructure.

To sum up, if the goals of the GPs are compared to the problems identified, a shift was visible away from the problems of unemployment, towards an increased importance of basic infrastructure and needs. In the productive sector, GPs set goals related to agriculture and allied activities, but not in the non-farm sector. Here, their mandate was limited, and macro-policy rather than GP-level intervention was needed. However, GPs did not attempt to exploit the mandate that they did have to the full. Equity-related goals were implied in the development of basic infrastructure, but others, such as alienation of land from tribals were out of purview, and needed state-level decisions.

GP Project Choices

In terms of actual projects, the emphasis had shifted still further towards basic needs and infrastructure, as against productive and employment generating activities. In this study, the three projects for which GPs had sanctioned the maximum amount of money every year, were identified for each GP across six years, leading to a list of 18 'largest projects' for each GP (Table 12). Of a total of 198 such largest projects across 11 GPs,[3] 67.2 per cent were concerned with the provision of basic needs and infrastructure, while 32.8 per cent were for productive and employment generation activities. Moreover, within the broad category of basic infrastructure, the predominant projects were for housing and roads, and nearly 31 per cent largest projects consisted of provision of housing. Similarly, even though the lack of roads, bridges, transportation, etc., were not identified as problems, these comprised 13.6 per cent of the largest projects. This prioritization was confirmed when the PRs and the FGDs were asked to identify the most important projects of the GP in the Ninth Plan and also its 'achievements'.[4] Though drinking water had been identified as the most important basic need, such projects comprised only 6.6 per cent of the largest projects. However, drinking water projects were identified as important projects in seven GPs and achievements in six. Possibly, when such projects had been taken up, even though amounts spent on them may have been small, the fact that they addressed urgent needs led to the perception of their being important as well as achievements.

The importance given to agricultural development as a significant goal in the GPs was not matched by the actual projects undertaken. From among the largest projects, a mere 19.7 per cent were concerned with agricultural development, irrigation and protection of water sources. Moreover, perceived achievements in agriculture, inspite of the priority given to the sector in stated goals, were conspicuous by their absence.[5] In parallel, when PRs and FGDs were asked what the shortfall of the GP had been, in seven GPs, failure in the productive sectors, especially agriculture, was identified. Clearly, as GPs gave concrete shape to their plans, they shifted towards what was simple to do. In contrast, agricultural development requires complex strategizing, beyond the capacity of the GPs. Some PRs and officials admitted to being perplexed because GPs were unable to impact agriculture in spite of many efforts (Table 13).

In the same vein, in two GPs in Wayanad, the inability to address

TABLE 12: 18 LARGEST PROJECTS OVER SIX YEARS IN THE PRIs*

	GP		Block		District	
	Total	% of Total	Total	% of Total	Total	% of Total
Basic needs and infrastructure						
Housing	61	30.8	21	38.9	13	24.1
Infrastructure						
Improvement/tarring of road	27	13.6	0	0	8	14.8
Other infrastructure**	16	8.1	2	3.7	6	11.1
Subtotal infrastructure	43	21.7	2	3.7	14	25.9
Electrification	8	4.0	2	3.7	1	1.9
Health	0	0	4	7.4	2	3.7
Sanitation	2	1.0	1	1.9	1	1.9
Drinking water	13	6.6	1	1.9	1	1.9
Anganwadis	5	2.5	0	0	0	
Education	1	0.5	2	3.7	4	7.4
Sub-total	133	67.2	33	61.1	36	66.7
Employment and productivity						
Irrigation	18	9.1	11	20.4	3	5.6
Protection of water sources	2	1.0	0	0	0	0
Agriculture development	19	9.6	3	5.6	2	3.7
Soil conservation	0	0	1	1.9	0	0
Subsidy for cows and goats to individuals	9	4.5	0	0	1	1.9

(Contd.)

TABLE 12 (Contd.)

	GP		Block		District	
	Total	% of Total	Total	% of Total	Total	% of Total
Sericulture	0	0	0	0	1	1.9
Training/self-employment for women	15	7.6	1	1.9	2	3.7
General employment programme	2	1.0	0	0	1	1.9
Industry	0	0	4	7.4	2	3.7
Sub-Total	65	32.8	20	37.0	12	22.2
Others						
Financial assistance to fisherwomen	0	0	0	0	5	9.3
Rehabilitation of agriculture labourers	0	0	1	1.9	0	0
Miscellaneous	0	0	0	0	1	1.9
Sub-Total	0	0	1	1.9	6	11.1
Total	198	–	54	–	54	–

Notes: * For each year the three largest projects in terms of the amount sanctioned were selected.

** These included drains for roads, development of SC colonies, meeting hall, cultural centre, stadium, PHC/hospital, agriculture office, panchayat office building renovation, fish market, improvement of bus stand.

TABLE 13: SHORTFALLS OF PROJECTS AS VIEWED BY PANCHAYAT REPRESENTATIVES AND THE PEOPLE

	No. of PRIs		
	GP	Block	District
Failure of project, lack of use	8	0	1
Incomplete projects	3	0	1
Poor selection of projects	2	0	0
Lack of impact on agriculture	6	1	1
No achievement in productive sector	1	1	0
Lack of impact on employment	2	0	0
Lack of people's participation	1	0	0
Failure to address sanitation problem in some areas	0	0	1
Lack of teamwork, coordination, ward-wise distribution of funds	0	2	1
Failure to rehabilitate the landless	1	0	0
Simple distribution of assets to individuals	1	0	0

the unemployment issue was viewed as a shortfall. However, some GP efforts were visible in the sphere of women's employment through the Kudumbashree programme. Though such projects constituted only 7.6 per cent of the largest projects, they were considered important in five GPs. Several GPs had collaborated with Kudumbashree groups and supported them. In contrast, other than women's employment programmes through Kudumbashree, only 1 per cent of the largest projects were concerned with employment generation in general. Notably, the fact that Kudumbashree groups were well organized and supported for livelihood activities through a network of organizations supported from the state level, appears to have enabled the GP to collaborate with them. It seems that GP representatives were not unwilling to engage in employment generation programmes, but they were not able to do so because these require complex strategizing. Where organizational and technical support was available, as in Kudumbashree, they had extended support.

The pro-people orientation of the GP, noted in the previous chapter, was confirmed by the fact that a large number of basic needs programmes, as also many programmes for agriculture and employment, were targeted towards deprived or marginalized groups. Table 14 shows that in the 72 largest projects of the Thrissur GPs, 43.1 per cent were

TABLE 14: TARGET GROUPS IN LARGEST PROJECTS IN THRISSUR AND WAYANAD

	Thrissur GPs	Wayanad GPs
Targeted and untargeted projects		
Total number of projects	72	72
Untargeted*	56.9%	47.2%
Targeted	43.1%	52.8%
Spread of targeted projects across social groups		
Below poverty line	41.9%	6.1%
SC	35.5%	0
ST	3.2%	52.6%
Women (all)	9.7%	26.3%
Below poverty line women	3.2%	7.9%
Children below 5 years	3.2%	7.9%
Paddy farmers**	3.2%	0

Notes: * Projects targeted at farmers of all categories have been included as untargeted, as they do not discriminate in favour of less powerful social groups.
** As paddy farmers tend to be poor, these have been included in the category of targeted.

targeted towards marginalized groups, and in the Wayanad GPs 52.8 per cent; were similarly targeted. The two largest target categories in Thrissur were BPL and SC families, while in the Wayanad GPs these were STs and women. In the Wayanad GPs, 52.6 per cent from among the largest projects were targeted towards the STs. Significantly, there were several instances when GPs had created infrastructure in SC and ST colonies, which had been neglected before decentralization. Moreover, expenditures in the SCP and TSP component were reasonably satisfactory (Table 17). This is in consonance with the finding in the previous chapter that one institutional characteristic of the GP was responsiveness to ordinary people.

Project Formulation and Implementation

As illustrated above, GP projects choices were influenced a great deal by their limited technical capacities. This was confirmed by the manner in which the GPs had formulated and implemented projects. In order to understand the processes of project formulation and implementation, brief case studies of sixteen projects across eight GPs of

Thrissur and Wayanad were undertaken. In each GP, one of the largest projects of the GP, and one project that GP representatives considered to be special in some way, were studied (see Boxes 5 & 6 for illustrations).

These case studies illustrate the manner in which the institutional strengths and weaknesses of the GP played out in its projects and

Box 5: Some Projects that did not Succeed

Wayanad GP3: Agriculture in dry lands (one of the largest projects)
The goal of this project was to increase cultivation in unused dry land. The project was formulated by the working group on agriculture in 1998–9. Paddy farmers' committees, pepper committees, and agriculture development committees also cooperated. The agriculture officer was the convener of this group and was responsible for formulating and implementing the project. The activities consisted of installing motor and pump-sets where water sources already existed, and digging wells and constructing tanks where they did not. The project was to be implemented by individual beneficiaries in their land.

Some interviewees believed that the project was taken up because of the stipulation to use a certain percentage of funds in the productive sector. The target beneficiaries were small land owners with less than 50 cents of dry land plots. However, when applications were invited, the number of applicants was below expectations, and the scope of the project had to be reduced. Moreover, some of the selected beneficiaries were not ready to implement the project. Consequently, there were time and cost overruns. Discussions with the FGDs revealed that most of the beneficiaries who did construct wells and tanks used them for drinking water purposes rather than for irrigation, and consequently the project had not benefited agriculture.

Thrissur, GP1: Making wasteland cultivable (a special project)
Because of the concentration of tile factories and excessive digging of clay, 40 hectares of paddy fields had degenerated into wasteland and waterlogged areas. The project proposed to clear water from these areas, and to make the land suitable for cultivation by levelling it as well as by making a few ponds. This, in turn, was expected to increase the productivity and employment in agriculture. As the first step, a meeting of the wasteland owners, who were expected to make a beneficiary contribution of around a third of the project cost, was convened, the scheme was explained, and their cooperation and contribution sought. A monitoring committee was constituted with representation of the GP, landowners and technical experts. The water was then pumped from the waterlogged areas by spending the GP's share of the money. However, the beneficiaries did not take up the next stage of the

work, i.e. levelling the land. In the meantime, water collected in the field again. This special project implemented with beneficiary cooperation thus failed.

Wayanad, GP4: Road construction (a special project)
The goal of this project was the construction of a road in the most undeveloped area of the GP. The suggestion came in a gram sabha. The working group formulated the project and a nine-member beneficiary committee was formed to implement it, with technical assistance from an engineer. The project was completed. A visit to the road, however, showed it to be in a pathetic condition, and rarely used. Further investigations revealed that the amount invested by the GP had been too small because of the ward-wise distribution of funds. Subsequently, another road was built in the area, while this one fell into disuse.

Thrissur GP: Housing project (one of the largest projects)
In the year 1999–2000, the government introduced the Swabhiman Housing Scheme to provide subsidy for houses for BPL families. COSTFORD (a semi-government organization) came forward as the promoter of this scheme in collaboration with the GPs in Thrissur district. As per the agreement, the panchayat was to pay one-third of the subsidy and COSTFORD, two-thirds of the subsidy to the beneficiaries. COSTFORD and the GP together formed an 'implementation committee' and trained the labourers and beneficiaries to manufacture bricks and other construction materials. The GP distributed its share of the first installment to 28 families. But due to technical and financial problems, COSTFORD could not distribute the second installment to those who finished the first stage of the work. As a result, 28 families, who started house construction during 1998 were left with only the first stage of their houses finished, with no hope of completing the work. This remained an unresolved issue for the GP, and the beneficiaries were extremely disappointed.

activities. As has been noted above, GP projects tended to focus on the basic needs of the people. Consequently, as GPs implemented their projects, they were often able to get support from the community. This was usually the dynamic of the successful projects: a basic community need was identified and addressed, and the community supported the implementation of the project. Success was most likely if complicated and alien techniques were not involved, but existing skills were tapped and supported. The example in Box 6 whereby the GP provided hous-

Box 6: Projects that Succeeded

Wayanad, GP2: Housing for ST families (one of the largest projects)
The goal of the project was to construct houses for homeless ST families. The implementing officer of this project was the GP secretary. Applications were collected through gram sabhas and the poorest applicants were selected. Beneficiaries contributed labour and constructed their own houses, while a committee of officials, PRs and working group members monitored the project. The major problem faced pertained to the transportation of materials to the house sites. This was handled by the GP and the project was completed in time.

Thrissur, GP 4: Protecting water sources (a special project)
The project envisaged protection, improvement and increase in the water storage capacity of ten canals and eighteen public ponds in different parts of the GP, in order to improve of irrigation facilities and enhance the groundwater supply by deepening, widening and strengthening the side walls of the canals and ponds. More than half the project cost was met through voluntary labour. When the project was completed, the availability of water from these sources increased during the summer and there was also an improvement in the water level of the wells near these canals and ponds.

Thrissur, GP2: Lift Irrigation Scheme (one of the largest projects)
This project was implemented with the two main goals of facilitating better irrigation facilities for agriculture and thereby increasing the labour days of farmers, as also the level of water in wells in two wards. As part of the project, water from an ever- flowing small stream was pumped through a motor into tanks and then flowed to a network of small canals that irrigated land. An individual gave free land for the construction of a motor shed near the stream, and retired engineers supervised the project. Beneficiaries contributed around a seventh of the amount. The project was successful, and benefits dry land farming.

ing to tribal families is one such case. However, even such projects could fail when the GPs either misjudged people's enthusiasm for the project, or because of technical lacunae. A striking example was the renovation of a canal in one GP, which was completed with the voluntary labour of 3,000 people, but was not useful because of technical problems. In fact, project failure was a recurrent problem in the GPs. When GP representatives considered the shortfalls and failures of the

GP, they were most likely to point to projects that had failed or where assets had been created but were of no use. Such failures were identified in eight GPs out of twelve. Among the eight largest projects studied, only two were successful. Among the 'special projects', four out of eight projects were successful and one was partly successful.

Productive sector projects posed a special challenge. GPs found it difficult to formulate appropriate projects in the productive sector, but as per state guidelines had to spend 30 per cent funds on such projects (Table 15). Expenditure trends showed that the GPs were sometimes not able to 'achieve' the stipulated minimum percentage of expenditure in the productive sector (Table 16). Moreover, in several cases, assets

TABLE 15: SECTORAL ALLOCATION FOR GENERAL SECTOR AND ELEVENTH FINANCE COMMISSION GRANT TAKEN TOGETHER IN THE TENTH PLAN PERIOD

(percentage allocation)

	Village panchayat	Block panchayat	District panchayat	Urban local government
Minimum ceiling for productive sector* (%)	30	30	25	10
Maximum ceiling for infrastructure sector (%)	30	30	30	50
Maximum ceiling for hospitals, schools, water supply and minor irrigation (%)	10	10	10	10
Minimum ceiling for Women Component Plan (%)	10	10	10	10
Children, disabled and aged** (%)	5	5	5	5
Minimum ceiling on slum development (%)	–	–	–	10

Source: Government of Kerala, 2002.

Notes: *Productive sector means projects relating to agriculture, animal husbandry, dairy development, fisheries, integrated watershed management, tiny and small industries, production of electricity through non-conventional energy sources, construction activities related to fish and other markets, manufacture of manure from solid waste (Government of Kerala, 2002).

**Funds for Anganwadi feeding are not included. These funds could first be set apart and then sectoral allocation could be made.

TABLE 16: PLAN EXPENDITURE IN 1998–9 AND 2001–2

	Total plan expenditure (Rs. in lakhs)	Productive sector (%)	Infra-Structure (%)	Service sector (%)	Agriculture (%)	Education (%)	Drinking water (%)
				1998–9			
Thrissur							
GP1	18.70	56.26	1.98	41.71	25.62	0.80	0
GP2	52.66	26.83	30.63	42.37	24.63	0	4.41
GP3	20.16	42.06	32.49	25.45	82.94	0.94	5.90
GP4	36.55	27.00	23.64	49.36	41.04	0.68	14.36
Wayanad							
GP1	41.71	33.42	19.06	47.52	28.27	0	18.34
GP2	79.49	17.71	26.15	56.13	14.15	0.82	1.02
GP3	41.13	35.89	30.42	33.70	15.75	2.87	3.84
GP4	93.26	25.76	34.85	39.40	2.94	2.7	13.51
Thiruvananthapuram							
GP1	NA	NA	NA	NA	NA	NA	NA
GP2	33.92	33.23	30.10	36.62	25.56	0.94	9.88
GP3	34.08	27.46	18.67	53.05	18.93	5.1	8.60
GP4	26.67	39.52	25.20	35.28	51.44	0.75	8.25

(Contd.)

TABLE 16 (Contd.)

	Total plan expenditure (Rs. in lakhs)	Productive sector (%)	Infra-Structure (%)	Service sector (%)	Agriculture (%)	Education (%)	Drinking water (%)
				2001–2			
Thrissur							
GP1	12.59	19.94	27.16	52.90	15.57	0	7.22
GP2	23.17	32.46	41.82	25.68	40.40	0	19.38
GP3	NA	NA	NA	NA	NA	NA	NA
GP4	15.14	42.07	38.57	20.07	14.73	1.62	3.89
Wayanad							
GP1	28.50	33.26	17.02	50.77	24.63	0	3.23
GP2	51.54	20.68	27.38	51.94	16.20	0	2.11
GP3	55.53	25.86	28.15	45.99	13.45	9.00	5.91
GP4	81.00	36.81	29.98	33.21	27.80	0.10	4.31
Thiruvananthapuram							
GP1	NA	NA	NA	NA	NA	NA	NA
GP2	NA	NA	NA	NA	NA	NA	NA
GP3	NA	NA	NA	NA	NA	NA	NA

TABLE 17: NINTH PLAN (1997–8 TO 2001–2) EXPENDITURE FOR GENERAL SECTOR, SPECIAL COMPONENT PLAN (SCP) AND TRIBAL SUB-PLAN (TSP) GRANTS IN THRISSUR AND WAYANAD PRIs

	Total		General sector		SCP		TSP	
	Total grant received (Rs. in lakhs)	% expenditure	Total grant received (Rs. in lakhs)	% expenditure	Total grant received (Rs. in lakhs)	% expenditure	Total grant received (Rs. in lakhs)	% expenditure
Thrissur								
GP1	142.70	81.43	106.76	80.13	35.94	85.28	0.0	—
GP2	305.31	83.10	220.57	85.61	73.89	75.41	10.85	85.16
GP3	301.03	83.82	220.57	85.41	70.98	78.49	9.48	86.92
GP4	210.26	85.57	175.15	87.31	34.57	76.54	0.54	100.00
Block	360.00	85.46	249.88	90.12	97.71	73.13	12.41	88.80
District	4958.82	81.98	3136.47	82.16	1757.34	81.57	65.01	84.34
Wayanad								
GP1	312.28	82.48	200.17	87.85	13.38	96.26	98.73	96.20
GP2	388.03	96.28	210.25	95.72	16.40	67.50	161.38	100.00
GP3	306.95	99.03	217.11	99.03	13.83	98.56	76.01	99.16
GP4	415.76	94.65	270.98	92.93	27.34	88.80	117.44	100.00
Block	1086.96	98.79	487.39	95.53	98.33	90.76	501.24	101.56
District	3820.76	93.45	1430.84	93.84	202.39	66.81	2187.53	95.68

created for productive purposes were actually used for other purposes. For example, a check dam-cum-bridge (one of the largest projects) was used as a bridge by a small number of families, but not used for irrigation. If the fact that assets created in the productive sector were used for other purposes is factored in, the expenditure in the productive sector would be still less. Not only was the provision of spending a certain sum of money on productive sector projects nullified in this manner, but assets that were not useful to a substantial number of people were sometimes created in an attempt to follow prescribed guidelines. In the case just described Box 5, successful housing projects would have been more worthwhile compared to a bridge that was rarely used. The other observed causes of failure included the ward-wise division of funds, which led to inappropriate financing of projects, and the fact that in collaborative projects, GPs could not deal effectively with other, larger agencies.

A Summing Up

In light of the institutional characteristics of the GP delineated in the previous chapter, the plan priorities and project outcomes are not surprising. The previous chapter had showed the GP to be an institution with strong roots in the community, including deprived groups. This section showed that the strength of GP projects lay in the development of infrastructure related to basic needs such as drinking water, roads and housing. GP projects also showed a fair concern for marginalized groups, both in the choice of projects and in targeting, and by addressing the needs of wards that had been neglected previously. However, the lack of technical and administrative skills illustrated in the previous chapter, contributed to a high degree of project failure. What emerged from this picture was a sort of thumb rule for success in GP projects: projects that addressed urgent needs of the people and were simple to execute were done best by the GPs. Consequently, there was some success in simple, social welfare projects such as provision of housing.

At the same time, GPs did not, or could not, take up productive sector projects, and when they did, were the least successful. In some cases, GPs did not spend the minimum stipulated amount for the productive sector; in other instances the stated goal was diverted to other purposes, and some projects simply failed. Here, there is need to go beyond the lack of technical capacities of the GP and ask what 'local economic development' as envisaged in the PPC means in the context of unemployment created because of paucity of industry, the declining competitiveness of commercial agriculture in global markets and shifting occupational preferences. These are problems that require macro-policy initiatives rather than GP-level interventions.

THE THREE SECTORS

This section focuses on the types of activities taken up by the GPs in three sectors, i.e. agriculture, school education and drinking water. This exploration allows us to understand in greater detail the role GPs can and do play, and how the overall socioeconomic context as well as macro-policy affects this role.

AGRICULTURE

As the above analysis shows, the crisis in agriculture was well recognized at the GP level. The specific problems of agriculture, stated in development reports as well as by various interviewees, were of a complex and structural type. One set of problems included unemployment caused by the decline in paddy cultivation, unfavourable prices for producers of cash crops in the global market, the fact that agriculture was not a preferred occupation, unavailability of labourers and extreme fragmentation of land. These problems needed state-level policy deliberations and macro-interventions rather than GP-level activities. A second set of problems was input related. These included the lack of irrigation, inadequate marketing and storage facilities and lack of training in modern agriculture practices. Of these too, several were not easily amenable to GP-level solutions. For example, marketing requires extended networks and a level of expertise that may or may not be available in the GP. It is not hard to see why, even though development of agriculture was stated as an important goal across the GPs, the number of projects in the sector did not match this goal.

An analysis of plan expenditure patterns for 1998–9 and 2001–2 showed that in 1998–9 out of 11 GPs for which expenditure figures were available, seven GPs and in 2001–2, out of eight GPs, seven GPs had expended between 11 per cent–30 per cent of plan funds on agriculture. In 1998–9 three GPs and in 2001–2 one GP had spent more than 30 per cent funds on agriculture (Table 16). The most significant activity was irrigation, followed by provision of inputs such as seeds and fertilizers (Table 18). However, these activities were set in the context of the larger problems described above, and it is hard to see how they could have resulted in a significant change in the agricultural scenario. GP initiatives were not likely to be effective unless the former were resolved. Additionally, benefits from projects undertaken could not be maximized because of lack of technical know-how, and irrigation projects were often used to augment sources for drinking water.

And in fact, the achievements and shortfalls in the agriculture sector, as stated in development reports and by PRs and in FGDs, showed that the perceived impact in the sector was small. The 'shortfalls' noted in several GPs, i.e. the inability to arrest the declining trend in agriculture, waning paddy cultivation, falling prices of pepper and coffee, and continuing low productivity, indicated an inability to solve core problems. Only some small changes were noted in six GPs, such as improvement in irrigation, some encouragement to cultivation of paddy, coconut, spices, and banana, construction of assets, pest control and an increase in the area under cultivation.

School Education

While scrutinizing the activities of the GPs in school education, two issues need to be kept in view. One, unlike in several other parts of the country, universal access and enrolment in elementary education has been one of the major successes of the 'Kerala model'. Two, as in the rest of the country, school education in Kerala is characterized by increasing privatization. Additionally, Kerala has a significant number of 'private aided' schools, i.e. schools which are managed privately, but for which the government provides salaries for teachers. The problems in school education identified in the sample GPs reflected this scenario, with the quality of schools and privatization of school education emerging as major concerns. Access to schools and drop out, critical issues in many parts of the country, were identified as problems in only two GPs situated in the tribal pockets of Wayanad.

Regarding the quality of schools, PRs and HMs pointed to shortage of teachers, inadequate school infrastructure as well as unsatisfactory classroom processes and low standards of achievement.[6] Here, there was some possibility of intervention by the GPs, but there were also important constraints. Curricular change as well as hiring and capacity building of teachers, etc., remained the domain of the state government.

TABLE 18: TYPES OF ACTIVITIES IN AGRICULTURE UNDERTAKEN BY THE GPs

(*Rs. in lakhs*)

	1998–9						2001–2					
	Thrissur		Wayanad		Thiruvanantha-puram		Thrissur		Wayanad		Thiruvanantha-puram	
	No. of projects	Expen-diture	No. of projects	Expen-diture	No. of projects	Expen-diture	No. of projects	Expen-diture	No. of projects	Expen-diture	No. of projects	Expen-diture
Total	35	49.48	47	32.26	4	13.81	24	16.71	40	45.09	4	17.49
		% of total for		% of total for		% of total for		% of total for		% of total for		% of total for
Crop production inputs	6	38.68	4	2.51	1	4.63	3	5.21	3	3.06	1	10.18
Agricultural implements	1	0.01	0	0	0	0	1	0.42	0	0	0	0
Irrigation	17	33.10	42	95.94	2	62.78	14	79.17	34	72.34	2	85.76
Non-irrigation infrastructure	1	0.73	0	0	0	0	3	6.22	0	0	0	0
Extension	2	1.43	0	0	0	0	0	0	0	0	0	0
Provision of finance	0	0	0	0	0	0	0	0	2	24.40	0	0
Soil conservation	1	4.04	0	0	0	0	0	0	0	0	1	4.06
Agri-processing	2	3.78	1	1.55	0	0	0	0	0	0	0	0
Others	5	17.64	0	0	1	32.59	3	8.98	1	1.00	0	

However, the school, while governed by centrally determined curricula and standards, is also a local institution amenable to local interventions, and several GPs (especially the 'best' GPs), had engaged successfully with lower primary schools (LPSs). GPs had attempted to improve school infrastructure by adding rooms, repairing buildings, buying equipment, and so on. Some GPs had also started pre-primary sections in schools. Additionally, GPs had provided various types of benefits to students including remedial coaching for SC/ST students, study tours and extra nutrition. Finally, as noted in the previous chapter, after decentralization, PTAs had become more active in several GPs, and had begun to support school activities. The reason for the increased activity of the PTAs, as one headmaster explained, was that parents and teachers could make proposals to GPs, which was sympathetic. Interviews with headmasters showed that these small and simple initiatives of the GPs had led to improved school functioning and had strengthened the school as an institution.

It would not, however, be correct to conclude that primary education was a high priority area for the GPs. In fact, the financial investment of the GPs in education was quite low. In 1998–9 investments in education in all the GPs were less than 3 per cent of their overall plan investments and in two GPs there was no investment at all. Similarly, in 2001–2, there was no investment in education in four GPs, and only in one GP was there any significant investment (9 per cent of the overall plan investment) (Table 16).[7] However, the GPs had improved the general administration of schools by providing relevant infrastructure and taking up small but meaningful programmes.

A second set of problems concerned privatization of education. Enrolment in government schools was reported to be declining in three GPs, as English medium private schools were preferred. In another three GPs, which did not have government schools, PRs said that the GP could not impact education, or that there was no guarantee that children from deprived groups would get admission. In one such GP in Thrissur, no priorities were set for education in the GP plan because there were no government schools. Moreover, state government officials, and not the GP, had powers for regulating private schools, such as enforcing fee norms. On the one hand, privatization was an important dynamic in school education, occupying an increasing space, which GPs confronted. On the other, it was an issue that needed to be deliberated and dealt with through macro-policy.

To sum up, GP interventions in education need to be seen against the fact that the school is affected by macro-policy on the one hand, and is a local institution on the other. To the extent that the school remained an artifact of macro-policy in terms of curricula, policy towards privatization of education etc., GPs were unable to impact it. But the GPs were able to address the needs of the school as an institution rooted in the community by augmenting need-based infrastructure, promoting some student activities and supporting the PTAs.

Drinking Water

As noted earlier, drinking water scarcity was identified as a problem in almost all the GPs. A more detailed scrutiny showed that the drinking water problem was more acute in SC colonies, tribal areas and in low lands, where many people from deprived groups live. Unlike the case of education, the plan expenditure pattern shows that GPs gave fairly high priority to drinking water (Table 16). In 1998–9 four GPs out of eleven had made an investment of more than Rs. 5 lakh in drinking water. In the same year in seven GPs out of eleven, investment in drinking water was more than 5 per cent of the plan funds. In 2001–2, investment was more than 5 per cent in three GPs out of eight GPs from which information was available. This priority given to drinking water was a consequence of the urgency of the issue for ordinary people. GPs, as institutions with close links to people, had responded to this problem. GPs had engaged actively with the problem of water scarcity by taking up water supply projects, installing of public taps, digging and protecting wells and providing safe drinking water through chlorination of wells.[8] But the effect of these was reduced because of incomplete projects and technical or financial snags.

However, as in the case of agriculture and education, several problems were not amenable to solutions by the GP. For instance, in one Thrissur GP, the water level was reported to be falling due to sand and clay mining and additionally, there was water pollution due to industrial waste—activities that could only be checked by the regulatory machinery of the state government. In Wayanad, even though there were drinking water schemes in most areas, there was scarcity of drinking water during the summer season as the water table had declined because of the shifting cropping pattern. Several of these mega-issues were beyond the scope of GP activities.

CONCLUSION

In Kerala, the attempt has been to facilitate local economic development through local strategies and action, and the GP has been the key institution in this endeavour. But GPs exist in a complex socio-economic scenario, which often requires macro-policy solutions. For instance, prices in global markets affected the profitability of cash crops of Kerala, and macro-policy, rather than GP-level solutions, appeared to be needed here. Similarly, the whole dynamic of privatization of education, as well as improving classroom processes go beyond the GPs. Consequently, the space for action by the GP seems more limited than the hopes *vis-à-vis* local economic development that led decentralization in Kerala would suggest.

At the same time, GPs were able to impact what could be addressed locally, such as improving school functioning and taking up small drinking water schemes. The impact of the GP was conditioned by its institutional characteristics. GPs were effective because they responded to the immediate needs of the people and could take up small, context-specific projects. Consequently, they addressed the drinking water situation and supported local schools. However, GPs were hampered by their limited technical and administrative skills, which resulted in an inability to conceptualize appropriate projects and project failure.

NOTES

1. Wayanad is included in the Government of India list of 'districts with no industries'.
2. Each GP in Kerala prepares a development report that describes its socioeconomic context, issues and development strategies. These development reports are prepared as per a detailed process articulated by the state government that includes consultations with the people and experts.
3. For one GP of Thiruvananthapuram information could not be obtained as GP records were not well maintained.
4. Housing projects were considered most important projects in ten GPs and seen as its achievements in seven. Roads were considered important projects in nine GPs and achievements in six.
5. In only three GPs, irrigation projects had been listed as achievements.
6. Studies have shown that the quality of education and achievement levels of students in Kerala are not different from those of the rest of the country in any significant way (NCERT, 1991). Attempts were made to improve the

quality of classroom transaction during the mid-1990s, but were not fully sustained.

7. The highest investment in these two years across the eight GPs was only Rs. 3 lakhs.
8. A major water supply project was undertaken in one GP in Thrissur at the cost of Rs. 90 lakhs, the first phase of which had been completed.

CHAPTER 7

Panchayati Raj Across the Tiers (Kerala)

In the 'which tier' question, that has engaged panchayati raj policy in India considerably, the village or gram panchayat has emerged as the most important tier in Kerala. But the overall impact of panchayati raj depends, not only on the most important tier, but on the extent to which the potential of each tier has been unleashed. On the one hand, the three tiers have varying potentials for participation, arising from their accessibility to the people, and on the other hand, for planning and organization, a consequence of size as well as administrative and technical support available. In this chapter, we shall scrutinize the 'other', i.e. block and district tiers in Kerala,[1] and delineate the dynamics of the three-tiered panchayati raj system.

THE RELATIVE IMPORTANCE OF THE THREE TIERS

Here, it is important to keep in mind the historical primacy of the village panchayat, the ambivalence about the district panchayat and the non-existence of the block panchayat in state policy. As Chapter 4 shows, till 1994, Kerala had only one tier of PRIs, i.e. the GP, which had existed on a continuous basis since the pre-Independence days in most areas. Opinion about developing strong district-level PRIs was divided when panchayati raj was first considered in the late-1950s. Subsequently, in the 1970s and 1980s, the creation of elected district boards was deliberated seriously, and in the early 1990s there was a short-lived attempt to empower them. On the other hand, the block panchayat was by and large absent in ideas as well as practice till the constitutional amendment. This lack of emphasis on the block panchayat appears logical, given the large size of the village panchayat in Kerala, and the small size of districts. It may be recalled that this essentially two-tier pattern corresponds to the recommendations of the Asoka Mehta Committee, as the large village panchayats of Kerala are akin to the mandal panchayats recommended.

In 1994, as the Kerala government passed conformity legislation to the constitutional amendment, a three-tier system of panchayats became mandatory and panchayats at the village, block and district level came into existence.[2] As panchayati raj got a new impetus in Kerala in the mid-1990s, because of the focus on people's participation and local planning, the centrality of the gram panchayat was reinforced, while the block and district level bodies were secondary. For instance, of the six phases of the PPC, the first four focused exclusively on the GP. Block and district panchayat presidents were invited for training only in the fourth round, and block and district plans were prepared in the fifth phase of the campaign. While this lack of emphasis on the block panchayat was consistent with earlier policy initiatives, the reduced importance of the district PRI marked a break.

The functions assigned to the three tiers reflect the centrality of the GP. This is clear from the division of developmental functions across three sectors, i.e. agriculture, school education and drinking water (see Annex 3). In addition, the GP is assigned several important civic functions as well as general functions to encourage people's participation, such as organizing campaigns, raising awareness on issues such as the environment, communal harmony, legal rights and other topics, organizing self-help groups, etc., which are not assigned to the higher tier PRIs. In contrast, the higher-tier PRIs are expected to provide technical assistance to the GP, and make their plans keeping in view the GP plans. Importantly, the GP has been envisaged as autonomous, and higher-tier PRIs have no supervisory powers over it.

The devolution of finances too has been in keeping with the primacy given to the GP. While GPs can raise taxes including property tax, profession tax, advertisement tax, entertainment tax and other non-tax revenues, the block and district panchayat cannot and are wholly dependent on government grants. Of the Ninth Plan funds that devolved to local bodies, 86.8 per cent funds devolved to rural local bodies and the rest to urban local bodies. From among the funds that devolved to rural local bodies, the share of the GPs was 63.3 per cent, of the block panchayats 18.9 per cent and of the district panchayat 17.7 per cent (GoK, 2002). This pattern of devolution is consistent with the PRI policy of Kerala, i.e. the primacy of the GP.

INSTITUTIONAL DYNAMICS

Representation

In the sample PRIs at all levels, out of a total of 257 PRs, 19.8 per cent belonged to SC and ST categories. While at first glance, this may appear to be an unremarkable outcome of the legal provisions for reservation, a comparison with the bureaucracy, where similar provisions for reservations for SCs and STs exist, highlights its significance. From among a total of 73 officials interviewed during this study in the same area, a mere 7.7 per cent belonged to the SC and ST categories. Though reservations exist in government jobs too, often, qualified candidates do not become available. This problem does not exist for elected candidates. In other words, reservation in the PRIs was more effective than reservation in the bureaucracy in ensuring opportunity for marginalized groups to participate in public institutions.

Among the PRIs, the GP appeared to provide most opportunity for representation of the marginalized groups. At the GP level, in areas where the population of SCs and STs was high, these groups formed a significant number in the panchayat committee and thus had greater opportunity to play a decision-making role. While the percentage of SC representatives was high in three GPs of Thrissur (more than 30 per cent), and the GPs of Wayanad had a significant number of ST representatives (in one Wayanad GP the representation of STs was more than 46 per cent), SC/ST representatives did not exceed 24 per cent in any of block or district panchayats [Tables 1 and 19]. In the same vein, GP PRs were economically less well off than the higher-tier PRs, while the district PRs were the best off (Table 2) and also older. Nearly a third of GP PRs were blue-collar workers and around 14 per cent were white-collar workers, but at the district level only 12.5 per cent were blue-collar workers and 37.5 per cent were white-collar workers. Nearly 70 per cent GP PRs owned neither cars nor motorcycles, and only 5 per cent owned a car. At the district level, two out of the six (33 per cent) PRs, from whom information was available owned cars, while only 3 (50 per cent) owned no vehicle. Additionally, in the district panchayat Wayanad, the president was a well-to-do businessman, an exception to all the other PRs interviewed in this study.[3]

However, the picture of the GP creating more space for the representation of deprived sections of the community was not consistent. In some ways, the block and district PRIs functioned in a more equitable manner. Unlike at the GP level, SC and ST as well as women panchayat

TABLE 19: COMPOSITION OF PANCHAYAT SAMITIS OF BLOCK AND DISTRICT PANCHAYATS

	Thrissur		Wayanad		Thiruvananthapuram	
	Block	District	Block	District	Block	District
No. of seats	10	27	13	15	12	25
% Women	40.0	40.7	46.2	33.3	33.3	36.0
% SC	20.0	14.8	–	6.7	8.3	12.0
% ST	–	–	23.1	20.0	–	–
% UDF	50.0	48.1	76.9	66.7	67.7	44.0
% LDF	50.0	51.9	23.1	33.3	33.3	56.0
Political control	Equal*	LDF	UDF	UDF	UDF	LDF

*President UDF.

representatives had been appointed chairpersons of block and district panchayat committees. Additionally, block and district level representatives were a little more positive than the GP representatives about women PRs. While a small minority of GP representatives had said that they opposed reservation for women, at the block and district level, no PR said so. Similarly, though at the GP level a small number of PRs made negative assessments of the performance of women representatives, at the block and district level none did. At the GP and block level, a majority of the PRs said that women had made no special contribution, but at the district level a majority of the PRs stated that women made a special contribution in changing social perceptions and to women's programmes.[4]

Functioning and Dynamics

PRIs at all tiers were characterized by stiff political competition along party lines. However, the GPs were politically more volatile. In contrast the fact that in two thirds of the sample GPs, the political party in power had changed after the previous election, in the three district PRIs, the party in power had been stable across the same elections. The block panchayats presented a picture in between. Political rivalry within the GP could also translate more easily into action. While the higher-tier PRIs resorted to complaints and inquiries, the GP PRs, along with these, also mobilized people for *gheraos* and other such activities. As compared to the higher-tier PRs, GP PRs were in close contact with their constituencies and could therefore mobilize public opinion more effectively.

Panchayat samitis at all tiers met regularly and frequently. But among the three tiers, the GP panchayat samitis were the most active *vis-à-vis* local issues such as taking action against anti-social elements, the drinking water situation, banning *pan masala*, and so on. Some GP samitis had made petitions to officials and the government about issues such as immunization, drinking water and placement of officials. In contrast, the block level meetings were totally routinized. Given the few responsibilities given to the block level panchayat, this was not surprising. At the district level issues such as drought and drinking water were discussed by the panchayat committee, and occasionally petitions were sent to the state government, but to a lesser degree than the GP. The standing committees were not particularly active at any level, but were more inert at the block and district level as compared to the GP. In one district panchayat the health and education as well as the welfare committees were defunct. The steering committees were defunct across the PRI system.

Allocation of resources among the constituencies of the PRs was the most major bone of contention across the three tiers. As in the case of the GP, in higher tier PRIs too, plan discussions centred on division of funds as per the priorities of panchayat members. As in the case of the GPs, there was a tendency to allocate funds equally to each member's constituency and several political representatives claimed that larger projects could not be undertaken as a consequence, and irrelevant projects were taken up sometimes. Matters related to planning and project implementation occupied most of the meeting time of the panchayat samitis.

Corruption was also a political issue across the three tiers. This concern with corruption across the three tiers needs to be seen against the fact that a major shift that the panchayati raj structure entails is that a much larger number of administrative decisions, such as tendering for projects, scrutiny of accounts, etc., take place in the context of political competition, where rivals constantly look for opportunities to criticize the incumbents. As this competition extends to implementation as well as selection of projects, corruption comes on to the centre-stage. The issues that had emerged in the GPs have been noted in Chapter 5. There were also allegations of misutilization of funds in the block and district panchayats in Wayanad. In the former case, the ombudsman was enquiring into the complaints and in the latter case, a sub-committee set up by the panchayat was making inquiries. Additionally, the block panchayat had also taken action against its secretary for misusing funds. But the GP engagement with corruption was more intense. In five out of twelve GPs, corruption had been made an election issue, but this was not the case in any block or district panchayat. At the GP level, projects were local, and known and seen on a day-to-day basis by PRs as well as the people. In this sense, the GPs were also more accountable than the higher tier PRIs.

Links with Society

The GP really differed from the other tiers in its closer relationship to society. The opportunity provided for participation at the GP level played a role. Particularly, some better organized groups such as Kudumbashree did influence the GP. But such groups also influenced the higher tier PRIs. The main difference between the GP and higher tier PRIs was the fact that GP PRs had closer contact with people. While GP representatives had frequent interactions with the people of their wards, this was not the case for block- and district-level PRs, who met the community only occasionally. People often petitioned the GP PRs, and GP PRs in turn attempted to mobilize them against opponents. This closer relationship between people and PRs influenced GP politics and its institutional character. The GPs were more responsive organizations. For example, PRs at different tiers perceived their role differently. While GP PRs gave priority to fulfilling basic needs of the people and the deprived sections, and spent a good deal of time interacting with them, many district PRs talked of 'development' in a more abstract and less people-centric way, and were also more likely to spend their time on work related to projects and office management.[5] People's participation played a smaller role than this dynamic.

ANOMALIES IN THE STRUCTURE

As noted above, the devolution of functions and finances has been consistent with the primacy given to people's participation and the GP in Kerala. This consistency of policy is, however, marked by several anomalies in practice, which we shall now attempt to understand.

THE DIVISION OF FUNCTIONS

Though the division of functions across the tiers reflects the primacy of the GP, it presents several anomalies, which arise from the fact that planning as well as implementation for development and other functions requires coordinated rather than independent action at several levels. For example, in agriculture, it is the function of the GP to encourage group farming, while the block panchayat is assigned the function of mobilizing agricultural loans and the district panchayat that of marketing. This division makes little logic in terms of pushing through meaningful agricultural development programmes, which would involve all the above activities together. Similarly, in education, lower primary schools are the domain of the GP, while upper primary and high schools are the domain of the district panchayat. Moreover, the lower primary sections of upper primary and secondary schools remain the domain of the district panchayat. This division too, is not logical. Notably, schools, whether up to the primary, upper primary or high school level, are institutions that serve the local population. While the GPs have the advantage of being able to maintain continuous contact with schools, obtain cooperation from parents and other members of society and address school-specific needs, higher tier PRIs do not, though the latter may be able to access more technical expertise. The logical functional division across PRIs would be of various types of activities *vis-à-vis* schools, and not the division of schools in terms of the level of education offered.

Administrative and Technical Capacity

The second anomaly arises from the availability of technical and administrative capacity, which does not match the functions assigned across the three tiers. In Kerala, as in other parts of the country, government institutions and officials (with very few exceptions) have been transferred to the tier at which they were located. As the availability of technical manpower within government is the strongest at the district level, and the weakest at the village level, there has been a fair disjunct between the functions assigned to the PRIs at different levels and the administrative and technical expertise available. The field study showed that the block panchayats were the best off in terms of staff available for rural development, because the pre-existing block development offices were well staffed (these offices had five or more extension officers as well assistant engineers and overseers along with support staff). The district PRIs were less well off, as the District Rural Development Agency had not been transferred to the district PRIs, and the GP had the least staff with respect to rural development. The personnel available at the higher tier PRIs were also better qualified.

A scrutiny of the profile of the PRI secretaries also showed that though the block and district PRIs performed less critical functions than the GP, they had better qualified and more experienced panchayat secretaries (Table 3). This was reflected in the manner in which PRI secretaries at the three levels perceived their role, i.e. block and district PRI secretaries emphasized coordination, implementation and supervision of developmental projects, while more than half the GP secretaries emphasized office management, organization of panchayat meetings, and so on. In terms of infrastructure and facilities too the block and district panchayats were better equipped. In fact, at the district level, fairly large amounts of funds had been spent on buildings.[6] Notably, no tier had a secretary who could play a leadership role and coordinate the work of various departments. Though district panchayat secretaries in Kerala were reasonably experienced, they were not senior enough to be able to lead other district officials. This situation was quite different from the Maharashtra and Karnataka models where senior chief executive officers were appointed to the zilla parishads.

In parallel, departmental capacity was also the least at the GP level. The structure of the three departments that have been followed in this study, i.e. agriculture, school education and drinking water, was such that more and better qualified personnel were available at the higher tier PRIs. In agriculture, the existing departmental offices and officials in agriculture included a Krishi Bhawan at each GP with an agriculture officer with 2–3 agriculture assistants; an assistant director with some clerical staff at the block level; and a fairly large departmental structure at the district level that included a joint director of agriculture as well as six deputy directors of agriculture with substantial staff. However, in terms of qualifications and training, the agriculture officials at the three levels were similar, as usually persons who join as AOs at the GP are promoted to the block and district level. In fact, more then a third AOs at the GP level had master's degrees while none of the district agriculture officers interviewed did (Table 7). In the departmental structure for school education, supervisory officials, i.e. an assistant education officer (AEO) at the block level and a deputy director of education at the district level existed at higher tiers but not at the GP level. As discussed in Chapter 5, the Kerala Water Authority was simply not structured to function at the GP level.

The consequence of the asymmetry between the functions assigned at various tiers and the departmental structure was that the bureaucracy at the block and district level had been distanced from the developmental activities of the PRIs. Several developmental functions were assigned to the GP, where the presence of the bureaucracy was small. The block and district PRIs had fewer functions. Additionally, at the higher tiers, the transfer of the bureaucracy was partial. In agriculture, while at the GP and block level the offices and officials stood transferred to the respective PRIs, only two deputy directors out of six (along with their staff) had been transferred to the district PRI (Annex 3). The block and district level officials of KWA too were not transferred to PRIs but remained part of the organization controlled from the state level. KWA officials implemented projects and gave advice as and when asked and were also members of the TAC. However, their interaction with the PRIs was quite limited and they did not see any major shifts in their role in the post-decentralization scenario. The transfer in case of the education department was quite limited in general, for though the schools stood transferred, teachers remained state government employees and the department responsible for various service matters as well as academic activities.

Relationship of Officials with PRs

Even when block and district officials were transferred to the PRIs, they were less involved with the PRIs compared to the GP-level officials. In agriculture, at the GP level, all AOs saw their role as implementing departmental as well as panchayat projects. At the block and district level, however, while all officials saw implementation of departmental schemes as their role, only half saw the implementation of panchayat projects as a role. In one district, panchayat-related projects had simply been handed over to one deputy director, and other departmental officials concerned themselves with departmental schemes only. Similarly, while at the GP level some AOs included formulation of projects for the panchayat and the development of agriculture in the GP area as their role, the block and district level officials did not. Moreover, while village officials had interacted with the PRIs in the implementation of projects, organizing gram sabha meetings and organizing farmers' day, the interaction of block and district officials was limited to TAC and working group meetings.

In school education, lower primary schools stood transferred to the

GP, while upper primary as well as high schools were transferred to the district panchayat. In case of LPSs, headmasters and PRs had collaborated to some extent on various projects to improve the schools. But in case of high schools transferred to district panchayats, headmasters had had little engagement with the district or any other PRI. At the same time, the district panchayat was simply not close enough to the schools. Instead, the district panchayat interacted with the deputy directors of education, who collaborated in planning, appraisal and implementation of projects. Here, the engagement of the GP was qualitatively different from that of the district panchayat. GPs could interact at the school level and take up school-specific activities, while the district panchayats functioned in a more centralized manner, with little contact with the schools. The situation at the block level was that, as no schools had been transferred to the block panchayat, the role of the AEOs who had been transferred to the block panchayat had shrunk.

As a rule, officials located at the block and district level provided support to their junior colleagues for departmental schemes, but not for PRI schemes, as PRIs in Kerala are envisaged as independent of each other and the higher tier PRIs are not expected to monitor the GP in any way. At all tiers, when departmental schemes were implemented, technical issues were discussed with higher-level officials. In agriculture, support was also available from the agriculture university at the district level. But for panchayat schemes, there was no clear modality for providing or getting technical support from within the government, as there was little contact among the three tiers, and the interaction of block officials with the GP was limited to the appraisal of its projects. This independent structuring caused some problems *vis-à-vis* accountability. For instance, the block panchayat in Thiruvananthapuram had allocated a project to a GP to implement. There had been complaints about beneficiary selection but since the GP was responsible for this activity, the block panchayat could not do anything. It appears that in attempting to ensure that the GP remains an autonomous organization, vital links that are needed among the various tiers have been ignored.

At all three tiers, PRs gave mixed views regarding officials. Around half said that their role was satisfactory but the other half was not satisfied. The PRI-official relationship had usually improved over time across the tiers. At the GP level, the dissatisfaction often arose from the performance of officials, i.e. that they caused delays, were not capable, and so on. At higher tiers, PRs mentioned lack of control over officials as a problem more frequently, though some GP representatives also complained about the lack of cooperation from officials. This is in consonance with the fact that GPs do not have skilled officials at their disposal (and therefore PRs complain about the lack of support), and the departmental transfer to the higher tier PRIs is limited and officials at the higher tiers were more senior and less willing to listen to the PRs (and consequently, PRs wanted more control over officials). The block and district officials were also more critical of PRs than the GP officials.

Technical Support from Other Agencies

Interestingly, the skewed distribution of the technical expertise available to lower tier PRIs existed for expertise available from civil society too. Interviews with resource persons who had engaged with PRIs at the GP and district level showed a greater degree of 'professionlization' in case of district RPs. All six of the RPs interviewed at the district level were post-graduates and worked in offices or were teachers or professors (Table 8). In contrast, almost half the RPs interviewed at the GP level did not have college education. The association of district-level RPs with the PRIs had also lasted longer (the political party in power had not changed in any of the sample district panchayats), against the sharp discontinuities in the involvement of RPs at the GP level. Only one district RP had stopped participating in PRI activities, other RPs had remained involved in plan and project formulation, training, working groups, TACs and monitoring committees. Similarly, it was also easier for higher tier PRIs to get support from NGOs, of which there were more at the district rather than GP level.

General Implications for Technical Support

The above discussion raises some important issues about technical expertise as a whole. In the panchayati raj system in Kerala, the devolution of functions at the GP level is the highest, and the state has attempted to match this with financial devolution as well. However, government departments have not been restructured in parallel. The 'fitting' of the panchayati raj structure into the existing administrative structure has led to a general distancing of expertise available within government from the whole panchayati raj system. The block panchayat simply does not perform very important functions and consequently the development staff that it has at its disposal is underutilized. At the district level, where the maximum qualified expertise exists, the role of the district panchayat remains limited on the one hand, and the transfer of departments has been partial on the other. This implies a *distancing of available technical resources from development initiatives* across the state. The government continues to pay its employees, but asks for less work from those placed at the block and district level.

As shown in earlier parts of this book, in national policy, the question of block and district level PRIs has been very central, and in several panchayati raj initiatives in the past, district PRIs have been the most important tier, because of the availability of administrative and technical manpower. In contrast, in Kerala, the vision of the block and district PRI tiers has not been articulated very clearly, except for the fact that the village panchayat has been protected from a situation where more centralized agencies of any kind, departments or higher tier PRIs, can dictate to it. The intention obviously has been that the GP should remain responsive and accountable to the people, and not to any other agent. However, as seen in the previous chapter, the lack of technical capacities makes it difficult for the GP to be effective in this endeavour. At the same time, the potential that exists in terms of technical and other expertise at the block and district level, especially the latter, has not got exploited.

PROJECTS ACROSS THE PRIs

The lack of clarity about the role and processes of higher tier PRIs, as well as the general distancing of technical and administrative expertise available within government was visible also in the planning process. The planning process prescribed at the block and district level was similar to that at the GP level (described in Chapter 5), with the difference that higher tier PRIs were expected to take into account the plans of the lower tier PRIs. But the process of doing this was not well defined. Investigations showed that higher tier PRIs had made their plans quite independently. Instead of discussing their plans in the gram sabha, higher tier PRIs were expected to hold discussions in the general body of the panchayat. While in one block and one district panchayat serious discussions about the approach to the plan had taken place, in others, there had been no discussion on the perspective and coordination of the plan, and funds had been distributed constituency-wise.

As in the case of the GPs, the block and district panchayats were free to select any official as their plan coordinator. Rather surprisingly, inspite of the availability of several experienced officials at these levels, the designated plan coordinators were officials who were junior and did not play a central role in developmental activities. Similarly, the technical expertise available in working groups at these levels was superior to that available at the GP level, but had not been utilized. The potential available at this level was illustrated in one district panchayat, where the education official had been extremely active in formulating several innovative projects that had been approved by the district panchayat. However, in general, the working groups had been inert. Not surprisingly, when PRs and officials at the block and district level were asked about their opinion of the planning process, they were more dissatisfied than the GP-level PRs and officials. While GP-level PRs and officials drew some satisfaction from the fact that people had participated in the process of planning, at the block- and district-level, this element was missing. Instead, there was dissatisfaction about inactive working groups, and the short time in which the plans had been prepared.

A scrutiny of the plan goals set across the PRIs showed that the goals of block- and district-level PRIs were similar to those of the GPs, with some difference in emphasis. Improving agricultural productivity was a goal in nearly all the PRIs. However, as per the functions devolved, promotion of industry was a goal more often at the district level. At the same time, compared to the GPs, higher tier PRIs had given low priority to basic needs and infrastructure. For instance, at the GP level, solving the drinking water problem was a goal in nine GPs out of eleven, but it was a goal in only one district panchayat and in no block panchayat. Similarly, building of roads and houses were stated as goals more often at the GPs than the block and district levels.

While there were a few differences in the pattern of goal setting, in terms of the actual projects undertaken, the similarities across the tiers were remarkable. For instance, among the largest projects, housing projects figured most often across the tiers, and along with other basic needs and infrastructure-related projects, formed between 61–8 per cent of the largest projects across the PRIs (Table 12). Thus PRIs at all tiers undertook the same types of projects. No PRI was really able to make a dent in the productive sector and employment generation. In most higher tier PRIs, strategic and innovative projects had not been attempted. Where they had, success had been mixed (see Box 7).

Box 7: Projects of the District Panchayat

A project which did not succeed: Rice Park

This project was launched by the district panchayat in 1998 with SCP funds to procure paddy regularly in the district through the paddy growers' associations, and subsequently to convert the paddy into rice with the help of a mechanized rice mill. The project was expected to provide employment to SC population, help paddy farmers get remunerative prices and increase the activities of paddy growers' associations. A society called the Ambedkar Society for Industrial Rural and Vocational Advancement was registered to run the project, and a rice mill and rice powder units were installed in a plot of land given by the state government. Various other equipment were also bought. However, the project did not function effectively; and there has been criticism about the large amount of money spent on it.

A successful project: Women's Transport Corporation

This project was started by the district panchayat in 1997 to enhance employment and empowerment of women. The panchayat gave financial assistance to a women's cooperative to purchase two buses and run a bus service on a particular route. The drivers and conductors of these buses are women, and as part of the project, given training in light and heavy motor driving. The project has proven to be a profitable venture and at the second stage a motor repair workshop has also been set up, and is also run by women who have been trained for it. The project provides direct employment to 16 women and is valued very much in the panchayat.

What was absent in the projects of higher tiers was strategic initiatives to address vital issues that could not be addressed at the GP level, or which supported the GP projects in some way. For example, in agriculture, district level agricultural officials said that macro-issues in the sector were ignored. This may have been addressed if the higher tier PRIs, especially the district panchayat, had been able to take advantage of the expertise available at this level. But as we have seen, this was not the case. At the same time, higher tier PRIs were not as effective as the GP on several local issues. For instance, while the GPs had made small but important interventions in primary schools, the engagement of the district panchayat with the schools transferred to it was much less.

CONCLUSION

The PPC attempted to adapt and embed the methodology of participatory planning for local development evolved in Kalliasseri to a larger panchayati raj structure, with the GP as the key PRI. The GP in Kerala derived its vibrancy as a consequence of being the focal point in process development and capacity-building activities of the state government as well as from its closeness to the people. It emerged as an organization responsive to the basic needs of the people. However, as the government bureaucracy had not been restructured to match the new role of the GP, it lacked the administrative and technical capacity to give these characteristics a more concrete and fruitful shape in the form of effective projects and activities. At the same time, it could not draw upon the type of resource support from civil society that KDS could.

As the block and district level panchayats came into existence, in tune with the constitutional amendment, the organizational picture was never really clear for these higher tier PRIs. These PRIs were not envisaged in the planning process followed in Kalliasseri, and nor was their role adequately clarified and elaborated during the PPC. At the same time, certain functions, finances, personnel, etc., were transferred to them. Given the existing structure of administration, the block and district panchayat, especially the latter, had much stronger technical and administrative capacities, and the potential for developing sounder projects. The block and district level could have been envisaged as providing technical support to the GP, as the resource persons did in Kalliasseri. But because of a concern with the autonomy of the GP, this potential had not been exploited. The result was that the panchayati raj system as a whole lacked the administrative and technical capacities required to give concrete shape to its own priorities.

NOTES

1. Block and district panchayats were studied along the same lines as the GPs as described in Chapter 5. There were however, some variations. For higher tier PRIs, FGDs and studies of grassroots associations were not relevant. Moreover, as the block panchayat played a very small role, resource persons were not interviewed and projects were not studied at this level. These activities were, however, undertaken for the district panchayat level. Additionally, officials at the district level, including the district collector, district planning

officer, deputy director panchayat and the officer in charge of performance audit were also interviewed.

2. There are 990 gram panchayats, 52 municipalities, 3 municipal corporations, 152 block panchayats and 14 district panchayats in Kerala.
3. These trends can only be seen as indicative, as the sample was small.
4. But at all tiers, women were seen as having special difficulties, not getting adequate recognition and support from colleagues and the political parties, having difficulties in attending meetings at night, being tied down by household work, and so on. With respect to their views about SC and ST representatives, the panchayat representatives at all three tiers were similar. At all tiers, PRs made positive as well as negative comments while assessing their contribution. PRs saw their lack of clout, education and experience as hindering their performance.
5. This difference was also visible for panchayat secretaries. When asked what the best part of their work was, GP secretaries were most likely to mention helping and serving people, while block and district panchayat secretaries were most likely to mention implementing panchayat projects.
6. For the two district-level PRIs for which this information was available, the amount spent was Rs. 60 lakh and Rs. 2 crore respectively.

PART 3

CHAPTER 8

Micro-institutions in Macro-structures

The panchayati raj dynamic, i.e. the emergence of PRIs as institutions with a particular pattern of characteristics, capable of and predisposed to certain types of interventions, in the context of Kerala's policy and socio-political background, has been the subject of investigation in the second part of this book. As the third part of this book begins with this chapter, the attempt will be to explore this dynamic in the wider Indian context. This exploration is critical for identifying key initiatives that need to be taken in the future, the subject of the next chapter. As the first part of the book showed, in Indian policy, PRIs have been viewed as institutions anticipated to promote socioeconomic development and equity, taking up context-relevant activities in a participatory manner, and also providing more responsive and accountable governance. There is, on the one hand, a need to comprehend the extent to which PRIs do in fact develop into such institutions, and on the other hand, what promotes or whittles development in this direction.

Some lessons are already visible from the experience of Kerala. Many features, such as the attempt to develop a public discourse on development, the process of participatory planning, etc., appear worth emulating. The shortfalls of Kerala policies, such as the inadequate technical capacity of PRIs, are equally striking. However, before extending these ideas across an all-India context, it is important to keep in view that the replication of Kerala policies elsewhere will not necessarily lead to the same outcomes. The institutional characteristics of the Kerala PRIs have emerged, not merely as a result of the state's panchayati raj policies, but as a consequence of *these particular policies being implemented in the specific sociopolitical context of the state.* In other words, policies *vis-à-vis* PRIs are important, but so is the larger sociopolitical context. For instance, in Kerala, the village panchayat has developed as an institution with strong alliances with ordinary people. This development is attributable to some extent to panchayati raj policies, such as the processes of participatory planning instituted during the PPC. But it is also a consequence of the wider social and political context of the state, its long tradition of redistributive and social welfare policies and strong civil society.

The exploration of the panchayati raj dynamic has to be based on the idea that while specific panchayati raj policies do shape PRIs, these can play out in different ways across varied contexts. And, it is this interplay of policies and contexts that needs to be understood in greater detail. In the first part of the book, various policy deliberations at the national and state level were highlighted, with a special focus on Maharashtra, Gujarat, West Bengal and Karnataka. In this chapter, the varying institutional characteristics of PRIs across India will be highlighted in a similar manner, with a special reference to these four states and Kerala, but some findings from the northern part of the country will also be drawn in. While the Kerala experience has been presented in detail in part two of the book, and includes a field study, the experiences of the other states are accessed through several major studies, and commentaries etc. that are, fortunately, available.

THE QUASI-LOCAL PANCHAYAT

An important point for understanding panchayat dynamics is that PRIs are quasi-local and quasi-autonomous institutions. On the one hand, PRIs are embedded in the larger social, political and administrative structure. For example, in Kerala, PRIs drew from the state's egalitarian (compared to the rest of the country) social context; their politics were affected by the competitive politics in the state as well as the ideologies and characteristics of various political parties; and the structure and functioning of the state bureaucracy impacted their activities and processes a great deal. In many ways, PRIs simply reflected the macro-governance structure.

On the other hand, however, PRIs have a dynamic of their own too. First, the independent dynamic of the PRIs is based on their existence as political entities. PRIs are not field offices of government departments but are political formations, wherein individual representatives have the support of voters of a particular area, just as they are candidates supported by centralized political parties. Additionally, this political formation is far more accessible to public scrutiny, debate and influence than the centralized structures of governance, and this feature has the potential to generate an independent dynamic. For example, in Kerala, though political competition in the GPs was organized along party lines, its PRs as well as people focused on local issues. This led to the emergence of new concerns, such as how resources were spread across wards, and sharpened the focus on others, such as corruption. Consequently, a new, local dynamic was also generated. Second, the legal framework, as well as the functions, functionaries and funds devolved to PRIs create the space through which the politics of the PRIs can be translated into specific projects and activities. The extent of devolution is a critical ingredient of PRI autonomy. While in Kerala, devolution has been substantial, as Chapter 3 shows, several state governments have simply not defined the sphere of PRI activities or devolved finances adequately.

To return to the original assertion, PRIs are 'quasi-autonomous', i.e. they have *only partial* autonomy from the larger, centralized governance structures; but there *is* also a degree of independence. PRIs thus present a tantalizing picture: they are embedded in the macro-governance structure, yet not totally defined by it. The understanding of the organizational dynamics within PRIs, consequently, is a complex exercise. It involves a simultaneous attention to the macro-context in which PRIs are situated, as well as an attention to their autonomous character. Policy documents often anticipate that democratic decentralization will deepen democratic practices, cut away at patronage-based functioning and rent seeking, result in more responsive and efficient functioning, and so on. But in fact, these outcomes are contingent on a far larger array of factors than the extent and form of democratic decentralization, i.e. the macro-structure in which PRIs are situated, the extent to which they reflect the dynamic of this structure or differ from it and generate a new dynamic, and the shape that the new dynamic within the PRIs takes. Below, an attempt is made to tease out the various strands of this equation and elucidate the range and pattern of this dynamic in the Indian context.

PRIs AND THE SOCIAL POWER STRUCTURE

Experience in several states shows that existing power relations in society influence PRIs considerably. The first phase panchayats tended to be elite dominated. For example, studies show that even in the successful panchayats of Maharashtra, the leadership of the zilla parishads was characterized by single caste dominance and affluent class orientation, and belonged overwhelmingly to the middle class peasantry (Inamdar, 1977). Reservation for SC/ST and women candidates has been the most important strategy for fighting elite domination. However, more recent studies confirm that domination by social elites continues to be an important feature of PRIs, in spite of reservations. In fact, PRIs appear to allow greater opportunity for the domination of social elites than centralized governments, because manipulation is easier. For instance, in UP, where iniquities are high and feudal social relations are prevalent, village elites set up proxy candidates from among lower castes and women in panchayat elections (Srivastava, 2006). A recent study from Karnataka shows that the customary panchayat comprising of senior caste leaders, usually headed by a person from the dominant caste, exercises considerable (though by no means complete) influence in the selection of candidates to contest election, and also influences the decisions of the village panchayat, including beneficiary selection (Pur, 2006). Studies from several states show that many elected women representatives tend to be relatives of powerful persons (men) (Nair, 1987; Westergaard, 1992). Reservation for women in recent years has resulted in a new term being coined, i.e. panchayat or sarpanch *pati* (husband). In such cases, a woman may be elected as the panchayat chairperson, but her husband may actually function as the village panchayat head, attending meetings and taking decisions.

But countering reservations in this manner is not possible in all states, especially where feudal patterns in social relationships have diminished in influence. Dreze and Sen (2002) point out that while in north India, local elites have been quite successful in wielding power in PRIs by setting up proxy candidates, in south India, this has not been the case. In Kerala, PRIs were not elite dominated and several village panchayat representatives belonged to the less well off sections of society, a characteristic that needs be seen against the backdrop of the active civil society and the high degree of politicization in the state.[1] And, panchayats may be one way through which reservation may become more effective in governance. For instance, in Kerala, reservations for SCs and STs had been far more successful in PRIs than in the bureaucracy, where minimum qualifications are necessary for recruitment against reserved posts (and such SC/ST candidates cannot be found).

In West Bengal, panchayats have been one modality through which a political party has succeeded in shifting political power away from social elites. Studies indicate that landlords and rich peasants have been kept outside the membership of the village panchayat, while the representation of poor and marginal farmers has been substantial, though that of sharecroppers has not been as per their share in the population (Bhattacharya, 2006; Kohli, 1987; Westergaard, 1992). However, this countering of elite domination has been effected through the mediation of a particular political party and *centralized* politics, and is not an outcome of panchayati raj *per se*. But the existence of decentralized structures appears to have made this possible in West Bengal. Thus, when supported by initiatives from the state level, village panchayats have been instrumental in shifting political power away from local elites.

Even if proxy candidates are not put up, the dynamic within the PRIs often reflects existing power relations in society. In the case of Kerala, a mild version was visible where members from reserved categories were viewed as weak and less capable. In other states, including West Bengal, several studies show that SC and women representatives are unable to assert themselves in PRI meetings (Bhattacharya, 2002; Westergaard, 1992; Crook and Manor, 1998; Nair, 1987). At the same time, high levels of social inequity can be conducive to an allocation of resources skewed in favour of more powerful groups. For instance, Bardhan and Mookherjee (2004) show in the case of West Bengal that panchayats failed to cater to the poorer sections in villages where the iniquities in literacy, ownership of eco-nomic assets and social disparities were high. However, the allocation of resources is mediated through the organizational dynamics within the PRIs as well. In this context, the continued presence of representatives from the marginalized sections of society may play an important role. While these representatives may be discriminated against or be proxy candidates in several instances, this is not always the case. Moreover, while representatives from reserved categories may behave in a subservient manner in general, they may still succeed in influencing decisions. For instance, a recent study of Rajasthan and West Bengal PRIs indicates that women panchayat presidents took up projects that answered women's needs, and SC panchayat presidents invested a larger share of public goods in SC hamlets (Chattopadhyaya and Duflo, 2004).

It is useful here to visit the 'which tier' question that has been so important in panchayat policy in India. The support for the village panchayat is often based on the argument that at this level participation is possible, and participation in turn is seen as promoting the voice of the marginalized. The question of the poor having greater voice at the lowest tier of local government is actually far more complex. There was some evidence of this being the case in Kerala, but the context here was of high level of literacy and awareness. In contrast, Crook and Manor (1998) note in the case of Karnataka that mandal councils were less egalitarian than zilla parishads, and councillors prevented their SC colleagues from influencing decisions and obtaining resources earmarked for SCs. At the same time, marginalized groups may have more voice at decentralized levels if they are concentrated in some areas, as they may come to control the local government and be able to look after their own interests. On the other hand, this would not hold true in cases where the marginalized are spatially dispersed, in which case such groups may be capable of organizing better at more centralized levels.

Existing social iniquities frame the PRI dynamic and exert a powerful influence on it. However, the extent to which PRIs develop as institutions that reflect existing iniquities or counter them, depends a great deal on the policy framework such as reservation, the nature of politics within the PRIs, and how panchayat representatives perceive their role. Kerala, where PRIs took up several projects that benefited marginalized groups, was characterized not only by the weakening of feudal relations in society, but also by a history of social welfare by the state, and in more recent policy, a focus during the PPC on inequity along with reservations. As a consequence, several PRs understood their role as addressing the needs of poor and marginalized communities. The intense political contest within the PRIs played out over the allocation of resources, ensuring that marginalized communities got their share. Below, we shall explore the relationship of politics and panchayats in greater detail.

POLITICS AND PANCHAYATS

The larger political party structure forms the background against which panchayat politics emerge, and in extreme cases panchayat politics may simply be an extension of state politics. In West Bengal, where one political party, i.e. the CPI(M), has been dominant for several years, and the village panchayat has been the institution through which the party has pushed its policies, village panchayats have functioned largely as extensions of the party. Panchayat election campaigns focus on the political party, so much so that the individual village panchayat candidates are introduced only a week or so before the elections. Once the panchayat is formed, the CPI(M) continues to play a very critical role in decision-making. Important issues are discussed before panchayat meetings among party members, and decisions of the panchayats (taken by voting), are often as per party directives (Bhattacharya, 2002 and 2006; Westergaard, 1992; William et al. 2003). As noted earlier, the village panchayats of West Bengal have been successful in implementing land reform and other pro-poor policies. However, this has happened because of the specific policies followed by the political party in power at the state level, rather than agenda-setting at the PRI level. The role of PRIs has been of successful collaboration with the state government to implement pro-poor policies.

There can be several long-term problems in such institutional arrangements, as they can collapse quickly if the party in power changes. The more troublesome outcome can be that PRIs become institutions where the *political* elite, i.e. those who are important within the political party, dominate. In fact, in West Bengal, party members mediate the access to governmental schemes for the poor, and favouritism in providing benefits along political party lines has been noted (Bhattacharya, 2002 and 2006; Westergaard, 1992; William et al. 2003).

In contrast, Kerala, where there was no continued dominance of a particular political party, provided a scenario of stiff political party competition. Though centralized political parties exercised considerable influence in this competition, it played out around local issues and concerns, and extended the scope of democratic politics to new arenas. As ward members fought for their fair share of panchayat resources, distribution of resources became more equitable over smaller units. Like the West Bengal PRIs, Kerala PRIs too reflected a pro-people orientation. The special feature in Kerala was that rent-seeking, i.e. the appropriation of resources by those responsible for managing them, also came under scrutiny as specific issues of corruption and other malpractices became good grounds to mobilize against opponents. Thus the political elites were contained along with social elites. This meant that the accountability of the panchayat increased. An interesting trend was that elected representatives who contributed in terms of their work (rather than those who belonged to a particular caste or political party) often came to have influence within the panchayat.

The importance of political competition for inducing better performance and accountability in the panchayat has been noted in other instances also. For instance, Bardhan and Mookherjee (2004) show that in West Bengal, land reform and other measures were more successful when there was a high level of political competition and the left was less certain about its re-election. Similarly, in Karnataka, in

PRIs where political competition was very high, there was greater accountability (Vijayalakshmi, 2006). Logically, increased accountability and effectiveness resulting from political competition, rather than the centralized programmes of one political party, are more likely to survive changes of political regimes and also rein in the power of political elites.

But political competition does not always lead to this result. The ground rules for political competition can change, and PRI politics can get organized around patronage and rent seeking, with enticements and intimidation replacing the democratic processes. This is often a dominant dynamic in the north Indian states. For instance, in PRI elections in Rajasthan, candidates invested heavily in election campaigns to reap richer rewards later, and gave various types of incentives to voters. Discussions among the electors during the elections revolved around the incentives provided by different candidates rather than their individual merit or plans for the panchayat (Kerbart and Sivakumar, 2005). High expenditure on village panchayat elections has also been observed in UP. Additionally, in several village panchayats, meetings of panchayat representatives have simply not been held, or members who dissented strongly in such meetings have been beaten up (Srivastava, 2006).

Two macro-contexts frame the establishment of competitive politics around patronage and rent-seeking. One, where the level of education is low and grassroots political and civic associations are not strong, as in much of north and east India, the likelihood of political competition getting organized around rent-seeking is a constant threat. In contrast, the orderly and regular meetings of the panchayat samiti and decision-making by vote in Kerala must be seen against the fact that PRs in Kerala tend to be educated and experienced in political and civic life. In this way, the general level of education in the state, as well as the existence of a large number of political and civic organizations, influences the nature of political interaction very directly. Two, even as awareness in civil society increases, politics may remain organized around patronage and rent-seeking if it is accepted by major competing political parties. In such cases, the 'choice' exercised by voters in selecting from among competing candidates (put up by different political parties), may be meaningless, as no matter what a particular party or candidate claims in terms of policy or priorities, the actual goal may be simple profiteering. Such politics are hard to penetrate as more ethical candidates are unlikely to be able to raise financial resources to win elections. Even if ethical individuals do get elected, they can be at some disadvantage in getting things done, as rent-seeking tends to be highly organized, and they may appear less effective than their more savvy counterparts. On the other hand, rival political representatives may choose to be silent about corruption because of an unstated consensus. When this type of politics takes root, the capacity of PRIs to address equity concerns, along with their accountability, is whittled.

The nature of politics that develops in a panchayat plays a central role in determining its institutional character. In cases where politics does get organized around genuine issues of public importance, as in many panchayats of Kerala, there are indications that PRIs become more responsive and less corrupt than centralized agencies and take up various pro-people projects. In Kerala, the fact that panchayat representatives were in close contact with the people, and that opponents could mobilize people around local issues, increased the responsiveness and accountability of the GPs. However, the emergence of a politics that promotes this cannot be taken for granted. In the Indian scenario in general, the question remains whether PRIs will at all become institutions that focus on *public* issues as against those where individuals simply maximize gains for themselves.

BUREAUCRACY

As noted in the previous chapters, even when there has been the most significant devolution of powers to PRIs, including that of Kerala, the management and control of the bureaucracy has remained centralized. State governments retain substantial control over the bureaucracy in terms of recruitment, disciplinary action (except for minor punishment in some states) and importantly, transfers and postings, which have been used liberally in recent years to promote personal loyalty and rent-seeking (Dwivedi, Jain and Dua, 1989; Potter, 1996; Rudolph and Rudolph, 1987). Consequently, the existing bureaucratic ethos tends to reproduce itself within the PRIs and the bureaucracy is one mechanism through which several existing governance practices are continued. Rent-seeking and other unethical practices, which have made strong inroads into the bureaucracy, are carried over to the PRIs. For example, a study of UP showed that rent-seeking nexuses between panchayat representatives and officials had been established in case of anti-poverty programmes, and corruption was almost mandatory as a certain sum had to be paid to the block-level officials (Srivastava, 2006). Similarly, a study based in Karnataka showed that panchayat representatives were drawn early into existing rent-seeking nexuses among officials and contractors (Vijayalakshmi, 2006).

At the same time, the concentration of professional capacities within the bureaucracy at centralized levels limits the capacity of PRIs to plan and implement projects effectively. This problem stood out sharply in Kerala, where several village panchayats, though serious about development, were not technically and administratively capable of planning and implementing effective projects. Studies on decentralization in other states such as Karnataka and West Bengal also note this fact (e.g. Bhattacharya, 2006; Crook and Manor, 1998). Technical and administrative capacities are the weakest at the level of village panchayats because of paucity of staff as well as the fact that officials who are transferred to these bodies are trained to carry out orders rather than take initiative. These problems exist at the district too, though to a lesser degree.

Given the problems that the existing bureaucracy brings to the PRIs, it is not unusual to find an implicit argument in a great deal of panchayati raj and decentralization literature that the bureaucratic structure is inherently anti-decentralization and anti-democratization and that 'bureaucracy' weakens local self-government. This assumption seems to have existed in the PPC in Kerala too. However, in actual fact, the Kerala study showed that 'protecting' the panchayats from the bureaucracy left the PRIs with weak administrative and technical capacities. At the same time, support from resource persons and NGOs was inadequate and mechanisms such as beneficiary committees, meant to replace the official-contractor nexus, were not successful. On the other hand, if a well-trained and ethical bureaucracy had assisted PRIs, the latter's capacity as well as accountability would have increased. For example in Karnataka, in district PRIs which had a large contingent of officials, and where capable and experienced officials functioned as chief secretaries of the panchayat, regulations were usually followed, while in mandal panchayats that employed just one bureaucrat, i.e. a secretary who was not well trained, they were often flouted (Crook and Manor, 1998). It is the low skills and poor modes of functioning within the bureaucracy, rather than the bureaucracy itself that pose a threat to decentralization. Across India, PRIs do not tap upon a capable and ethical bureaucracy, and the situation in the northern and eastern states is most problematic.

Though the bureaucracy represents more continuity than change, one shift that does occur as PRIs are strengthened is that government officials function under conditions of increased interaction with politicians, i.e. panchayat representatives. The direction of change that this augers depends upon the type of politics that take hold within the PRIs. Where panchayat representatives themselves are involved in rent-seeking nexuses, the availability of officials who have previous practice and experience can merely ease the process. However, if the political formation within the PRI has developed along more ethical lines, then PRs are likely to be able to impact the bureaucracy accordingly.

MACRO-POLICY

Panchayats exist in the context of national and state macro-policies which frame their activities and projects. In fact, in many states, panchayats are largely known as agencies that implement various state and central government schemes and policies. However, even when panchayats simply implement government schemes, they change them, as they politicize implementation. Village panchayats in West Bengal developed as institutions that could be effective *vis-à-vis* land reforms, in a way that the bureaucracy could not have been. This politicization can have several consequences, depending on the nature of local politics. In several schemes implemented by PRIs the location of assets, selection of beneficiaries, etc., are decentralized, and these decisions can change the overall character of the scheme on the ground, even if it remains the same on paper. Whether it is better or worse depends on the character of the local institution.

What is interesting to note, however, is the importance of macro-policy even when PRIs are given the 'autonomy' to take up their own programmes and projects, as in Kerala. The Kerala study showed that the larger socioeconomic context and macro-policy were critical in defining the sphere of activities in which PRIs could be effective. For instance, in Kerala though several activities *vis-à-vis* agriculture stood transferred to the PRIs, the main problems in agriculture arose as a consequence of unfavourable global prices for producers, shifting crop patterns, occupational preferences, fragmentation of land and other factors. As long as macro-policy did not address these, the programmes undertaken by panchayats, e.g. irrigation, were not effective in alleviating either farmer distress or agricultural unemployment. Similarly, even though lower primary schools stood transferred to the GPs, the activities of the GPs *vis-à-vis* such schools were limited by the fact of increasing privatization of primary education (which could only be addressed by state government policy), and the fact that curricula, textbooks and teacher training—critical ingredients of school quality—remained with the state governments. PRIs could improve school buildings and take up a few programmes, but these were a small part of a larger picture. In other words, institutional capacities, i.e. the extent to which PRIs could actually address a problem, were a function of the macro-policy context, among other things.

In Indian policy, the question of decentralization has not yet been discussed in any detail in the context of the liberalized economy that has become more closely knit with the global economy, and where the sphere of the private sector has expanded considerably. As institutions, the capacity of PRIs to engage with these powerful actors is small, and only national and state governments have the potential to regulate their operations and negotiate the terms of engagement. In fact, the devolution to PRIs of functions and activities, in situations where other powerful actors that are not democratically accountable play an important role, can have the impact of reducing *any* form of state intervention, and thereby whittling rather than expanding the democratic space.[2] For example, in the absence of an adequate macro-policy in agriculture, decentralization can increase helplessness as PRIs face unfavourable outcomes of larger events and processes, but are unable to address the causes or evolve effective strategies to protect local interests.

At the same time, there exists the possibility of PRIs exerting a pro-people pressure on the state itself, as PRIs are also forums where local demands can be articulated. The fact that PRIs are political institutions raises the likelihood that they will resist decisions that go against popular interest and build upon those that address people's needs and aspirations and solve pressing local problems. However, in many states, the local politics within PRIs may not be of a type that facilitates such activity. Even in Kerala, while there were instances where PRIs petitioned the state government or exerted pressure on private actors in favour of community interests, this happened rarely, and the more common picture was that of helplessness of PRIs to deal with more powerful agencies.

PEOPLE'S PARTICIPATION

Some of the strongest arguments in favour of panchayati raj are based upon the possibility of participation of the people in the activities of local government. As illustrated in Chapter 3, participation has been expected to allow the poor to demand their share of resources, increase accountability of PRs and lead to the formulation of context-specific and need-based projects, i.e. counter several problems of centralized institutional functioning. As the discussion below shows, participation can go someway towards these goals, but there are several riders. First, effective participation only emerges in some contexts, which have to be carefully created. Second, the impact of participation is far more limited than is often assumed.

The gram sabha is the most important forum of participation, expected to assist in planning and implementation through voluntary contribution and by scrutinizing and questioning the decisions of the panchayat. But the actual experience of the gram sabha has been disappointing across the country. The question of the gram sabha becoming a forum where the poor can exercise influence needs to be seen against the fact that power-relations within society along the lines of caste, class, and gender are integral to the gram sabha. The participation of marginalized communities and women in gram sabha meetings has often been reported to be small and these groups do not wield much influence (Bhattacharya, 2002; Behar, 2003; Crook and Manor, 1998; Jafri and Singh, 2006; Jain, 1997; Joshi, 1995). Recent studies, as well as the Kerala study, also show another trend: that gram sabhas are attended most by potential beneficiaries, i.e. those living below the poverty line (Ghatak and Ghatak, 2002). But this does not mean much *per se,* as potential beneficiaries would collect in any other office or institution also, and may not attempt to influence the village panchayat in any other way.

Gram sabha as a forum for accountability also has significant limitations. Thin gram sabha attendance has been reported even among the states that have decentralized substantially, including Kerala. Gram sabha attendance needs to be seen in the context that people lack time, may lose a day's wages if they attend meetings and may lack faith in the utility of the gram sabha (Bhattacharya, 2002; Behar, 2003; Jafri and Singh, 2006; Jain, 1997; Joshi, 1995). Most villagers also usually lack the skills to examine accounts and papers placed before them. Moreover, PRs can jettison gram sabhas if these become too uncomfortable. For instance, in Karnataka, when villagers demanded explanations for unfulfilled election promises and raised questions about processes followed by the mandal panchayats, the councilors first began to organize meetings in a manner so that people could not attend and ultimately, in most places, abandoned the gram sabha (Crook and Manor, 1998).

However, the gram sabha can contribute to transparency in some conditions. For example, in Kerala, the beneficiary selection process has been made transparent by involving the gram sabha. An important point to be noted here is that people took interest in the beneficiary selection process because it affected them personally. Secondly, this transparency was an outcome of instituting a detailed *process.* In other words, the general placement of documents, etc., before the gram sabha may not help much in increasing accountability, as no one, except political opponents, benefits from scrutinizing accounts. Political opponents might undertake this exercise, but this may depend on the one hand, on the extent to which their own activities can stand such scrutiny, and on the other, on whether they actually gain an advantage by exposing corruption or maladministration. Where rent-seeking is accepted by all major political parties, even political opponents may not expose it.

Finally, the idea that participation will lead to more context-specific projects getting formulated is also valid in a very limited way. Gram sabhas appear to be good forums for articulating demand, and provide valuable information about what needs to be done. But they are far less successful in identifying appropriate solutions. Though in policy documents gram sabha meetings are often envisaged as forums for people to discuss developmental issues with a problem solving orientation, this is an exception rather than the rule. For instance, the West Bengal study quoted above showed that most people who attended gram sabhas hardly spoke, and the topics of discussion centered on political opponents pointing out the failures of the incumbents (Ghatak and Ghatak, 2002). Moreover, project identification needs technical skills that may not be available.

In recent years, there has been a new thrust towards organizing participation outside the PRI structure through community-based associations of several types, such as users' committees, SHGs, and so on. One critique of such associations has been that they can be used to reduce the influence of PRIs and subvert the democratic process. For example, in the case of Andhra Pradesh—a state that has promoted such associations with great vigour—it has been argued that the lack of institutional clarity of such groups has been used to extend and deepen the political party control (Powis, 2003). Another criticism has been that as the membership criteria of such groups is often loose, they become venues where socially powerful groups exercise authority. For instance, in Karnataka, village forest committees (VFCs) were formed to take decisions regarding access to forest resources and to promote the participation of excluded sections, but in reality, many of the VFCs comprised only the landed elites (Narayan, 2003). The counter argument is that self-help groups can strengthen PRIs rather than be its competitors (Bandhyopadhyaya, Yugandhar and Mukherjee, 2003).

Both these assertions are true, depending on the context. In some circumstances, community-based associations can strengthen the panchayat and increase its capacity for action, though in other conditions they can be manipulated to weaken them. Two factors appear important for the outcome. First, where PRIs are empowered institutions, as in the case of Kerala, such associations do not appear to pose a threat. To the contrary, the best community-based associations in Kerala, Kudumbashree and PTAs, strengthened the panchayat. Kudumbashree was successful in offering a modality through which the GP could channel resources to create credit and employment opportunities for poor women. It is doubtful if the panchayats would have paid the same attention to women's credit and employment without the programme. Similarly, it is through organized participation that in the West Bengal, panchayats magnified the impact of popular policies and programmes. However, the scenario can be the opposite where such groups have been organized without a parallel empowering of the panchayats.

Second, while these groups have the potential to strengthen PRIs, the processes within such groups are of considerable importance for this outcome. Lack of focus in terms of activity as well as loose membership criteria make such groups vulnerable to manipulation by elites. In such cases, the groups can be used to counter the more democratic processes of the PRIs or subvert them to various ends. Moreover, as the Kerala case showed, the availability of such forums can promote and support the manipulative tendencies within PRIs.

CONCLUSION

The above discussion shows that to get a grasp of the 'panchayati raj system' in a particular state, merely understanding specific panchayati raj policies, i.e. the manner in which a particular state has devolved functions, funds or functionaries, or the various processes developed, is not adequate. It is equally necessary to focus on the social structure and mobilization, the nature of politics in the state, the capacity of its bureaucracy and its overall policy environment, as these are as important as specific panchayati raj policies in determining the type of the panchayati raj institutions that take root. Panchayats tend to reproduce this macro-governance structure, and moreover, the space created for an independent dynamic of PRIs to emerge is also, to a fair extent, contingent on this macro-environment.

A very major issue *vis-à-vis* PRIs in India is the organization of politics around patronage dispensation and rent-seeking. To the extent that this remains a dominant dynamic, the benefits that can flow from the extension of political competition to new arenas are vitiated. At the same time, there is little evidence that the nature of participation that exists in most PRIs counters this trend in any significant way. Patronage-based functioning and rent-seeking chip away at the political space that belongs to public issues, such as development and equity, and weakens the panchayat as a public institution. Moreover, rent-seeking also reinforces elite domination. Panchayat elections become forums where 'investments' are made for future rewards, and only the well off can make such investments. The incentive for the powerful to 'capture' the panchayat increases if rent-seeking is possible, because of possible material benefit.

NOTES

1. Similar results were reported in a study of democratic local governance in six countries, i.e. Bolivia, Honduras, India (Karnataka), Mali, Philippines, Ukraine. In some areas of Philippines local bosses simply dominated the local governments, but in Latin America, where civil society was more developed, the distribution of benefits was equitable (Blair, 2000).
2. Slater (2000) argues that since the late 1980s, with the global deployment of neo-liberal ideas on fiscal decentralization and cutting back of the central state's capacity to intervene economically and socially, more institutional importance has been given to the local or municipal level of government. In such situations where the effectiveness of central state intervention in the economies of peripheral societies is curtailed and there is a proliferation of financially weak local governments, large firms with dynamic investment strategies can operate with fewer checks and controls.

CHAPTER 9

PRIs as Opportunity

Panchayati raj has been promoted for long-term, ideological and strategic reasons, as well as for short-term political calculations, and strong initiatives have emerged when it has been seen to serve both these ends. The more serious reasons for promoting PRIs include facilitating context-relevant socio-economic development, addressing poverty by giving the marginalized an opportunity to participate, and improving governance by deepening democratic practices as well as increasing accountability and responsiveness to the people. But PRIs are embedded in the existing socio-political and policy context, and these influence the organizational features of PRIs to a very large extent, so that more often than not, PRIs tend to reproduce the larger dynamic (and its problems), rather than become sites for the emergence of a new ethos driven by participation and local goals. An argument can therefore be made that we may expect nothing from panchayati raj other than the continuation of what already exists.

However, this conclusion is not warranted, as our analysis shows that in some contexts, PRIs can emerge as more responsive and transparent organizations compared to centralized government, because competitive politics are extended to new arenas of governance and because their links to society are closer. The emergence of PRIs as responsive, accountable and equitable structures of governance is thus a distinct possibility. But it is not a predetermined outcome. This possibility is likely to be realized in the context where social relations are equitable, civil society empowered and politics competitive as well as ethical. Paradoxically, where this is not the case, and where, PRIs, seen in Indian policy as the solution to the problems of centralized government, are most 'needed', the likelihood of a new ethos tends to be smaller.

The simple extension of the above argument can be that changes in the macro-governance structure are first necessary, e.g. if corruption is weeded out of Indian government, it will be stemmed in PRIs too, and if society becomes more egalitarian and politically active, PRIs will be parallelly transformed. Without doubt, such changes in politics, society and the bureaucracy will affect and alter the PRIs. But such macro-level change is not the subject of this book, which is to explore the significance and potential of decentralization. Moreover, it may be recalled from Chapter 2, that since the mid-1980s in Indian policy, PRIs have been seen as the solution to the problems of the macro governance structures. To suggest that these should be changed to change the PRIs is to run around in circles.

As noted above, in some macro-contexts, PRIs do emerge as institutions making space for the kinds of expectations voiced in policy discourses. However, since contexts cannot be replicated, the relevant question here is whether the favourable effect produced by the larger context in some instances, can in some way be simulated through policy interventions. In asking this question, an important shift is made in viewing the emergence of PRIs as responsive, accountable and effective institutions as an *opportunity* rather than merely a possibility. An opportunity, like a possibility, retains the character of tentativeness, i.e. of a process that may or may not come to fruition. But the critical conceptual shift here is that the idea of opportunity contains the prospect of *interventions* to change the scenario, as against the inevitable outcome shaped by a larger context.

In this chapter, the attempt is to identify strategies for maximizing the opportunity presented by the PRIs. This is done in two steps. First of all, if PRIs present an opportunity, then the precise nature of this opportunity needs to be understood accurately for it to be exploited fully. As was argued in the beginning of this book, the expectations from PRIs tend to be diverse, and some of these are not justified by experience. Unrealistic expectations that defy logic and experience confuse the debate and lead to strategies that do not bear fruit. At the same time, they often divert attention away from strategies that can be effective. To be effective, panchayati raj policies need to maximize realistic opportunities, and below, the contours of such realistic opportunities are explored. This exercise leads to the next step, i.e. the identification of strategies to maximize these realistic opportunities.

CONTOURS OF THE OPPORTUNITY

The expectations from PRIs in Indian policy may be divided into three broad, though interrelated categories. The first category that emerged early on after independence and has persisted since, is of overall socio-economic development, i.e. that panchayats will plan and implement projects that lead to rural and agricultural development in their area. The second category is that of poverty alleviation, i.e. that PRIs will act in favour of the marginalized sections of society, formulate context-specific strategies to alleviate poverty and implement them effectively. The third category comprises what may broadly be called governance, whereby PRIs are expected to be more responsive and accountable than centralized agencies, and hence deliver social services more effectively. As noted earlier, these categories are interrelated (and to some extent overlapping). For instance, improvement in governance is a precondition for the capacity of PRIs to impact poverty alleviation as well as overall socio-economic development. But still, these separate categories are useful for understanding the scope of opportunity presented by the PRIs, as they represent three broad strands of expectations visible in panchayat policy.

The opportunity of the creation of a governance structure through PRIs, which is an improvement on the more centralized government institutions, seems a central one, a precondition for effectiveness in other spheres. Experience shows that in appropriate conditions, PRIs can be more transparent and accountable, as well as responsive to people's needs than centralized government structures. The possibility of greater accountability and reduced corruption derives from the extension of competitive democratic politics to new arenas, i.e. from the spheres of policy formulation at the central and state level to implementation at the grassroots. It is a useful plank on which political opponents can campaign, and public opinion can be mobilized because of the increased visibility of the decisions as well their direct impact on people's lives. The possibilities contained in this shift should not be underrated, as the appropriation of state resources by state elites themselves, and their misallocation to suit a rent-seeking agenda, is a very central problem in India, and can waylay the best designed developmental or poverty alleviation programmes. This opportunity is exploited best when there is a high degree of political competition, and where rent seeking is excluded from competitive politics because of a high level of awareness within civil society. This opportunity is also maximized in cases where the ethics of the bureaucracy have not been eroded.

Another important opportunity that PRIs provide is of more responsive government, particularly with regard to the immediate needs of the people, because of the much closer contact between political decision-makers and the people, and the centrality of local problems. For instance, PRIs have been effective in West Bengal during flood relief (Ghosh and Kumar, 2003), in transmitting early warnings of disaster in Karnataka (Crook and Manor 1998), and the Kerala experience points in the same direction. With decentralization, the accessibility of the governance structure to the people increases. The number of persons to whom citizens can complain increases, and as these persons are local, the cost of making a complaint or petition goes down. This characteristic of PRIs can counter official apathy to a large extent. The responsiveness of PRIs seems to be especially high in case of problems that are perceived as urgent needs of the people, as in case of floods and droughts, or problems of daily living such as provision of drinking water. Even rent-seeking PRIs may perform these tasks better than centralized agencies, because of the moral pressure that emanates from within the community. A skilled bureaucracy makes it more possible for PRIs to be effective is addressing such needs.

While PRIs promise a superior ability to deal with urgent local problems, their capacity to promote long-term socioeconomic development appears to be more limited. There are no examples where, independent of macro-policy, PRIs have successfully negotiated the overall socio-economic development of a region over a period of time. As has been argued previously, regional socio-economic development often demands macro-policy initiatives rather than micro level interventions, especially in the context of growing linkages with larger economies and wider markets (Rao, 1989). For instance, in Kerala, though at the panchayat level the major problems recognized were those of production and unemployment, PRIs could not address the complex scenario from which these emanated. Even where micro-level initiatives can be effective, it is often difficult to access appropriate technical know-how at decentralized levels, particularly at the level of the village panchayat.

In general, because of limited expertise available, PRIs tend to adopt simple solutions. For example, in Karnataka, PRI plans became fragmented lists of pet schemes rather than integrated sets of mutually reinforcing proposals, and the councilors had a strong bias towards construction projects (Crook and Manor, 1998). The problem of inadequate expertise at the PRI level can be solved to some extent, but it is not possible to make available to a large number of PRIs the type of expertise that can be accessed by central and state level institutions. The capacity of PRIs to bring about local economic development also needs to be viewed against the fact that PRIs respond to popular pressure rather than long-term strategic goals, more so than centralized agencies, where institutions that follow longer term goals can be more easily created. For example, in Karnataka, the main elements of district plans were selected because councilors favoured them for political rather than developmental reasons, and councilors did not take up projects that were considered 'not needed' by the villagers (Crook and Manor, 1998). The Kerala experience is similar. The reluctance of PRIs to levy taxes may also be seen in this light, as tax collection is not popular.

The extent to which PRIs are capable of addressing inequity and poverty without strong state-level initiative is similarly small. As in the case of overall socio-economic development, the limitations of PRIs in countering iniquities and poverty also arise from the fact that local solutions to the problem of poverty simply may not exist. For instance, in Kerala, PRIs set a pro-poor agenda, but were able to make a dent only in terms of providing basic infrastructure for deprived groups, and could not address the all-important question of livelihoods. Similarly, PRIs may not be able to, and also lack the incentive to deal with, the needs of migrant populations, an important concern, as such people are often from among the poorest strata in India.

While decentralization *per se* does not lead to local economic development and reduction of poverty, this scenario can change dramatically with appropriate macro-policy. The West Bengal experience shows that if strong initiatives at the macro-level exist, PRIs are capable of *magnifying* the impact of such policies. They can do so by suiting such policies to the local context, by providing a forum where stakeholders can participate and contribute, and by doing a better job of some processes such as beneficiary selection, which require local knowledge. Consequently, questions regarding the capacity of PRIs to impact local economic development as well as poverty need to be posed in light of existing macro-policies. Where appropriate macro-policies are in place, these can be made more effective if empowered PRIs collaborate.

One way in which panchayats can counter inequity better than centralized agencies is in regional terms, because fund allocation takes place over smaller units. When allocations are more centralized, whole villages or groups of villages may be ignored. However, in a decentralized system, as has been visible in the case of Karnataka as well as Kerala, if a transparent formula is put in place, government funds can be allocated more equitably through PRIs across villages and even wards within villages. Political competition can add to this trend. For example, the Kerala study showed that ward representatives were vigilant about getting the fair share for their constituencies and the village panchayat provided basic infrastructure to wards that had previously been neglected. This more nuanced distribution of resources takes on special significance at the village panchayat level, where different castes or socio-economic groups may reside in separate wards, and equity across wards may also represent equity across such groups.

However, such regional equity can be ensured only in the context of transparent distribution of grants from the state government, and the design of transfers becomes critical in establishing the effects of decentralization on poverty (Bird and Rodriguez, 1999). The absolute transparency of the transfer is critical. For instance, Bardhan and Mookherjee (2004) show that in the case of West Bengal, villages with greater social and political clout tended to corner more funds. And where PRIs raise their own resources, the outcomes can be the opposite. Crook (2003) argues that decentralization, if it enhances political and fiscal autonomy of territorial sub-units, is likely to exacerbate uneven development between richer and poorer areas unless balanced by central equalization schemes.

To sum up, the most important opportunity provided by panchayats appears to lie in facilitating responsive and transparent government. The potential of PRIs to address long-term socioeconomic development and reduction of overall poverty exists in the context of appropriate macro-policies. Given appropriate macro-policies, PRIs can magnify their impact, but decentralization *per se* does not guarantee either overall development or eradication of poverty. There are also limits to what PRIs can achieve in terms of local economic development and poverty reduction because at decentralized levels, it is not possible to provide the technical expertise that can be garnered at the central and state level.

MAXIMIZING THE OPPORTUNITY

Above, an attempt has been made to sketch the realistic possibilities that PRIs embody. However, as the previous chapter shows, this opportunity is not realized easily, because PRIs are shaped by the larger sociopolitical structure. Additionally, it is most difficult to foster effective PRIs where they are needed the most, i.e. areas where social inequities are high and the functioning of government unsatisfactory. The important question for panchayati raj policy therefore is whether, and how, this cycle, i.e. the micro-institution of the panchayat mimicking the macro-structure and reproducing its problems, can be broken by appropriate policy initiatives or government action.

The idea of PRIs as opportunity has frequently been implied in several policy discussions and documents, especially as the question of institutional design has been discussed and as state panchayati raj policies have been formulated. However, these discussions have often revolved around a small set of issues, such as which tier of PRIs is the most appropriate, whether elections should be direct or indirect, who should be the chief executive office of the PRI, etc. But our analysis shows that the dynamic of institutional outcomes is far more complex. The organizational characteristics of PRIs depend upon the *interplay* of the existing social relations, political ethos, the macro-policy environment, the characteristics of the bureaucracy, etc., with the finer points of institutional design.

Consequently, a reinvestigation into the most pertinent policy thrusts based on the complexity of the panchayati raj dynamic is vital. This necessitates the rearticulation of old concerns and formulation of strategies derived from the complete, rather than partial, picture. For example, a much-discussed question in policy *vis-à-vis* panchayati raj has been, whether elections of PRI representatives should be direct or indirect. As seen in Chapter 3, these deliberations contain the idea that more meritorious, and possibly less corrupt, candidates will be able to win direct elections, whereas in indirect elections more wily candidates would have an advantage. However, corruption in PRIs is a larger systemic issue which concerns political parties as well as the bureaucracy, and it is unlikely that one type of election or the other can counter it effectively. At the same time, elimination or reduction of corruption from PRIs is a key concern, as it has the potential for altering the basic nature of PRIs in the sense of whether they develop as genuine public institutions, or merely become outfits for individual profiteering. What is needed here is the articulation of policy initiatives that recognize the critical importance of whittling corruption and effectively countering the influences that propel the PRIs towards it.

In other words, effective strategies *vis-à-vis* PRIs need to address the complexity of the PRI dynamic rather than ignore it. They need to impact the most central and critical factors that shape the PRIs, rather than tinker with details. Below, four such key, strategic interventions are identified.

Clarification of the PRI Space

A critical precondition for effective decentralization is a more precise identification of issues and problems that are amenable to PRI-level interventions. An important problem here is that the functions devolved to PRIs often tend to be very wide, such as 'agriculture' or 'employment generation' or, when these are sub-divided and narrowed down, the basis for the division remains obscure (as seen in the case of Kerala). This lack of definition leads to a lack of clarity about the PRI role, and subsequent inaction. This issue can be addressed to some extent by a realistic clarification of the role that PRIs can play in various sectors.

The articulation of the PRI role frequently runs into two types of problems. The first of these is the 'devolution' to PRIs of functions and areas, which actually require macro-policy interventions, and are not amenable to micro-level strategies. The second is the devolution of functions that exceed the technical and administrative capacity of the PRIs. Both these set the stage of institutional 'failure' of PRIs, as they are faced with problems in which they cannot intervene. In addition, the devolution of functions where macro-policy interventions are necessary leads to a parallel inattention to these sectors in macro-policy as these are considered 'devolved'. In such cases, the net effect (of decentralization) tends to be a lack of policy, or an inadvertent policy emerging out of inaction.

The exaggeration of the role that PRIs can play, and 'more' decentralization in the form of the devolution of an ever-greater number of functions, consequently, does not achieve the goals of expanding and deepening the democratic space, or provide solutions to 'local' problems. In fact, the overall impact of unrealistic devolution can be of increased helplessness in terms of an institution that is ineffective, as well as an absence of needed macro-policy response. What is critical is an *accurate* articulation of the role of PRIs, in terms of problems that can be resolved through micro-policy response and the technical capacities of PRIs. It needs to be recognized that constant stock taking of such devolution is also necessary. PRIs exist in a shifting socio-economic scenario, which demands a constant reassessment of their role. For instance, sectors that once required more straightforward interventions suited to domestic markets may demand complex strategies in the context of global markets. On the other hand, technologies may change and become more user-friendly and accessible, allowing greater management at the PRI level.

While areas that need macro-policy interventions are often devolved to PRIs, the activities in which PRIs perform better than centralized agencies are inadequately devolved. As illustrated in the previous chapters of this book, if adequate administrative and technical expertise exists, PRIs show a great deal of potential for responding to the most urgent needs of the people and for planning and implementing social welfare initiatives such as housing for the poor, basic infrastructure, provision of drinking water and so on. Such activities and programmes generate popular enthusiasm on which PRIs can capitalize by eliciting participation from the people and consequently perform better than centralized agencies. They are also capable of the context-specific responses that are required in such situations. This responsiveness can be built upon by devolving an increasing number of such functions to PRIs. This would ultimately lead to a substantial increase in state capacity to effectively intervene in social welfare.

It is reasonable to argue that activities that can be devolved best to PRIs are those that generate popular enthusiasm and are amenable to local and technically uncomplicated solutions (or solutions that match the existing technical capacity of PRIs). In contrast, the devolution of sectors and activities that respond to global rather than domestic markets, as well as those that require complex, technical solutions can be a meaningless exercise which can lead to a reduced state capacity for problem solving and association of institutional failure with PRIs. As yet, the devolution of functions has not matched up to this complexity. Devolution is either minimal, so that PRIs become agencies that implement pre-formulated schemes and cannot adapt them to suit local needs, or as in the case of Kerala, PRIs have responsibility in spheres where macro-policies are needed, resulting in failure and lack of action.

The implication of the argument made so far is not that PRIs need to be kept out of the picture for problems that require macro-policy responses and technically complex solutions. In fact, experience shows that PRIs can participate in and enhance macro-initiatives. The PRI and macro-policy combination can be made fruitful in two ways. First, if a modality is created where PRIs can 'demand' a macro-policy initiative, they can become forums where the felt and immediate needs of the people can be voiced. These can then be translated into an appropriate macro-policy response. In other words, PRIs can become important sites for articulation of people's needs and impact macro-policy. The important issue here is the creation of processes whereby

PRI demands can be legitimately articulated and incorporated into the macro-policy.

The second way in which PRIs can combine with macro-policy is to enhance policies that may be centrally conceived (as in the case of land reform in West Bengal). While there is need to be wary of the case where PRIs simply implement tightly structured programmes, there is also need to be cautious about devaluing the 'mere implementation' role of PRIs. As argued in the previous chapter, PRI collaboration in macro-policy initiatives is never identical to implementation through the bureaucracy. PRIs tend to expand and adapt the macro-policy response to make it relevant to their context and suit local priorities. If centralized policy initiatives and programmes are structured in a way that the options available to PRIs are increased, then irrelevant macro-policies are likely to be weeded out and relevant ones strengthened. This is possible if flexibility is built into programme structure and collaboration is sought from PRIs, as in the case of Kudumbashree in Kerala. This type of design of centralized programmes, to allow for choices and flexibility at the PRI level, is consequently, critical.

To sum up, a clearer articulation of the PRI space requires a constant assessment of areas amenable to macro and micro-initiatives as well as the technical complexities involved. Devolution to PRIs is meaningful only in the context of such clarity. Additionally, 'implementation' by PRIs of programmes and policies conceived at the central or state level needs to be seen, not just in terms of PRIs following central directives but also in the context of adapting these to local needs and eliciting popular participation, and thereby making them far more meaningful and effective. However, this is possible if these programmes themselves are structured in ways that allow options and transformation.

Accountability Mechanisms

Frequently, expectations from decentralization get grounded because PRIs tend to mirror rather than transform the patronage-based, rent-seeking practices within the larger system.[1] Only in a small number of cases does the opportunity created by political competition at the grassroots and increased visibility of the decision-making process translate into an institution that is more accountable.[2] At the same time, the use of PRIs for personal profiteering destroys their capacity to function as forums for genuine debates and decisions about public issues. The Indian experience of panchayati raj confirms the view that 'in order for political competition to have positive effects; it must be constrained by mutually accepted ground rules', and that 'Unless force and corruption can be made marginal to the repertoire of competitive strategies, increased political competition has adverse effects' (Evans, 1996: 1127–8). In India, political competition creates an opportunity, but the opportunity is waylaid because of the inability to establish ground rules to channel political competition into genuine policy development and performance *vis-à-vis* stated goals.

As argued, the flouting of ground rules regarding rent-seeking and profiteering has deep roots in the Indian state. Political parties are themselves riddled with these predicaments, and therefore do not address them in any significant way at the PRI level. Since the ethics of the bureaucracy too have been eroded, PRI officials may also not uphold the rule of law, and can in fact, facilitate the establishment of rent-seeking networks. In fact, at the PRI level, some processes of accountability such as legislative discussion and debate are absent, while others such as audit, supervision and media scrutiny are poorly developed. Such lacunae can be used to good effect to strengthen unethical practices.

As noted in Chapter 3, the problems within the government set-up in India have led several panchayati raj proponents to stress accountability to the people rather than to centralized authorities. But experience shows that participation does not *per se* improve accountability significantly. In Kerala, ground rules are followed in many PRIs in the context of an educated populace, high political participation and strong civic traditions. But such contexts do not exist in most parts of India and may take decades to develop, if they develop at all. We have visited in Chapter 3, the initiatives of the Mazdoor Kisan Shakti Sangathan, an NGO working in Rajasthan, which has initiated public hearings (*jan sunwais*) to hold panchayats accountable. However, while such initiatives may succeed with the support of committed NGOs, there is little evidence that the gram sabha can ensure accountability without such support. As argued in the previous chapter, panchayat representatives may simply not hold gram sabha meetings, and the latter, when held, may not be effective in intervening in PRI decisions.

There is some cause for intervening to create appropriate 'ground-rules' in PRI politics. The option worth exploring is whether the effect of contexts such as that of Kerala can be mimicked in a more direct fashion by policy initiatives. To some extent, a greater focus on the education of PRI representative as well as the people about the political process and panchayati raj can have an effect. But this may not be adequate. People may resent unethical practices within PRIs, but may not be able to impact decisions if *appropriate mechanisms* for doing so are not available. At present, if citizens want to protest corruption, there is usually no forum where they can be sure of being heard. Even in Kerala, the field study showed that in one GP, corruption was a dominant and uncontested dynamic.

Putting in place strong independent accountability mechanisms is therefore critical for the future of panchayati raj. In some ways, this recommendation is not original and the establishment of the ombudsman, audit processes, and so on are recommended frequently in policy documents. But these initiatives are often not seen as *central.* Suggestions related to accountability usually appear towards the end of policy documents, and occupy only a small amount of space. Moreover, the scope of action for audit as well as the ombudsman tends to be quite narrow, i.e. going through accounts or inquiring into complaints when made. In parallel, actual initiatives in this direction have been minimal. Even in Kerala, where an ombudsman has been set up, there are long delays in inquiring into complaints and often citizens who make complaints do not follow them up (Vijayalakshmi, 2006). In contrast, the emphasis here is on the *centrality* of processes of accountability to the whole panchayati raj project and the importance of defining the scope of these processes to address the *core issues* of panchayat functioning. The scope of accountability mechanisms needs to go beyond financial audits and ensure instead that on the one hand, legitimate political processes such as regular and orderly conduct of panchayat and gram sabha meetings, democratic decision-making (in contrast to beating up dissidents) and abiding by the decisions are followed, and on the other that dispensation of patronage and rent-seeking are made marginal to PRI processes. If quasi-judicial bodies are set up to ensure that these 'ground-rules' are followed, the likelihood of a real political dialogue emerging over public issues will be greater. This is desirable and valuable in itself, and is likely to lead to the emergence of more responsive and effective governance.

Often, the risk anticipated in setting up powerful accountability mechanisms is the possibility of their becoming mechanisms for control by centralized governments. This has indeed been the experience in the past in India. However, so far, the accountability structures have usually been under the direct control of state governments. But if these are independent bodies, the outcomes can be different. For instance, the Indian experience with judicial and quasi-judicial independent authorities has been positive in several ways. The higher judiciary and the Election Commission are examples of institutions that have successfully insisted on the ground rules in several instances. There is no reason why similar institutions cannot be created for panchayats too. For instance, committees of officials and members of the judiciary, the members of which cannot be changed by the government of the day, can go into the workings of various PRIs and take action to stem unethical practices as well as ensure that the panchayat functions in a systematic fashion.

The mandate of such bodies can be such that they are not allowed to interfere with the actual decisions of the PRIs, but only ensure that legitimate political processes are followed. The intervention of such bodies may be limited to the following issues:

- Whether or not appropriate processes are followed, such as holding of panchayat and gram sabha meetings, whether opponents are harassed in any way, whether decisions taken by the panchayat are actually followed.
- Prevention of corruption and financial accountability.

If the agenda of accountability is limited to ensuring that legitimate political processes are followed, the 'interference' of these bodies will not reduce PRI autonomy but strengthen it. By supporting legitimate political practices, these bodies would guard against the subversion of politics for private ends, and thereby augment the autonomy of the PRIs as public institutions. The existence of such mechanisms or bodies would also lend support to other actors struggling with the same issues. If strong mechanisms for whittling unethical practices are put in place, political rivals are likely to take recourse to these. If there is a modality by which people can demand that gram sabhas be held, they may do so. Moreover, civil society organizations working in this area would have a forum for voicing as well as following their concerns.

However, a few considerations need to be kept in view. First, the composition and terms of reference of such bodies have to be thought through carefully, so that they are not amenable to manipulation. A simple official overview or supervision, say by the BDO of the village panchayat, is not a solution, as officials are controlled directly by state governments. Second, it is important that these bodies follow judicial and quasi-judicial processes, so that simple interference by centralized authorities can be checked. At the same time, these bodies must have teeth, so that they can intervene effectively. For example, such bodies may need to be authorized to make inquiries proactively on their own account, as against simply waiting for complaints to be made. Rather than only go into the processes of individual PRIs, their scope of work may include policy advice and recommendations too, to the extent that these strengthen the legitimate political processes of the PRIs.

Developing PRIs as accountable institutions where corruption is minimized can have very wide spin offs for governance in India in general, and may be seen as a strategic intervention in the macro-structure too. As a better alternative governance structure emerges, it is likely that the unethical practices within existing institutions will be questioned more. At the same time, creating mechanisms that enforce the rule of law is simpler at the level of PRIs than at more centralized levels, where power is entrenched and concentrated. For instance, the public hearings held by the Mazdoor Kisan Shakti Sangathan in Rajasthan as well as the initiative of the organization to put up candidates who run panchayats in an ethical manner (Khera, 2005) are activities that are much more possible at the level of the PRIs than in case of elections to the national and state legislatures. And, given the fact that PRIs do not have influence over investigating and supervising agencies as central and state governments do, it will be easier for these agencies to act objectively.

Organizing Participation

The third strategy for strengthening PRIs involves maximizing the advantages of participation, and the close links that can be forged at the PRI level with people. As seen earlier, the mere existence or even empowerment of village panchayats and holding gram sabhas does not guarantee participation. The community in India is divided and hierarchical, so that gram sabhas as well as other types of community-based associations are often dominated by social elites. Moreover, gram sabhas are not as effective as is often anticipated because they tend to be thinly attended, and people often lack the motivation and skills needed to scrutinize panchayat accounts and decisions. Clearly, a more strategic organization of participation, i.e. the development of mechanisms and processes whereby people can participate effectively in a sustained manner is necessary.

Community-based associations of some types, i.e. those with clear goals leading to tangible individual or community benefit, with membership criteria and processes that are not open to manipulation by powerful people, and with some organizational and technical support, offer a promising way of organizing participation. However, such associations can whittle the democratic space if they become elite dominated and if the PRIs are disempowered. On the other hand, when such associations are made up of marginalized groups and not used to disempower PRIs, they do not usurp local democracy but can strengthen it. Such groups are able to pressurize the PRIs to undertake projects and tasks as per their needs on the one hand, and increase the capacity of the PRIs to implement such projects on the other. In fact, such groups may successfully counter elite domination within PRIs. The logical strategy in this scenario would be for governments as well as NGOs and activists to organize less powerful groups around their needs, on the one hand providing administrative and technical support and on the other demarking a clear relationship between these groups and PRIs.

Finally, while expectations from the gram sabha may need to be moderated and made more realistic, the potential that it does have needs to be exploited to the fullest. The Kerala experience illustrates two important strategies. The first of these is public education *vis-à-vis* socioeconomic development and the role of PRIs. The ineffectiveness of the gram sabha springs to some extent from the fact that the role of the panchayat itself is inadequately understood. Thus gram sabhas often make 'wish lists' of projects much beyond the capacity of the panchayat, but fail to focus on the legitimate demands that they can make, i.e. appropriate use of resources, their non-partisan allocation, efficient service delivery, and so on. In other words, gram sabhas do not seem to automatically start making relevant and meaningful demands, but may have to be educated in doing so. Second, the development of processes of consultation between the PRIs and the people's needs is also vital. The Kerala attempt of developing a process for participatory planning is a significant step in this direction. A clearer articulation of other processes, e.g., beneficiary selection by the community, would similarly facilitate participatory democracy.

Technical and Administrative Capacities

A final significant policy initiative that needs to be taken is the enhancement of the technical and administrative capacities of the bureaucracy to assist the PRIs. At present, the technical and administrative capacities of PRIs, especially of village panchayats, constrain their capacity to implement their own agenda. The Kerala study showed that even when political representatives were keen to select projects as per local needs, project failure remained a constant risk. To quote Peter Evans once again, 'Incentives derived from political competition are hard to actualize without an adequate administrative structure' (Evans, 1996: 1127).

Here, it is important to recognize that PRIs do not need to be 'protected' from the bureaucracy, but to be equipped with the appropriate personnel.[3] The fact that the motivation and ethics of the bureaucracy have been eroded does not diminish the need for appropriate technical and administrative support. While voluntary expertise can be useful and can augment the technical resources of the GP, it cannot *substitute* for a skilled bureaucracy, whose services are assured and which is accountable. For instance, if a bureaucracy that is well trained in social welfare can be created at the local level, it can increase the overall capacity of PRIs to deliver these services. Significantly, the provision of a well-trained bureaucracy goes beyond the simple transfer of existing officials to PRIs. It may require a shake-up of the structure of several departments. Intensive retraining would clearly be needed to make officials capable of advising PRIs and executing their decisions.

A question that often emerges *vis-à-vis* local government is whether the officials working within them should be accountable to the political representatives only, so that they become more committed to the PRI rather than following the departmental agenda. As noted in Chapter 3, this question has been approached with some caution in Indian policy. Here, two points need to be considered. First, that a political dynamic based on public issues rather than private profiteering is not guaranteed in PRIs, so that the complete shifting of control over officials to PRIs is unlikely to solve the problems within the bureaucracy. Second, the experience of totally politicized bureaucracies in developing countries has been harsh (Cameron, 2001). At the present juncture in India, there does not seem to be a simple solution to this issue. The more prudent course of action appears to be to focus first on facilitating a better political ethos in the PRIs, and simultaneously develop a bureaucratic set up more suited to their role. The transfer of control of the bureaucracy to PRIs will be meaningful only subsequently.

CONCLUSION

The attempt in this book has been to capture the complex and fascinating dynamic of grassroots democracy in India, and to delineate, in the context of this dynamic, critical policy steps. Panchayats present an intriguing picture of institutions embedded in the larger social and governance structure, but also capable of generating a new dynamic which has the potential for impacting the macro-structure. How this can be brought about has been a consistent concern in Indian policy. In this book, the attempt has been to *widen* the scope of this discussion by recognizing the complexity of the panchayati raj dynamic. This wider understanding enables more *focused* policy formulation to address core concerns. The way forward is not in the minutiae and details but in some strategic interventions, i.e. a clearer demarcation of macro-policy and panchayat level concerns, an insistence on the 'ground rules' of politics, the development of mechanisms and processes for participation, and the development of a technically skilled bureaucracy.

NOTES

1. A similar experience is reported from Bangladesh, where financial resources to local governments were increased and there was participation. However, the popularly elected chairpersons could not be held accountable and corruption and patronage in allocations ensued (Crook and Manor, 1995).
2. The experience in Africa is similar. Though there are examples of decentralized government enhancing participation, without appropriate accountability mechanisms, this has not led to greater responsiveness towards the poor (Crook, 2004).
3. Reviewing the experience of local governments in Latin America, Bird and Rodriguez (1999) point to the need for getting more professional and better paid staff for the efficient delivery of services.

ANNEXES

ANNEX 1: DETAILS REGARDING THE FIELD STUDY IN KERALA

TABLE A: INTERVIEWS CONDUCTED

	No. of persons interviewed										
	Panchayat representative				Panchayat secretaries				Resource persons		
	GP	Block	District	Total	GP	Block	District	Total	GP	District	Total
Total	43	8	8	59	12	3	3	18	23	6	29
Male	29	5	5	39	11	3	2	16	22	6	28
Female	14	3	3	20	1	0	1	2	1	0	1
General	28	6	5	39	12	3	2	17	21	6	27
SC	9	1	2	12	0	0	0	0	2	0	2
ST	6	1	1	8	0	0	1	1	0	0	0

	Agriculture department				Education department					Drinking water (KWA)				Overall Total
	GP	Block	Districts	Sub-total	LPS HMs	HS HMs	Block	District	Sub-total	Block	District	Sub-total	Others*	
Total	12	3	3	18	9	10	2	3	24	1	2	3	10	55
Male	6	2	2	10	6	5	1	2	14	0	2	2	10	36
Female	6	1	1	8	3	5	1	1	10	1	0	1	0	19
General	12	2	3	17	7	10	2	3	21	1	2	3	9	50
SC	0	1	0	1	1	0	1	0	2	0	0	0	1	4
ST	0	0	0	0	1	0	0	0	1	0	0	0	0	1

*These included officials who dealt with panchayats in various capacities such as district panchayat officers, district planning officer. Officialsin charge of performance audit and district collector.

TABLE B: GENDER AND CASTE CATEGORIES OF PERSONS INTERVIEWED

	Total no. interviewed	Female	SC	ST
PRs	59	20	12	8
Officials*	73	21	4	2
RPs	29	1	2	0

*This includes panchayat secretaries, departmental and other officials.

TABLE C: SHORT CASE STUDIES CONDUCTED

Community-based associations		Projects	
Type of association	No. of GP level case studies	Largest Projects GP level	8
Kudumbashree (women's group)	4	Largest project at district level	2
Agriculture related	3	Special projects at GP level	8
School related	2	Special projects at district level	2
Health related	1		
Beneficiary committee	1		
Ward committee	1		
Total	12	Total	20

ANNEX 2: INFORMATION ABOUT THE SAMPLE PRIs

TABLE A: POPULATION CHARACTERISTICS OF SELECTED SAMPLE DISTRICTS (KERALA) AS PER CENSUS 2001

Indicators	Thrissur	Wayanad	Thiruvanantha-puram	Kerala
Total population (2001) in lakhs	29.75	7.87	32.35	318.41
Male (%)	47.8	50.0	48.3	48.6
Female (%)	52.2	50.0	51.7	51.4
SC (%)	11.19	4.3	11.5	9.8
ST	0.16	17.4	0.7	1.1
Literacy rate (%)	90.3	85.3	89.3	90.9
Male Literacy rate (%)	95.11	89.8	92.7	94.2
Female literacy rate (%)	89.71	80.7	86.1	87.7
Hindu (%)	59.2	50.2	68.1	56.2
Muslim (%)	16.4	26.9	13.3	24.7
Christians (%)	24.2	22.5	18.4	19.0

Source: http://www.censusindia.gov.in, GoK, Economic Review 2005.

TABLE B: POPULATION CHARACTERISTICS OF SAMPLE VILLAGE PANCHAYATS

	Thrissur				Wayanad				Thiruvananthapuram			
	GP1	GP2	GP3	GP4	GP1	GP2	GP3	GP4	GP1	GP2	GP3	GP4
Indicators	1	2	3	4	1	2	3	4	1	2	3	4
Total population (1991)	18,664	29,874	22,200	25,353	28,573	23,151	30,442	37,045	26,201	25,306	24,735	24,735
% Male	49.0	50.4	49.2	49.1	51.9	51.0	50.0	49.8	52.6	49.5	48.5	52.6
% Female	51.0	49.6	50.8	50.9	48.1	49.0	49.8	50.2	47.4	50.5	51.5	47.4
% SC	11.2	14.0	12.0	8.2	2.8	4.0	2.7	4.3	16.9	6.6	10.9	8.4
% ST	NIL	1.9	0.02	1.6	21.5	38.6	15.0	16.7	0.04	1.2	0.3	0.03
Literacy rate (1991)	88.8%	94.0%	95.0%	92.2%	84.1	72.5	84.8	83.9	89.8	91.62	87.1	90.3
Male	93.0%	92.0%	94.8%	95.5%	88.6	78.0	89.0	88.6	94.9	94.8	96.1	92.2
Female	84.8%	84.7%	89.7%	90.0%	79.1	66.8	80.6	79.3	84.1	88.4	82.3	86.7

Source: Records available with village panchayats.

TABLE C: BASIC FACTS ABOUT THE SAMPLE GRAM PANCHAYATS

	GP1 (SC/ST-headed)	GP2 (Woman-headed)	GP3 (General male-headed)	GP4 (Well-functioning)
Thrissur				
Location	10 km from block HQ	12 km from block HQ	6 km from block HQ	11 km from block HQ
No. of villages covered fully	1	2	2	1
No. of villages covered partly	1	0	0	0
Year when set up	1977	1962	1952	1953
Grade	Special	Special	Special	Special
Number of wards	11	15	12	14
Majority party in 1995	LDF	LDF	UDF	LDF
Majority party in 2000	LDF	UDF	LDF	LDF
Wayanad				
Location	11 km from block HQ	12 km from block HQ	9 km from block HQ	5 km from block HQ
No. of villages covered fully	2	1	2	2
No. of villages covered partly	0	2	1	0
Year when set up	1962	1971	1961	1971
Grade	Special	Special	Special	Special
Number of wards	15	13	16	18
Majority party in 1995	LDF	LDF	LDF	LDF
Majority party in 2000	UDF	LDF	UDF	UDF

(Contd.)

TABLE C (Contd.)

	GP1 (SC/ST-headed)	GP2 (Woman-headed)	GP3 (General male-headed)	GP4 (Well-functioning)
Thiruvanathapuram				
Location	4 km from block HQ	In block HQ		6 km from block HQ
No. of villages covered fully	1	1	1	1
No. of villages covered partly	1	1	0	0
Year when set up	1952	1953	1953	1952
Grade	Special	Special	First grade	First grade
Number of wards	14	14	13	14
Majority party in 1995	LDF	UDF	LDF	LDF
Majority party in 2000	UDF	UDF-LDF equal	LDF	UDF

TABLE D: BASIC FACTS ABOUT BLOCK AND DISTRICT PANCHAYATS

District Panchayats	Thrissur	Wayanad	Thiruvanathapuram
No. of blocks	17	3	12
No. of GPs	92	25	78
Population of largest GP	48,056	56, 530	68,968
Population of smallest GP	9,216	9,114	12,440
Average GP population	25,317	27,124	29,111
Year when set up	1995	1995	1995
Majority party in 1995	LDF	UDF	LDF
Majority party in 2000	LDF	UDF	LDF

Block panchayats	Block in Thrissur	Block in Wayanad	Block in Thiruvanathapuram
No. of GPs	6	8	8
Year when set up	1995	1995	1995
Majority party in 1995	UDF	UDF	LDF
Majority party in 2000	Equal*	UDF	UDF

*President UDF.

ANNEX 3: FUNCTIONS AND FUNCTIONARIES OF THE THREE-TIER PRIs IN KERALA ACROSS THREE SECTORS

GP	Block	District
Agriculture *Functions*:		
1. Land development and managment: Cultivate waste and marginal lands, ensure optimal utilization of land, soil protection 2. Improvement of agriculture practices: Production of organic manure, establishment of nurseries, encourage horticulture and vegetable cultivation, fodder development, seed protection, farm mechanization 3. Organization of people: Encourage cooperative and group farming, organize SHGs among farmers 4. Institutional: Management of Krishi Bhawans	1. Management of watersheds within the panchayat area 2. Support to GP: Arrange agriculture inputs required for schemes at village level 3. Extension and training: Training of farmers and conduct of agricultural exhibitions 4. Agriculture finance: Mobilize agricultural loans 5. Encouragement of sericulture	1. Watershed management for watersheds covering more than one block 2. Improvement of agriculture practices: Provide for agricultural inputs, pest control, promotion of commercial crops, cultivation of ornamental plants 3. Institutional: Running agricultural farms 4. Marketing: Marketing of agricultural products 5. Technical: Soil testing, application of bio-technology, conduct of locally appropriate research and development 6. Organization of people: Popularization of innovative projects, promotion of agricultural cooperatives

Officials and Institutions transferred Krishi Bhawans located in the GPs. In each Krishi Bhawan one Agriculture Officer and 2–3 Assistants	One post of Assistant Director and auxiliary posts	1. Two posts of Deputy Director and and auxiliary posts 2. Post of District Soil Conservation Officer and auxiliary posts 3. One Assistant Executive Engineer and connected posts 4. Soil testing laboratories in the district 5. District Agriculture Farm and Nursery 6. District Sales Counter
Education 1. Management of government primary and pre-primary schools 2. Implementation of literacy programmes 3. Management and promotion of reading rooms and libraries	Management of Government Industrial Training Institutions	1. Management of high schools and higher secondary schools (including lower and upper primary schools attached), technical schools, vocational training centres 2. Management of District Institute of Education and Training 3. Coordination of central and state sponsored programmes

(Contd.)

ANNEX 3 (Contd.)

GP Block	Block	District
Officials and Institutions transferred		
Government lower primary schools in the GPs	Assistant Director Education	4. Upper primary schools and high schools. One section from the Deputy Director's office
Drinking water		
Setting up and management of water supply schemes in the GP area		Implementation of water supply schemes covering more than one GP
Officials and institutions transferred	Nil	Nil

ANNEX 4: SOCIO-ECONOMIC SITUATION IN THE GPs

THRISSUR DISTRICT

GP1

People worked in agriculture as well as tile factories and wood-packing industries, and more than a hundred families were engaged in making gold ornaments. The main crops were coconut, paddy, areca nut and banana. The GP had small-scale plastic units, timber processing units, and tile and brick making units.

There was lack of irrigation and area under paddy was declining because of clay mining. Unemployment was a major problem, because of decline in paddy cultivation as well as shutting down of tile factories. Most land holdings measured less than one hectare. Suicide of factory owners was also reported. At the same time, labourers came from the neighbouring Tamil Nadu to work in tile factories and the construction sector. People from Bihar came to work in the gold ornament industry. 55 per cent families were registered as living below the poverty line. The poorest people were SCs and farm labourers. Many SCs were daily wage earners in farms and tile factories.

All the schools (5 LPS, 2 UPS and 1 HS) of the GP were private aided, so that the panchayat could not invest funds for infrastructure development. In most of the wards, there was severe water scarcity. Though there were drinking water schemes, they were riddled with technical problems.

GP2

The chief occupations of the people were agriculture and work in quarries. The main crops were coconut, paddy, rubber and nutmeg. The average land holding was 0.96 hectares. Lack of irrigation was a problem in agriculture. There were no significant industries, but there were around 50 stone quarries. Unemployment was a major issue, but labourers from Tamil Nadu and Orissa came to work in the construction sector and did other menial work. 52 per cent families were registered below the poverty line.

In terms of educational facilities, the GP had 5 LPSs (2 government and 3 private aided), 4 UPS (2 government and 2 private aided), and one government-supported HS. The GP had helped improve infrastructure facilities in government schools and introduced a few projects for improving the quality of education.

Scarcity of drinking water was a major issue. Though there were adequate water sources in the hilly areas, these had not been tapped fully.

Illicit consumption and production of alcohol was a problem in the GP.

GP3

People of the GP were engaged in agriculture and worked in brick units. The main crops were paddy, coconut, nutmeg, areca nut, banana, and tapioca. There were several industries including chemical industries. Most landholdings were below one hectare. The area under paddy was declining because of large-scale clay mining and lack of irrigation facilities. There was a strong sand mining mafia that subverted the authority of the panchayat. Root wilt and Mandari diseases affected coconut farming.

People from Tamil Nadu, Karnataka and Nepal come to work in tile factories and other industries. Pollution caused by the chemical industry was identified as a major problem. Because of illegal sand mining, about which the authorities did not take action, the amount of cultivable land had reduced and the water level had declined. There were 27 per cent families registered below the poverty line. The poorest people were SCs, who were mainly unskilled workers.

There were no government schools in this panchayat, and so no projects could be taken up in the education sector. The quality of water was poor because of a high level of salinity. In some areas there was scarcity of water and a few drinking water projects had been started.

GP4

The chief occupations were agriculture and work in tile factories, textile mills and small spinning units. The main crops were paddy, coconut, banana and rubber. There was a sharp decline in paddy cultivation and growing interest in rubber and banana cultivation. Most land holdings were below one hectare. Agricultural labourers from a neighbouring district came as farm labourers.

The GP had textile mills, small-scale spinning units and brick and tile factories. Labourers from Tamil Nadu, Andhra Pradesh, Maharashtra and Karnataka came to work in the tile factories. Tile factories and spinning mills were closing down and industry was declining, leading to increasing unemployment. 68 per cent families lived below the poverty line.

There was only one government managed school in the GP, i.e. a high school run by the GP. The GP had constructed a new building for this school and provided computers and scholarships to poor students. There was acute drinking water scarcity. Two projects implemented during the Ninth Plan had solved the problem partially. Scarcity of drinking water, drought and lack of irrigation were identified as major problems.

WAYANAD

GP1

The main occupation of people was agriculture. There were few non-farm activities and no large and medium scale industries. Small industries included one printing press, one milk chilling unit, one cattle feed unit, a spice powder unit, a chemical unit and so on. The number of educated unemployed was increasing.

The main crops were coffee, pepper, areca nut, coconut, paddy, banana and rubber. 59.82 per cent of the total area was under cash crops. This caused water scarcity. Irrigation facilities were inadequate. There had been a decline in the prices of agricultural produce, which had led to a decrease in production of cash crops and increased unemployment in the farm sector. Problems due to unemployment such as illicit liquor production and consumption, excessive alcoholic consumption, anti-social activities like theft had followed.

Most people had between 0.5–1.0 hectare land. Estate owners were the well-off group. STs, especially Paniya and Kattunaikkars, were the poorest people with no or little land. They worked as agricultural labourers or on estates. Other ST groups had an average of 0.25 cents of land. Many BPL families were engaged in Kudumbashree activities. There was no notable migration from the GP. Migrant labourers come to the GP for coffee plucking, construction of roads, and so on from Mysore and Tamil Nadu.

There were ten schools in the government and government aided sector and three in the private sector. The number of schools was inadequate and for many children schools were located far away. Infrastructure facilities, teaching quality and examination results were poor. Private schools were perceived as better, but a majority of the people could not afford the high fees.

Drinking water scarcity was one of the major problems faced by this GP. The reasons for the scarcity included shift in the cropping pattern (from paddy to banana and areca nut), ineffective water conservation measures and a high level of drought. ST colonies faced health problems due to the scarcity of clean drinking water. Conversion of paddy fields into residential plots and for banana and areca nut cultivation had had adverse effect on watersheds.

GP2

The main occupation of the people was agriculture. There were very few non-farm activities and no major industries. The main crops were coffee, paddy, pepper, coconut, banana and ginger. A majority of the land holdings were between 0.5–1.0 hectares. Land under paddy had been converted to other crops such as ginger, banana, etc., resulting in a lower water table. The agricultural situation was characterized by falling prices and low rainfall. The low price for agricultural commodities had led to loss of employment and income for farmers and farm labourers and increased poverty, particularly among the ST population. This had been exacerbated by the loss of traditional occupations and alienation of land. People from this GP migrated to Tamil Nadu as well as Karnataka for employment, though there was also in-migration from elsewhere.

64 per cent families were registered as BPL, most of whom were STs engaged in agriculture. The SC population was relatively better off. There were 846 families without homes and 261 families lived in the forest. There was an adverse male-female ratio (1000 : 960). In general, settler farmers were the wealthiest group. Among STs, Kurumas were better off.

There were twelve government schools, three aided school and one unaided school. Some areas lacked access to educational facilities, which was compounded by the poverty and illiteracy of parents. School infrastructure was inadequate. There was incessant water shortage, even in areas that had abundant supply earlier, due to the shifting of cropping pattern, environmental destruction, excessive sand mining of rivers and lack of water conservation measures. ST families were the worst affected, as there were few viable water supply schemes in tribal areas.

GP3

The main occupation of the people was agriculture. A few people also worked in granite quarries, but there were no major industries. The main crops were coffee, pepper, areca nut, paddy and coconut. A majority of the holdings were less than half acre. The agricultural situation was characterized by falling prices and low rainfall. The problems of the agricultural sector had resulted in high incidence of poverty, particularly among the ST population. This had been exacerbated by the loss of traditional occupations and land alienation.

66.6 per cent families were estimated to be below the poverty line. STs were the poorest group, the SC population was relatively better-off and settler farmers were the most affluent. People migrated to Tamil Nadu as well as Karnataka for employment. There was also in-migration from these states.

There were 12 government schools, one school set up by the panchayat, one aided and six unaided schools. In general, schools were available within reasonable distances, except for tribal pockets where drop-out rates were high.

GP4

The main occupation of the people was agriculture. Non-farm activities were very few, comprising mainly construction works and government jobs. There were no major industries. The main crops were paddy, coffee, pepper, coconut, tea, ginger, areca nut, rubber and banana. Small industries included hollow brick units, furniture, rice and flour mills etc.

Paddy cultivation had declined because of low prices and water scarcity. Several paddy fields had been converted to cash crop cultivation and also into residential plots. In parallel there had been a decrease in the prices of pepper and coffee, and disease had affected pepper and coconut production very adversely. Agricultural workers were the worst affected group. About 50 per cent of the landowners had more than half a hectare land. The poorest people were some ST groups such as Paniyas, Naikkans and Uralis, and poor people in the general category. They were engaged in agricultural labour. Among the STs, Kurumas and Kurichias were landowners and farmers. Estate owners were the most prosperous group. Agricultural labourers migrated to Karnataka seasonally. Labourers also come to the GP from Karnataka and Tamil Nadu for construction work and agriculture.

The number of educated unemployed was rising. A few people (mainly Muslims) worked in the Gulf countries. The GP had the largest number of SHGs under Kudumbashree in the district. Eighty-eight micro-enterprises had been started by poor women under Kudumbashree. These included photostat shops, candle making and mushroom cultivation.

There were fifteen schools in the panchayat area: thirteen schools in the government /aided sector and two in the unaided sector, both English medium. The infrastructure facilities and number of teachers were inadequate in government schools. ST students often dropped out. The student strength in the government schools was declining because of unaided English medium schools and drop-out of ST students.

Drinking water scarcity was a major problem, with a worsening drought situation.

There was illicit liquor production and consumption and increased usage of *Pan Parag*, etc.

THIRUVANANTHAPURAM

GP1

The chief occupations of people were agriculture, small industries and service sector jobs. The main crops were paddy, coconut, plantain, tapioca and rubber. There was fragmentation of land and paddy fields had been diverted to other uses. There was lack of proper irrigation facilities and marketing. The main non-farm activities included small-scale trade and services, cane work, lime shell, reed work, oil extraction from coconut, pottery, furniture manufacturing, saw mills, jewelry making, quarrying.

Unemployment was a major problem and people migrated to the Gulf as labourers. SCs were the poorest people. Their main occupations were casual labour in agriculture, and cane and coir work.

The GP had five government LPSs, one government UPS and two aided high schools. The number of unaided schools was increasing and there was a shortage of teachers in government schools. Drinking water shortage though prevalent was not acute.

GP2

The main occupations of people were agriculture, cattle rearing, rubber tapping, bamboo and reed work. There were some industries such as a graphite factory, soldering lead company and rubber plants. The main crops were paddy, plantain, coconut, tapioca and rubber. The area under paddy cultivation had declined, while there was an increase in rubber cultivation. Plantain had also become a profitable crop. Share-cropping was practiced and there was a shortage of labourers. Some of the problems of this sector included lack of marketing facilities, increasing cost of cultivation, low social status of farmers and low productivity of coconut.

SCs were the poorest people and were engaged in agricultural labour, bamboo and reed work. Women worked as housemaids and home nurses. There was labour migration to Bombay and Banglore for menial jobs. There was also in-migration of labourers from Tamil Nadu for casual labour.

The GP had eleven government LPSs, three UPSs and two HSSs. Problems identified included lack of adequate infrastructure, lack of teaching aids, shortage of teachers, and poor examination results.

There was a water supply scheme as well as public taps and wells. There was water shortage in some areas, particularly SC colonies.

GP3

The main occupations of people were agriculture, bamboo and reed work, and rubber tapping. More than half the land holdings were less than one hectare.

The main crops were rubber, coconut, paddy, plantain, tapioca, pepper, vegetables, cashew, areca nut, ginger and betel vine. There was a decline in the area of paddy cultivation and increase in the area under cash crops like rubber, pepper, garden nurseries and plantain. The problems of agriculture included lack of irrigation and marketing facilities, decline in the price of agriculture products, lack of training in modern agriculture practices, and low social status attributed to farming.

Other occupations included small-scale trading, services, government employment, business, casual labour, brick making, pottery and quarrying. There were no industries. The poorest people were from SC and ST communities. Their main occupations were bamboo and reed work, collecting firewood and other forest produce and casual labour. There was migration of men as menial workers to other parts of the country. Illicit liquor brewing and selling was a major social problem in the GP.

The GP had five LPSs, three UPSs and two HSs. There was shortage of school teachers and lack of infrastructure facilities.

There was no water supply scheme in the GP and open wells were the main water source. Water shortage was a major problem, particularly in SC colonies. Due to sand mining in the river, the groundwater level had sunk.

GP4

The chief occupations of people were agriculture, cattle rearing, quarrying, brick making, bamboo and reed work, casual labour, domestic labour, and work in cashew factories.

The main crops were rubber, paddy, coconut, plantain, betel vine, tapioca, cocoa and areca nut. 50 per cent of the land holdings were below half a hectare. Area under paddy cultivation had been declining. Plantain cultivation brought good profit, but the lack of marketing and storage facilities were bottlenecks. Interest in agriculture was declining and agriculture labourers were not available. The cost of cultivation was increasing and there was a lack of irrigation facilities.

About 30 per cent of the people were registered as BPL. SCs, among the poorest, were reed workers. There was labour migration to the Middle East and other parts of the country. Women migrated to the Middle East as domestic helps.

The GP had five LPSs, three UPSs and one HS. Problems identified included erosion of quality in education, lack of sufficient furniture in schools and competition from unaided English-medium schools.

Bibliography

Acharya, P. (1994), 'Elusive New Horizons: Panchayats in West Bengal', in *Economic and Political Weekly*, vol. 29(5), 29 January, pp. 231–4.

Ahluwalia, M.S. (2000), 'Economic Performance of States in Post Reform Period', in *Economic and Political Weekly*, vol. 35(19), 6 May, pp. 1637–48.

Association of Voluntary Agencies for Rural Development (1962), *Panchayat Raj as the Basis of Indian Polity: An Exploration into the Proceedings of the Constituent Assembly*, New Delhi: AVARD.

Bagchee, S. (1987), 'Poverty Alleviation Programmes in the Seventh Plan: An Appraisal', in *Economic and Political Weekly*, vol. 22(4), 24 January, pp. 139–48.

Bailey, F.G. (1965), 'Decisions by Consensus in Councils and Committees', in *Political Systems and the Distribution of Power*, ed. Michael Banton, London: Tavistock Publications.

Bandhopadhyaya, D. (2003), 'Twelfth Finance Commission and Panchayat Finances', in *Economic and Political Weekly*, vol. 38(23), 7 June, pp. 2242–3.

Bandhopadhyaya, D., B.N. Yugandhar and Amitava Mukherjee (2002), 'Convergence of Programmes by Empowering SHGs and PRIs', in *Economic and Political Weekly*, vol. 37(26), 29 June, pp. 2556–61.

Bardhan, P. and D. Mookherjee, (2004), 'Poverty Alleviation Efforts of West Bengal Panchayats', in *Economic and Political Weekly*, vol. 39(9), 28 February, pp. 965–74.

Bardhan, P. (2001), 'Sharing the Spoils: Group Equity, Development, and Democracy', in *The Success of India's Democracy*, ed. Atul Kohli, Cambridge: Cambridge University Press.

Bardhan, P. (2000), 'Local Governments and Delivery of Public Goods in Governance', in *Decentralization and Reform in China, India and Russia*, ed. Jean-Jacques Dethier, Boston: Kluwer Academic Publishers.

Bardhan, P. (1978), 'Authoritarianism and Democracy: First Anniversary of New Regime', in *Economic and Political Weekly*, vol. 13(11), 18 March, pp. 529–32.

Basu, K. (1993), 'Structural Reform in India, 1991–3', in *Economic and Political Weekly*, vol. 28(48), 27 November, pp. 2599–2606.

Behar, A. (2003), 'Madhya Pradesh: Experiment with Direct Democracy: Time for Reappraisal', in *Economic and Political Weekly*, vol. 38(20), 17 May, pp. 1925–7.

Bhattacharya, Buddhadeb (1969), *Evolution of the Political Philosophy of Gandhi*, Calcutta: Calcutta Book House.

Bhattacharya, B.B and S. Sakthivel (2004) 'Regional Growth and Disparity in India: Comparison of Pre- and Post-Reform Decades', in *Economic and Political Weekly*, vol. 39(10), 6 March, pp. 1071–7.

Bhattacharya, D. (2006), 'Writers' Building and the Reality of Decentralized Rural Power', in *Local Governance in India*, ed. Niraja Gopal Jayal, Amit Prakash and Pradeep K. Sharma, New Delhi: Oxford University Press.

Bhattacharya, Moitree (2002), *Panchayati Raj in West Bengal: Democratic Decentralization or Democratic Centralism*, Delhi: Manak Publishers.

Biju, M.R. (1998), *Dynamics of New Panchayati Raj System: Reflections and Retrospect*, New Delhi: Kanishka.

Bijukumar, V. (2004), 'Developmental State and Party Politics in India: Form Consolidation to Crisis', in *Review of Development and Change*, vol. 9(2), July–December, pp. 163–83.

Bird, R. and Edgard H. Rodriguez (1999), 'Decentralization and Poverty Alleviation: International Experience and the Case of the Philippines', in *Public Administration and Development*, vol. 19(3), pp. 299–319.

Blair, H. (2000), 'Participation and Accountability at the Periphery: Democratic Local Governance in Six Countries', in *World Development*, vol. 28(1), pp. 21–39.

Buch, N. (2004), 'Let the Sun Shine on the Grassroots Too: 73rd Constitutional Amendment: Story of Implementation and Deviations', in *New Issues in Panchayati Raj*, ed. D. Bandhopadhyaya and Amitava Mukherjee; published for Task Force on Panchayati Raj, Rajiv Gandhi Foundation, New Delhi: Concept Publishing Company.

Cameron, Robert (2003), 'Politics-Administration Interface: The Case of the City of Cape Town', in *International Review of Administrative Sciences*, vol. 69(1), March.

Centre for Development Studies (CDS) (1975): *Poverty, Unemployment and Development Policy: A Case Study of Issues with Reference to Kerala*, United Nations, reprinted by the Centre for Development Studies, Thiruvananthapuram.

Chakraborty, B. and Mohit Bhattacharya (eds.) (2003), *Public Administration: A Reader*, New York: Oxford University Press.

Chambers, R. (1994), 'Participatory Rural Appraisal (PRA): Analysis and Experience', in *World Development*, vol. 22(9), September, pp. 1253–68.

Chandrashekhar, R. (1989), 'Panchayati Raj Bill: The Real Flaw', in *Economic and Political Weekly*, vol. 24(26), 1 July, pp. 1433–5.

Chattopadhyaya, R. and Esther Duflo (2004), 'Impact of Reservation in Panchayati Raj: Evidence from a Nationwide Randomized Experiments', in *Economic and Political Weekly*, vol. 39(9), 28 February, pp. 975–8.

Chattopadhyaya, S.P., Krishna Kumar and K. Rajalakshami (1999), *Panchayat Resource Mapping to Panchayat Level Planning in Kerala*, Kerala Research

Programme on Local Level Development, Thiruvananthapuram: Centre for Development Studies.

Chaturvedi, A. (1987), 'Inter-Departmental Dynamics: Relations between Four State Government Departments at the District Level', in *Economic and Political Weekly*, vol. 22(9), 28 February, pp. M9-M19.

Chaudhry, P.K. (1969), 'Panchayati Raj in Action: A Study of Rajasthan', in *Rural Sociology in India*, ed. A.R. Desai, Bombay: Popular Prakashan.

Chibber, P. (1995), 'Political Parties, Electoral Competition, Government Expenditures and Economic Reform in India', in *The Journal of Development Studies*, vol. 32(1) October, pp. 74–96.

Conyers, D. (1986), 'Future Directions in Development Studies: The Case of Decentralization', in *World Development*, vol. 14(5), May, pp. 593–603.

Corbridge, S. and John Harris (2001), *Reinventing India: Liberalization, Hindu Nationalism and Popular Democracy*, Cambridge: Polity Press.

Crook, Richard C. (2003), 'Decentralization and Poverty Reduction in Africa: The Politics of Local-Central Relations', in *Public Administration and Development*, vol. 23(1), pp. 77–88.

Crook, Richard C. and James Manor (1995), 'Democratic Decentralization and Institutional Performance: Four Asian and African Experiences Compared', in *Journal of Commonwealth & Comparative Politics*, vol. 33(3), pp. 305–34.

——— (1998), *Democracy and Decentralization in South Asia and West Africa*, Cambridge: Cambridge University Press.

Dantwala M.L. and J.N. Barmeda (1985), 'Rural Development', in *Public Policy and Policy Analysis in India*, ed. R.S. Ganapathy et al., New Delhi: Sage.

Das, M.K. (2000), 'Kerala's Decentralized Planning: Floundering Experiment, in *Economic and Political Weekly*, vol. 35(49), 2 December, pp. 4300–3.

Dayal, I., Kuldeep Mathur and Mohit Bhattacharya (1976), *District Administration: A Survey for Reorganization*, New Delhi: Macmillan.

Dhar, P.N. (2003), *The Evolution of Economic Policy in India: Selected Essays*, New Delhi: Oxford University Press.

Dhawan, R. (1989), 'Implications of Panchayati Raj', in *Mainstream*, vol. 27 (44), 29 July, pp. 6–9.

Dreze, J. and Amartya Sen (2002), *India: Development and Participation*, New Delhi: Oxford University Press.

——— (1996), *India: Economic Development and Social Opportunity*, New Delhi: Oxford University Press.

Dreze, J. (1990), 'Poverty in India and the IRDP Delusion', in *Economic and Political Weekly*, vol. 25(39), 29 September, pp. A95-A104.

D'Souza, J.B. (1999), 'Local Self Government and Citizens', in *Economic and Political Weekly*, vol. 34(42), 16–23 October, pp. 2984–6.

Dube, S.C. (1969), 'Community Development: A Critical Review', in *Rural Sociology in India*, ed. A.R. Desai, Bombay: Popular Prakashan.

Dwivedi, O.P., R.B. Jain and B.D. Dua (1989), 'Imperial Legacy, Bureaucracy and Administrative Changes', in *Public Administration and Development*, vol. 9(3), July, pp. 253–69.

Eaton, K. (2001), 'Political Obstacles to Decentralization', in *Development and Change*, vol. 32(1), January, pp. 101–27.

Economic and Political Weekly (1991), 'Debasement of District Councils in Kerala', vol. 26(49), 7 December, pp. 2793–4.

Economic and Political Weekly (1992), 'Structural Adjustment: Second Thoughts Within Government', vol. 27(13), 28 March, pp. 623–5.

Evans, Peter (1995), *Embedded Autonomy: States and Industrial Transformation*, Princeton: Princeton University Press.

——— (1996), 'Government Actions, Social Capital and Development', *World Development*, vol. 24(6), June, pp. 1119–32.

Franke, Richard W. and Barbara H. Chasin (1992), *Kerala: Development Through Radical Reform*, San Francisco: Institute for Food and Development Policy.

——— (1998), 'Kerala: A Valid Alternative to the New World Order', *Bulletin of Concerned Asian Scholars*, vol. 33(3), July, pp. 25–8.

George, K.K. (1990): 'Kerala's Fiscal Crisis: A Diagnosis', in *Economic and Political Weekly*, vol. 25(37), 15 September, pp. 2097–2105.

Ghosh, A. (1992), 'One Year of Narsimha Rao Government: A Balance Sheet', in *Economic and Political Weekly*, 1–8 August.

——— (1989), 'The Panchayat Raj Bill', in *Economic and Political Weekly*, 1 July.

——— (1988), 'Decentralized Planning: West Bengal Experience', in *Economic and Political Weekly*, 26 March.

Ghosh, B. and Girish Kumar (2003), *State Politics and Panchayats in India*, New Delhi: Centre de Sciences Humaines and Manohar.

Government of India (2005), Report of the Twelfth Finance Commission, New Delhi.

——— (2004), *A Compendium of Resolutions of the Seven Round Tables of Ministers In-Charge of Panchayati Raj* (July–December 2004), Ministry of Panchayati Raj.

——— (2002), 'National Human Development Report 2001', *Planning Commission*, Government of India.

——— (2001), *A Consultation Paper on Review of the Working of the Constitutional Provisions for Decentralization (Panchayats)*, Vigyan Bhawan Annexe.

——— (2001a) *Report of the Task Force on Devolution of Powers and Functions upon Panchayati Raj Institutions*, Ministry of Rural Development.

——— (2000), *Report of the Eleventh Finance Commission*, New Delhi.

——— (1992), *Eighth Five-Year Plan*, Planning Commission.

——— (1986), 'A Draft Concept Paper on Revitalization of Panchayati Raj Institutions for Democracy and Development', Committee for the Concept Paper on Panchayati Raj Institutions, Department of Rural Development.

——— (1985a), *Seventh Five-Year Plan*, Planning Commission.

——— (1985b), *Report of the Committee to Review Existing Administrative Arrangements for Rural Development and Poverty Alleviation Programmes* (*CAARD*), Department of Rural Development, Ministry of Agriculture.

——— (1984), *Report of the Working Group on District Planning*, Planning Commission.

——— (1980), *Sixth Five-Year Plan*, Planning Commission.

——— (1979), *Report of the Working Group on Block Level Planning*, Planning Commission.

——— (1978), *Report of the Committee on Panchayati Raj Institutions, Department of Rural Development*, Ministry of Agriculture and Irrigation.

——— (1965), *Report of the Committee on Panchayati Raj Elections*, Ministry of Community Development and Cooperation.

——— (1963), *Report of the Study Team on the Position of Gram Sabha in Panchayati Raj Movement*, Ministry of Community Development and Cooperation.

——— (1958), *A Study of Panchayats*, Planning Commission.

——— (1957), *Report of the Study Team for Community Development and National Extension Service*, Planning Commission.

——— (1956), *Second Five-Year Plan*, Planning Commission.

Government of Kerala, *Economic Review*, various years.

——— (2002), *Guidelines for the Preparation of the Tenth Five-Year Plan by Local Governments*. G.O. dated 6.6.2002.

——— (1997), *Final Report of the Committee on Decentralization of Powers*.

——— (1994), *Kerala Panchayat Act*, Kochi: Swami Law House.

——— (1979), *The Kerala District Administration Act 1979*.

——— (1971), *The District Administration Bill 1971*.

——— (1968), *Report of the Select Committee on the Kerala Panchayat Raj Bill 1967*.

——— (1967), *Report of the Administrative Reorganization and Economy Committee 1965–7*.

——— (1958), *Report of the Administrative Reforms Committee*, A Government of Kerala Publication.

Gray, H. (1969), 'The Problem', in *Rural Sociology in India*, ed. A.R. Desai, Bombay: Popular Prakashan.

Guha, Ramachandra (2005), 'Verdicts on Nehru: Rise and Fall of a Reputation', in *Economic and Political Weekly*, vol. 40(19), 7–13 May.

Gulati, I.S. (1994), 'Speech at International Congress of Kerala Studies'.

Hanumantha Rao, C.H. (1992), 'Agriculture: Policy and Performance', in *The Indian Economy: Problems and Prospects*, ed. Bimal Jalan, New Delhi: Penguin.

Hargopal, G. and C.H. Balaramulu (1981), 'Bureaucratic Culture in Panchayati Raj Institutions', in *Quarterly Journal of Local Self Government*, vol. 11(3), January–March, pp. 164–75.

Herring, R.J. (1989), 'Dilemmas of Agrarian Communism: Peasant Differentiation, Sectoral and Village Politics', in *Third World Quarterly*, vol. 11(1), January.

Hewitt, V. (1989), 'The Congress System is Dead: Long Live the Party System in Democratic India?' in *The Journal of Commonwealth and Comparative Politics*, vol. XXVII(2), July, pp. 157–71.

Hirschmann, D. (1981), 'Development or Underdevelopment Administration? A Further Deadlock', in *Development and Change*, vol. 12, pp. 459–79.

Hirst, P. (1996), 'Democracy and Civil Society', in *Reinventing Democracy*, ed. Paul Hirst and Sunil Khilnani, Oxford: Blackwell.

Inamdar, N.R. (1977), 'Maharashtra', in *Patterns of Panchayati Raj in India*, ed. G. Ram Reddy, New Delhi: Macmillan.

Isaac, T.M. Thomas and Richard W. Franke (2000), *Local Democracy and Development: People's Campaign for Decentralized Planning in Kerala*, New Delhi: Left Word.

Issac, T.M. and P.K. Michael Tharakan (1995), 'Kerala: Towards a New Agenda', in *Economic and Political Weekly* 30(31–2), pp. 1993–2004.

Issac, T.M. et al. (1995), *The Kalliasseri Experiment*, Mundur: Integrated Rural Technology Centre.

Issac, T.M. and S. Mohana Kumar (1991), 'Kerala Elections, 1991: Lessons and Non-Lessons', in *Economic and Political Weekly*, 21 November.

Jafri, A. and Vikas Singh (2006), 'Mainstreaming Gender in District Plans in Madhya Pradesh', in *Local Governance in India*, ed. Niraja Gopal Jayal, Amit Prakash and Pradeep K. Sharma, New Delhi: Oxford University Press.

Jain, L.C., B.V. Krishnamurthy and P.M. Tripathy (1985), *Grass Without Roots: Rural Development Under Government Auspicies*, New Delhi: Sage.

Jain, R.P. and O.P. Dwivedi (1990), 'Administrative Culture and Bureaucratic Values in India', *Indian Journal of Public Administration*, vol. 26(3), July–September, pp. 435–50.

Jain, S.P. (1997), 'The Gram Sabha: Gateway to Grassroots Democracy', in *Journal of Rural Development*, vol. 16(4), pp. 557–73.

Jayal, N.G. (1997), 'The Governance Agenda: Making Democratic Development Dispensable', in *Economic and Political Weekly*, 22 February.

Jenkins, R. (1999), *Democratic Politics and Economic Reform in India*, New York: Cambridge University Press.

Jha, P.S. (2002), *The Perilous Road to the Market*, New Delhi: Rupa.

Jha, S. (2002), 'Strengthening Local Governments: Rural Fiscal Decentralization in India', in *Economic and Political Weekly*, 29 June, pp. 2611–12.

Jha, S.N. and P.C. Mathur (1999), *Decentralization and Local Politics: Readings in Indian Government and Politics*, New Delhi: Sage.

Joseph, M. (2003), 'Performance of the Southern States: A Comparative Study', in *Economic and Political Weekly*, vol. 38(37), 13–19 September.

Joshi, G.V. (1995), 'Gram Sabha in Karnataka: A Non Starter?', in *Kurekshetra*, April.

Kannan, K.P. (1990), 'Kerala Economy at the Crossroads?', *Economic and Political Weekly*, 1–8 September, pp. 1951–6.

——— (1995), 'Public Intervention and Poverty Alleviation: A Study of Declining Incidence of Rural Poverty in Kerala, India', in *Development and Change*, vol. 26, pp. 701–27.

Kannan, K.P. and K.S. Hari (2002), 'Kerala's Gulf Connection: Remittances and their Macroeconomic Impact in Kerala's Gulf Connection', Thiruvananthapuram: Centre for Development Studies.

Kannan, K.P. and K. Pushpangan (1988), 'Agricultural Stagnation in Kerala: An Exploratory Analysis', in *Economic and Political Weekly*, 24 September, pp. A120–8.

Katzenstein, M., Smitu Kothari and Uday Mehta (2001), 'Social Movement Politics in India: Institutions, Interests and Identities', in *The Success of India's Democracy*, ed. Atul Kohli, Cambridge: Cambridge University Press.

Kaviraj, S. (1997), 'The General Elections in India', in *Government and Opposition*, vol. 32(1), pp. 3–24.

——— (1996), 'Dilemmas of Democratic Development in India', in *Democracy and Development: Theory and Practice*, ed. Adrian Leftwich, Cambridge: Polity Press.

——— (1991), 'On State, Society and Discourse in India', in *Rethinking Third World Politics*, ed. James Manor, New York: Longman.

——— (1988), 'A Critique of the Passive Revolution', in *Economic and Political Weekly*, Special Number, November.

——— (1984), 'On the Crisis of Political Institutions in India', in *Contributions to Indian Sociology*, New Delhi: Sage.

Kerbart, E. and Sowmya Sivakumar (2005), 'Panchayat Elections in Rajasthan: A View form the Field', in *Economic and Political Weekly*, vol. 40(8), 19–25 February, pp. 723–5.

Khanna, B.S. (1999), *Rural Local Government in India and South Asia*, New Delhi: Deep and Deep.

Khera, R. (2005), 'Bringing Grassroots Democracy to Life', in *Economic and Political Weekly*, vol. 40(8), 19–25 February, pp. 725–8.

Kohli A. (1997), 'Crisis of Governability', in *Politics in India*, ed. Sudipta Kaviraj, New Delhi: Oxford University Press.

——— (1994), 'Centralization and Powerlessness: India's Democracy in a Comparative Perspective', in *State Power and Social Forces: Domination and Transformation in the Third World*, ed. Joel S. Migdal, Atul Kohli and Vivienne Shue, New York: Cambridge University Press.

——— (1989), 'Politics of Economic Liberalization in India', *World Development*, vol. 17(3), pp. 305–28.

——— (1987), *The State and Poverty in India: The Politics of Reform*, Cambridge: Cambridge University Press.

——— (1983), 'Parliamentary Communism and Agrarian Reform: The Evidence from India's West Bengal', in *Asian Survey*, vol. XXIII, no. 7, July.

——— (1993), 'Democracy amid Economic Orthodoxy: Trends in Developing Countries', in *Third World Quarterly*, vol. 14(4).

——— (1997), 'Crisis of Governability', in *Politics in India*, ed. Sudipta Kaviraj, New Delhi: Oxford University Press.

Kothari, R. (1990), *State Against Democracy: In Search for Humane Governance*, London: Aspects Publications.

Krishnaswamy, K.S. (1993), 'Karnataka's New Step Backwards', in *Economic and Political Weekly*, 1 May, pp. 847–9.

Kumar, Mohana S. (1993), 'Literacy Movement in Kerala: One Step Forward, Two Steps Backwards', in *Economic and Political Weekly*, 9 October.

Leftwich, A. (1993), 'Governance, Democracy and Development in the Third World', in *Third World Quarterly*, vol. 14(3).

Lindberg, S. (1992), 'Peasants for Democracy? Farmers' Agitations and the State', in *India in When Democracy Makes Sense*, ed. Lars Rudebeck, AKUT, Working Group for the Study of Development Strategies, Uppsala University, Sweden.

Lok Sabha (1992), Joint Committee Report of the Constitution (72nd Amendment) Bill, 1991.

Mahajan, G. (1999), 'Civil Society and its Avtars: What Happened to Freedom and Democracy?', in *Economic and Political Weekly*, 15 May.

Maheshwari, A. (2002), 'Economic Reforms and Rural Poverty', in *Economic and Political Weekly*, 27 April.

Manor, J. (2001), 'Madhya Pradesh: Experiments with Direct Democracy', in *Economic and Political Weekly*, 3 March, vol. 36(9), pp. 715–16.

——— (1999), *The Political Economy of Democratic Decentralization*, Washington, D.C.: World Bank.

——— (1995), 'The Political Sustainability of Economic Liberalization in India', in *India: The Future of Economic Reform*, ed. Robert Cassen and Vijay Joshi, New Delhi: Oxford University Press.

——— (1992), 'Panchayati Raj and Early Warnings of Disaster', in *Economic and Political Weekly*, 22 May, pp. 1019–20.

March, J.G. and Johan P. Olson (1984), 'The New Institutionalism: Organizational Factors in Political Life', in *American Political Science Review*, vol. 78, pp. 734–49.

Mathew, George (1999), 'Decentralized Institutions: Government and Voluntary Sector', in *Economic and Political Weekly*, vol. 34(9), 27 February, pp. 529–33.

——— (1994), *Panchayati Raj: From Legislation to Movement*, New Delhi: Concept.

——— (1996) 'Panchayati Raj in India', in *Development Policy and Adminis-*

tration: Readings in Indian Government and Politics-1, ed. Kuldeep Mathur, New Delhi: Sage.

Mathur, K. (2003), 'Strengthening Bureaucracy: State and Development in India', in *Public Administration: A Reader*, New Delhi: Oxford University Press.

——— (1996), 'Designing Poverty Alleviation Programmes: International Agencies and Indian Politics', in *Development Policy and Administration: Readings in Indian Government and Politics-1*, ed. Kuldeep Mathur, New Delhi: Sage.

——— (1995), 'Politics and Integration of Integrated Rural Development Programme' in *Economic and Political Weekly*, 14–21 October.

Migdal, J.S. (1994), 'The State in Society: An Approach to Struggles of Domination', in *State Power and Social Forces: Domination and Transformation in the Third World*, ed. Joel S. Migdal, Atul Kohli and Vivienne Shue, New York: Cambridge University Press.

Miller, D. (1992), 'Deliberative Democracy and Social Choice', in *Prospects for Democracy*, ed. David Held, Cambridge: Polity Press.

Mishra, S.N. (1981), *Rural Development and Panchayati Raj*, New Delhi: Concept.

Mitra, Subrata K. (2001), 'Making Local Governments Work: Local Elites, Panchayati Raj and Governance in India', in *The Success of India's Democracy*, ed. Atul Kohli, Cambridge: Cambridge University Press.

Mitra, S.K. (1991), 'Room to Maneuver in the Middle: Local Elites, Political Action and the State in India', in *World Politics*, vol. 43(3), April, pp. 390–413.

Mukherji, Nirmal (1996), 'Decentralization Below the State Level', in *Development Policy and Administration: Readings in Indian Government and Politics-1*, ed. Kuldeep Mathur, New Delhi: Sage.

Mundle, S. and M. Govinda Rao (1992), 'Issues in Fiscal Policy', in *The Indian Economy: Problems and Prospects*, ed. Bimal Jalan, New Delhi: Penguin.

Nair, J. (1987), 'Karnataka: Zilla Parishad Elections', in *Economic and Political Weekly*, 24 January, pp. 122–3.

Nair, N.D. Gopinath (2000), *People's Planning in Kerala: A Case Study of Two Village Panchayats*, Discussion Paper No.16, Discussion Paper Series, Kerala Research Programme on Local Level Development, Thiruvananthapuram, Centre for Development Studies.

Namboodiripad, E.M.S. (1994), 'Inaugural Address', International Congress of Kerala Studies.

Narayan, J.P. (1970), *Communitarian Society and Panchayati Raj*, Varanasi: Navachetana Prakashan.

Nayak, P.B. (1992), 'Sharpening Inequities', in *Economic and Political Weekly*, 11–18 April, pp. 823–8.

Nossiter, T.J. (1988), *Marxist State Governments in India: Politics, Economics and Society*, London: Printer Publishers Ltd.

——— (1982), *Communism in Kerala: A Study in Political Adaptation*, Berkeley: University of California Press.

——— (1978), 'State Level Politics in India: 1975–7: The Emergency and its Aftermath in Kerala', in *Journal of Commonwealth and Comparative Politics*, vol. 1b(1), March.

Oommen, M.A. (2005), 'Twelfth Finance Commission and Local Bodies', in *Economic and Political Weekly*, vol. 40(20), 14–20, pp. 2022–6.

———, (2004), 'Fiscal Decentralization in Kerala', in *Fiscal Decentralization to Rural Governments in India*, World Bank, New Delhi: Oxford University Press.

——— (1999), 'Panchayat Finance and Issues Relating to Inter-Governmental Transfers', in *Decentralization and Local Politics: Readings in Indian Government and Politics*, ed. S.N. Jha and P.C. Mathur, New Delhi: Sage.

——— (1992), 'The Acute Unemployment Problem of Kerala: Some Exploratory Hypothesis', *IASSI Quarterly*, vol. 10(3), pp. 232–55.

Oommen, M.A. and Mahi Pal (1994), 'MPs' Local Area Development Scheme', in *Economic and Political Weekly*, vol. 29(5), 29 January, pp. 223–5.

Palharya, S. (2003), 'Decentralized Governance Hampered by Financial Constraint', in *Economic and Political Weekly*, 15 March, pp. 1024–8.

Parameswaran, M.P. (1998), 'Kerala "Model"—What Does it Signify?', *Bulletin of Concerned Asian Scholars*, vol. 30(4).

Parayil, G. (1998), 'The Perils of Trying to be Objective Without Being Reflexive: The Kerala Model Revisited', *Bulletin of Concerned Asian Scholars*, vol. 30(3), pp. 28–31.

Parel, Anthony J. (ed.), *M.K. Gandhi: Hind Swaraj and Other Writings*, Cambridge: Cambridge University Press.

Patnaik, P., C.P. Chandrasekhar and Abhijit Sen (1996), 'The Proliferation of the Bourgeoisie and Economic Policy', in *Class Formation and Political Transformation in India*, ed. T.V. Sathyamurthy, New Delhi: Oxford University Press.

Pillai, Mohanan M. (1990), 'Wither State Sector Enterprises in Kerala', in *Economic and Political Weekly*, 17–24 February, pp. M9–M16.

Pandya, J.N. (1981), 'Panchayati Raj in Gujarat', *Quarterly Journal of Local Government*, vol. LI(3), January–March, pp. 151–6.

Patnaik, P., C.P. Chandrashekhar and Abhijit Sen (1996), 'The Proliferation of the Bourgeoisie and Economic Policy', in *Class Formation and Political Transformation in Post-Colonial India*, ed. T.V. Sathyamurthy, New Delhi: Oxford University Press.

Patnaik, P. (1985), 'New Turn in Economic Policy: Context and Prospects', in *Economic and Political Weekly*, vol. 21(23), 7 June, pp. 1014–19.

Potter, D. (1996), 'The Prime Minister and the Bureaucracy', in *Development Policy and Administration: Readings in Indian Government and Politics-1*, ed. Kuldeep Mathur, New Delhi: Sage.

Powis, B. (2003), 'Grass Roots Politics and the Second Wave of Decentralization in Andhra Pradesh', in *Economic and Political Weekly*, 28 June, pp. 2617–22.

Pur, K. (2006), 'Selection by Custom and Election by Statute: Interfaces in Local Governance in Karnataka', in *Local Governance in India*, ed. Niraja Gopal Jayal, Amit Prakash and Pradeep K. Sharma, New Delhi: Oxford University Press.

Putman, R. (1993), *Making Democracy Work: Civic Traditions in Modern Italy*, Princeton: Princeton University Press.

Rao, V.M. (1989), 'Decentralized Planning: Priority Economic Issues', in *Economic and Political Weekly*, vol. 24(25), 24 June, pp. 1399–1405.

Rahul (1992), 'Rhetoric Versus Reality: The State, Jawahar Rozgar Yojna and People's Participation', in *Economic and Political Weekly*, 19–26 December, pp. 2692–3.

Rajaraman, I. (2000), 'Fiscal Features of Rural Local Government in India', in *Governance, Decentralization and Reform in China, India and Russia*, ed. Jean Jacques Dethier, Boston: Kluwer.

Rajaraman, I. and Garima Vashishtha (2000), 'Impact of Grant on Tax Effort of Local Government', in *Economic and Political Weekly*, vol. 35(30), 12 August, pp. 2943–8.

Reddy, G. Ram (1977), *Introduction in Patterns of Panchayati Raj in India*, ed. G. Ram Reddy, New Delhi: Macmillan.

Ramachandran, V. (1988), *Report of the Measures to be Taken for Democratic Decentralization at the District and Lower Levels*, Government of Kerala.

——— (2000), 'Kerala', in *Status of Panchayati Raj in the States and Union Territories of India*, Institute of Social Sciences, New Delhi: Concept.

Ramachandran, V.K. (2000a), 'Human Development Achievements in an Indian State: A Case Study of Kerala', in *Social Development and Public Policy: A Study of Some Successful Experiences*, ed. Dharam Ghai, Geneva: United Nations Research Institute of Social Development and Macmillan.

Rammohan, K.T. (2000), 'Assessing Re-assessment of the Kerala Model', *Economic and Political Weekly*, vol. XXXV.

Rani, G. (1999), 'State Finance Commissions and Rural Local Bodies: Devolution of Resources', in *Economic and Political Weekly*, 19 June, pp. 1632–9.

Ray, A. and Jayalakshami Kumpatla (1999), 'Zilla Parishad Presidents', in *Karnataka: Their Social Background and Implications for Development in Decentralization and Local Politics: Readings in Indian Government and Politics*, ed. S.N. Jha and P.C. Mathur, New Delhi: Sage.

Ray, A. (1992), 'New Economic Policy and Indian Federalism', in *Economic and Political Weekly*, 25 January, pp. 147–50.

——— (1988), 'The Sarkaria Commission's Perspective: An Appraisal', in *Economic and Political Weekly*, 28 May.

——— (1987), 'New Panchayati System in Karnataka: Elections and After', in *Economic and Political Weekly*, 14 January, pp. 262–4.

——— (1985), 'Delivery Systems for Rural Development: A Field View of Institutional Linkages', in *Public Administration and Development*, vol. 5, no. 4, pp. 353–62.

——— (1982), 'From Consensus to Confrontation: Federal Politics in India', in *Economic and Political Weekly*, 2 October.

Rondinelli, D.A., James S. MacCullough and Ronald W. Johnson (1989), *Analysing Decentralization Policies in Developing Countries: A Political Economy Framework* in *Development and Change*, vol. 20, pp. 57–87.

Rudolph, Lloyd I. and Susanne Hoeber Rudolph (1987), *In Pursuit of Lakshmi: The Political Economy of the Indian State*, Chicago: University of Chicago Press.

Sambrani, S. (1979), 'Mythologies of Area Planning', in *Economic and Political Weekly*, Review of Agriculture, 23–30 December, pp. A135–9.

Samoff, J. (1990), *Decentralization: The Politics of Interventionism* in *Development and Change*, vol. 21, pp. 513–30.

Saradamoni, K. (1994), *Kerala: Society and Politics*, Speech at International Congress of Kerala Studies.

Sethi, J.D. (1989), 'Panchayats: Democracy or Dictatorship', in *Mainstream*, 15 July.

Sharma, R. (2003), 'Kerala's Decentralization: Idea in Practice', in *Economic and Political Weekly*, vol. 38(36), 6 September. See also revised version published in *Decentralization: Institutions and Politics in Rural India* (2007), ed. Satyajit Singh and Pradep K. Sharmam, New Delhi: Oxford University Press.

Sheth, D.L and Harsh Sethi (1996), 'The NGO Sector in India: Historical Context and Current Discourse', in *Development Policy and Administration: Readings in Indian Government and Politics-1*, ed. Kuldeep Mathur, New Delhi: Sage.

Shetty, S. L. (2003), 'Growth of SDP and Structural Changes in State Economies: Interstate Comparisons', in *Economic and Political Weekly*, vol. 38(49) 6 December, pp. 5189–200.

Shiviah, M., K.V. Narayana Rao, L.S.N. Murty and G. Mallikarjuniah (1976), *Panchayati Raj: An Analytical Survey*, Hyderabad: National Institute of Community Development.

Singh, S.K. (1999), 'Self Governance for the Scheduled Areas', in *Decentralization and Local Politics: Readings in Indian Government and Politics*, ed. S.N. Jha and P.C. Mathur, New Delhi: Sage.

Slater, D. (2003), 'On the Spatial Dynamics of Democratic Politics: Analysing the Bolivian Case', in *Development and Change*, vol. 34(4), pp. 607–32.

——— (1989), 'Territorial Power and the Peripheral State: The Issue of Decentralization', in *Development and Change*, vol. 20(3), July, pp. 501–31.

Smith, B.C. (1985), *Decentralization: The Territorial Dimension of the State*, London: George Allen and Unwin.

Srivastava, R. (2006), 'Panchayats, Bureaucracy and Poverty Alleviation in Uttar Pradesh', in *Local Governance in India*, ed. Niraja Gopal Jayal, Amit Prakash and Pradeep K. Sharma, New Delhi: Oxford University Press.

Srivastava, S.S. and Rajesh Tandon (2005), 'How Large is India's Non-Profit Sector?', in *Economic and Political Weekly*, vol. 11(19), 7–13 May.

Srivastava, Jayati (2005), 'NGOs at World Trade Organization: The Democratic Dimension', in *Economic and Political Weekly*, vol. 11(19), 7–13 May.

Streeten, P. (2002), 'Empowerment, Participation and the Poor', Background Paper for HDR 2002, Human Development Report Office, United Nations Development Programme.

Subrahmaniam, K.K. (1990), 'Development Paradox in Kerala: Analysis of Industrial Stagnation', in *Economic and Political Weekly*, 15 September.

Subramaniam, V. (2003), 'Administration in the Eighties: Major Trends and Challenges', in *Public Administration: A Reader*, New York: Oxford University Press.

Swaminathan, M. (1990), 'Village Level Implementation of IRDP: Comparison of West Bengal and Tamil Nadu', in *Economic and Political Weekly*, 31 March, pp. A17–27.

Tanzi, V. (2000), 'Some Politically Incorrect Remarks on Decentralization and Public Finance', in *Decentralization and Reform in China, India and Russia*, ed. Jean-Jacques Dethier, Boston: Kluwer.

Tharamangalam, J. (1998), 'The Perils of Social Development without Economic Growth: The Development Debacle of Kerala, India', *Bulletin of Concerned Asian Scholars*, vol. 30(1), pp. 23–34.

Tornquist, O. and P.K. Michael Tharakan (1996), 'Democratization and Attempts to Renew the Radical Political Development Project: Case of Kerala', in *Economic and Political Weekly*, 13(20), 27 July.

Tornquist, O. (1992), 'Communists and Democracy: Two India Cases and One Debate', in *When does Democracy Make Sense*, ed. Lars Rudebaeck, AKUT, Working Group for the Study of Development Strategies, Uppsala: Uppsala University.

United Nations Development Programme (2000), *Decentralization in India: Challenges and Opportunities*, New Delhi: Human Development Resource Centre.

Vakil, F.D. (1977), *Gujarat in Patterns of Panchayati Raj in India*, ed. G. Ram Reddy, New Delhi: Macmillan.

Vankatarangaiya, M. and P. Pattabhiram (1969), *Local Government in India: Select Readings*, Bombay: Allied.

Varshney, A. (1995), *Democracy, Development and the Countryside: Urban Rural Struggles in India*, New York: Cambridge.

Venugopal, K.R. (2001), *India Panchayati Raj Report 2001*, Hyderabad: National Institute of Rural Development.

Varghese, B.G. (1977), 'Voluntary Action: A New Mission for the New Missionaries', in *Voluntary Action*, January–October.

Vijayalakshmi, V. (2006), 'Transparency, Accountability and Governance: Local Government in Kerala and Karnataka', in *Local Governance in India*, ed. Niraja Gopal Jayal, Amit Prakash and Pradeep K. Sharma, New Delhi: Oxford University Press.

Wallace, P. (1978), 'Centralization and Depoliticization in South Asia', in *Journal of Commonwealth and Comparative Politics*, vol. 16(1), March, pp. 4–21.

Webster, N. (1996), 'Panchayati Raj in West Bengal: Popular Participation for People or the Party?' in *Development Policy and Administration: Readings in Indian Government and Politics-1*, ed. Kuldeep Mathur, New Delhi: Sage.

Westergaard, K. (1992), 'Local Government in Bengal: Steps Towards Democracy?' in *When Democracy Makes Sense*, ed. Lars Rudebeck, AKUT, Working Group for the Study of Development Strategies, Uppsala University.

Williams, G., Rene Veron, Stuart Corbridge and Manoj Srivastava (2003), 'Participation and Power: Poor People's Engagement with India's Employment Assurance Scheme', in *Development and Change*, 34(1), pp. 163–92.

Williams, D. and Tom Young (1994), 'Governance, the World Bank and Liberal Theory', in *Political Studies*, 1994.

World Bank (2004), *Fiscal Decentralization to Rural Governments in India*, New Delhi: Oxford University Press.

——— (2000), *Overview of Rural Decentralization in India*, vols. 1 and 2.

——— (1994), *Governance: The World Bank Experience*, Washington D.C.: World Bank.

——— (1992), *Governance and Development*, Washington D.C.: World Bank.

Yadav, Y. (1993), 'Towards an Indian Agenda for the Indian Left', in *Economic and Political Weekly*, 9 October, pp. 2199–2201.

Yugadhar, B.N. and B.Y. Raju (1992), 'Government Delivery Systems for Rural Development', in *Economic and Political Weekly*, 29 August, pp. M123–7.

Zachariah, K.C., E.T. Mathew and S. Isuyadaya Rajan (2002), *Migration Patterns and their Socio-Economics in Kerala's Gulf Connection*, Thiruvanathapuram: Centre for Development Studies.

Index